IS THE HOMOSEXUAL MY NEIGHBOR?

REVISED AND UPDATED EDITION

A Positive Christian Response

LETHA DAWSON SCANZONI + VIRGINIA RAMEY MOLLENKOTT

HarperSanFrancisco
A Division of HarperCollinsPublishers

GRATEFUL ACKNOWLEDGMENT is made for permission to reprint material from the following sources: W. H. Auden, *Collected Longer Poems* (New York: Random House, 1969). Reprinted by permission of Random House, Inc; *Am I Running with You, God?* by Malcolm Boyd. Copyright © 1975, 1977 by Malcolm Boyd. Reprinted by permission of Doubleday & Company, Inc; "The Age of Anxiety," in W. H. Auden, *Collected Poems,* ed. Edward Mendelson (New York: Random House, 1976). Used by permission of Random House, Inc; *Homophobia: A Weapon of Sexism* by Suzanne Pharr (Little Rock, AR: Chardon Press, 1988).

Unless otherwise noted, Scripture quotations contained herein are from *The New Revised Standard Version* of the Bible, copyrighted © 1989 by the Division of Christian Education of the National Council of Churches of Christ in the United States, and are used by permission. All rights reserved.

Scripture quotations identified as NEB are from *The New English Bible.* © The Delegates of the Oxford University Press and the Syndics of the Cambridge University Press, 1961, 1970. Reprinted by permission.

Scripture quotations identified as NIV are from *The New International Version* © 1973 by the New York Bible Society International. Published by the Zondervan Corporation.

Scripture quotations identified as KJV are from the King James Version of the Bible.

Library of Congress Cataloging-in-Publication Data
Scanzoni, Letha.
    Is the homosexual my neighbor? : a positive Christian response / Letha Dawson Scanzoni, Virginia Ramey Mollenkott. — Rev. and updated ed.
        p. cm.
    Includes bibliographical references and indexes.
    ISBN 0-06-067078-9 (pbk.)
    1. Homosexuality—Religious aspects—Christianity.
I. Mollenkott, Virginia R.   II. Title.

95 96 97 98 RRD H 10 9 8 7 6 5 4 3

▼▼▼▼▼▼▼▼▼▼

Contents

▼▼▼▼▼▼▼▼▼▼

Preface

"THE QUESTION that makes up the title of this book shouldn't be necessary." With these words we began the original edition of *Is the Homosexual My Neighbor?* The question shouldn't be necessary, we said, because Jesus made it clear that every person is our neighbor. And the Bible likewise makes clear our responsibility to our neighbor: "You shall love your neighbor as yourself."

Yet, all too often, the Bible is brandished as a weapon to clobber gay and lesbian people. Claiming to be doing the will and work of God, some Christians are hurting their neighbors, bearing false witness against them, and assaulting their dignity and sense of self-worth. It was in the hope of alleviating such hurtfulness (which harms us all) that we wrote the first edition of this book, and our purpose remains the same as we send out this updated edition—a radical revision and expansion that both we and our publisher felt was called for in these changing times.

The need for such a book is perhaps even more urgent today than in 1978, when it was first published. Almost daily, the media report news about homosexual people or homosexuality in general (including new research findings). Gay men and lesbian women are featured on television talk shows. Their stories are told in award-winning Broadway plays and musicals, as well as in movies and TV documentaries. They are discussed on radio call-in programs. They may even show up in the comics pages of the newspaper. (In 1993, Canadian cartoonist Lynn Johnston's sensitive and sympathetic story line about a gay teenager's "coming out" to his parents and a close friend ran for a month as part of her popular, family-oriented "For Better or for Worse" comic strip, resulting in the strip's cancellation by numerous newspapers.)

As we go to press, a governmental commission on gay and lesbian people in the military decided on a "don't ask, don't tell, don't pursue" policy that forces people into the constricting closet yet again. Hawaii's state supreme court has just become the first in the nation to open the door to legalized same-sex marriages, compelling family-law experts to debate what this could mean for other states when the final ruling is made. Norway, following Denmark's lead, is in the process of passing legislation recognizing same-sex unions as equivalent to heterosexual marriages. Russia has just repealed the Soviet-era law that had declared male homosexuality a crime punishable by imprisonment. The United States Senate has recently confirmed Roberta Achtenberg as assistant secretary of housing and urban development, making her the first self-affirmed lesbian woman to hold such a high federal office. Yet, as gay and lesbian people continue to gain visibility, political clout, and increasing recognition of their personhood and many contributions to society, they find themselves facing a tremendous backlash of fear, hatred, and well-financed efforts to deny them civil-rights protection and declare them special objects of God's wrath.

AIDS, the terrible disease that has cut short the lives of so many gay men, was completely unknown when this book was first published. It now affects millions of people throughout the world regardless of sexual orientation, and only uninformed people now refer to the disease as a "gay plague." But because it has touched so many lives in the homosexual subculture, gay and lesbian people continue to exercise a leadership role in dealing with the disease. They pressure government and the medical establishment to develop effective vaccines and treatment as rapidly as possible, they disseminate warnings about high-risk sexual behavior, and they provide loving care for people with AIDS, who have often been ostracized by others.

As with the first edition, we hope that individuals, church study groups, and students in institutions of higher learning will find this book helpful in dealing with the inevitable questions surrounding a subject so misunderstood and, consequently, so often perceived as threatening. Our combined backgrounds in literature, sociology, religious studies, and human sexuality have enabled us to explore the topic in depth from many different angles. And our personal histories, not fully shared in the first edition, have provided a further angle of vision.

▼ THE STORY BEHIND THE BOOK

We, the authors, first met in 1973 at a theological seminary where we both had been invited to speak at a symposium on women and the church. But for years before that time, we had been reading and appreciating each other's books and articles, sensing a kinship of spirit in our outlooks on life. Both of us stressed a solid integration of faith and learning, both of us were interested in ethics, and both of us wanted to promote compassionate love and honest justice in a world filled with hate, exploitation, greed, and oppression. After the symposium ended, we continued our discussion of such mutual concerns through long and frequent letters.

It isn't surprising, then, that our correspondence sparked the idea of collaborating on a book. At first, we planned a book on general ethical principles applied to various contemporary social issues of concern to Christians: abortion, euthanasia, pornography and censorship, capital punishment, divorce, and world hunger, to name a few. We planned to treat homosexuality as only one section in this cluster of social issues. In distributing the work between us, we agreed that Letha would write the chapter on homosexuality because she had already researched the topic for both her sex-education book for parents and a college sociology textbook she had just finished coauthoring. Because she lived in Bloomington, Indiana, at the time, she had access to the latest human-sexuality research from the Kinsey Institute at Indiana University. Virginia began the chapters on divorce and censorship, drawing upon her background as a professor of literature and a specialist in the work of John Milton, who centuries earlier had written on these topics as well. Both of us would draw upon our long years of studying the Bible.

Then, in August 1975, Virginia traveled to Letha's home not only to discuss the book but to share something she had seldom shared with anyone—the news that she herself was a lesbian Christian and had been aware of her homosexual orientation since her earliest memories. It was not easy for Virginia to disclose this information about herself, and it was not easy for Letha to receive it.

For Letha, the issue had theretofore been abstract and theoretical. She had been able to write about it objectively and nonjudgmentally—even empathetically—for the college textbook. But now it had to be considered "up close and personally" and in relation to her Christian faith and understanding of Scripture. She also realized, at the deepest level, that she would at some point have to take an unpopular public stand that could be costly to her Christian writing and speaking ministry.

For Virginia, there was the agonizing experience shared by countless other gay and lesbian people as they watch and wait for a friend's response to the disclosure of their homosexuality. Will there be censure, condemnation, rejection? Or will there be acceptance?

At a much later time, as the two of us looked back on that moment, Virginia said she remembered the color draining from Letha's face in shock over the revelation, the news having been a total surprise. Letha mistakenly took that comment as a criticism and, feeling hurt, reacted defensively in a subsequent letter, trying to explain the cognitive dissonance she felt. She said Virginia hadn't known what she was thinking at the time. "Mostly it had to do with friendship and appreciation for you, and a sense of God's call to something new so that my life would never be the same again," Letha wrote. She continued:

> My feelings were not those of condemnation, as you thought. But it meant a great deal had to be worked through, and doing so I feel helped in later writing. I don't see how you

can condemn a person for physical signs of honest emotional reaction. I'm a person, not a zombie or a robot. I feel, and I feel deeply. And what was happening was that the *gap* [referred to on page 51] was being pushed away and not you, and it was the beginning of a whole new outlook. Can you understand? (I'm crying as I write this.)

Virginia responded by explaining her own reaction. "I did not say that I knew WHY you went pale. I only said that it is a terrible thing to be a person who has news to tell that can drain the blood out of a good friend's face," she wrote. Continuing to bare her heart, she told Letha:

I can fully recognize that your shock came from the gap's being pushed away in your mind, and I have often expressed appreciation for the fact that in the long run, you did work through things so that the *gap* has been pushed away rather than the friendship's being dissolved. I am fully aware of all that; but it cannot change the fact that for me it is a dreadful thing to know that I am a person who can cause such trauma to a good and decent and loving Christian person. I did not say, nor have I ever thought, that you went pale in *condemnation* of me. It is the fact that I have to turn you pale at all that is distressing to me, not the reason for the paleness.

Stating that she felt Letha had failed to understand what she had been trying to say to her, Virginia reiterated the distress she experienced because of church and societal reactions to homosexual people:

NO MATTER WHY you went pale, to me it is awful to be the sort of person who has to deliver such psychic blows to another Christian in the process of being honest about who I am. I was talking about *my* identity, my wish that I could be acceptable without trauma to others. I was not accusing you of being condemning, nor was I being so audacious as to assume that I knew your motives. I was trying to express

my inner agony at being a person who is not acceptable
until after another person I admire has gone through all
kinds of painful changes in order to be able to *accept me
without deserting their moral standards.* (You accepted me
all along; but at first you were "accepting the unacceptable"
out of a gracious instinct; only after much struggle did full
acceptance become possible.) I was saying that I wish I
had been CREATED ACCEPTABLE. It isn't your fault that
I was not. I am crying now so I guess I'd better change the
subject.

And so through tears, prayers, inner and outer struggles, Scripture searching, discussions by mail and telephone, and study in a variety of disciplines, we forged ahead with work on the ethics book, all the while learning from each other. Letha was helped to see through Virginia's eyes what it is like to live as a homosexual Christian experiencing the intense pain that societal and church attitudes constantly inflict on God's gay and lesbian children. And by watching Letha's struggles, Virginia was able to see firsthand how difficult it can be to move from the safety of silence and the relative detachment of scholarly objectivity to the taking up of so unpopular a cause as homosexual personhood within a heterosexist church.

"I'm very glad I talked to you about it all," Virginia wrote Letha shortly after sharing her news, "because until I did, I had forgotten just how 'outcast' I really am because of my nature—or would be, if all were known. It is hard to believe, when one is somewhat removed from evangelical everyday contacts, just how *damned* one would be. I know it, yet I also know of how devoted I am to Christ, and I keep forgetting that my devotion isn't what would matter to most people. Your extreme soul-searching and your caution and your fear on the topic have painfully alerted me to my true status in Christendom. And after all it is better to be realistic about such things."

When Letha was seeing Virginia off at the airport following that first visit, Virginia said Letha reminded her of Huck Finn in his struggles of conscience—the story we recount in chapter 2. And Letha was eventually able to tell Virginia, "You are my 'Peter vision,'" referring to the biblical account of Peter's vision of the sheet (also discussed in chapter 2). But, like Peter, Letha underwent much inner turbulence over the new truth being shown her. "About three-fourths of me accepts it as such [that is, a new understanding from God], and I find myself saying, 'That was a pretty tricky thing You did to me, Lord!'" Letha wrote in one of her letters. "And I have to smile as I add, 'But I can't think of any possible way in all the world that could have been a more effective way to convince me." She continued:

> But then the remaining quarter of me starts fighting back and, like Peter, I find myself saying, "Not so, Lord. You don't change your mind about things like that. And how can I be sure this is from You?" See what I mean by struggles? Part of it is the loneliness of it all, knowing that one cannot discuss it or seek counsel from other Christians because they wouldn't understand. Yet feeling the loneliness is good for me, I think, because it helps me identify more with others who feel alone. After all, if we're going to be talking about "incarnational theology" we've got to be willing to live it, as Jesus did, and identify with the oppressed, the needy, the outcast, and the downcast.

Letha often reread the note Virginia had written upon returning to New Jersey after that first visit. "I deeply appreciated your personal understanding and affirmation of who I am," Virginia had said. "On the topic we discussed so much, has it occurred to you that you currently are at the place where many of the most humane evangelicals are about women—in practice, *acting* as if women were equals, *wanting* to see women as equals before God, yet unable to theorize that way because they feel the Bible says no? You wrote *All We're Meant to Be* chiefly for those people. Maybe a future book will offer the same liberating affirmation to another oppressed group of Christians and will help to break down some of the prejudice against them."

Letha also remembered the dream Virginia had had the night after sharing her news; it so vividly dramatized the anguish and fear homosexual Christians often endure at the thought of revealing their sexual orientation in view of the way they have been stigmatized, ostracized, and persecuted. In the dream, Virginia was standing, ready to give a speech, behind the stage curtain of a large auditorium at the fundamentalist university from which she had graduated years before. But as the curtain opened, instead of seeing the audience that was waiting to hear her, she found herself staring into the huge barrel of a rifle pointed directly at her face. (It was a horrible nightmare, but the imagery was apt. The May 1993 issue of *Lear's* magazine featured an interview with a minister who boasted of his Bible training at that same school, saying he had learned both to load and shoot the "Gospel gun"!)

There was much more to think about and discuss together as Letha began the chapter on homosexuality in Christian perspective for the projected ethics book. Although she had never knowingly talked with a homosexual person before, the topic was not entirely new to Letha because she had been corresponding with a woman who had once felt it was her mission to convert homosexual people to both Christ and heterosexuality. But then the woman had totally changed her mind and her ministry, after meeting what she called some of the "most solid, mature Christians" she had ever known, Christians she described as having "both the fruits and the gifts of the Spirit in great abundance," many of whom were living in committed couple relationships. Surprised at her correspondent's changed mind, Letha had debated the topic with her in several letters, arguing biblical passages and natural law, but all the while realizing there was much more to learn. At one point, hoping to clarify the issue in her own mind, Letha drafted a preliminary version of what later became the chart in our chapter 9, asking her friend if *this* summarized what she was proposing— an entirely different ethical model. And, of course, such an alternative view was exactly what was being proposed. In response to Letha's request for further information to share with a college Sunday-school class she was co-teaching on social issues, the woman had sent cassette tapes in which she outlined the biblical basis for her changed view. Letha hesitantly shared the tapes and letters with Virginia during that first visit and in subsequent correspondence, knowing they might be helpful and encouraging to Virginia, but realizing that she, Letha, was not yet ready herself to take such an accepting position—at least, not publicly. This prompted Virginia to write:

> Letha, dear Letha, I'm sorry to think of the heavy responsi-
> bility and the struggle my very existence has brought into
> your life—or at least has brought to a head in your life. . . .
> I am deeply appreciative of the struggle you have gone
> through and the warmth of your personal acceptance even
> when theoretical acceptance and moral approval could not
> yet be a part of you. I am grateful to God for the long corre-
> spondence you have held on the subject with A., for without
> that you could never have responded to me as positively as
> you did. Besides, I have learned a few things from A.'s in-
> sights, and I want to take some notes on her letters before
> returning them to you. . . . She has thought things through
> much better than I ever have done, largely I think because
> I was personally involved, and I have never been very strong
> in anything that might amount to self-defense. (That's why
> I was so slow to get going on the women's issue—because
> I had an interest in female equality, and therefore somehow
> felt I shouldn't fight for it. Really sick socialization, I'd say.)

But there was no turning back for either of us now. A few weeks after Virginia's visit, Letha wrote to tell her that "David's English class is studying *Huck Finn* right now" (referring to Letha's then fourteen-year-old son, who had accompanied us to the airport). Rereading David's copy of the book, thinking back on the parting conversation, and trying to put everything together was making it hard for Letha to concentrate on her writing and speaking responsibilities. She tried to work, "but you had presented a challenge and it kept returning to my mind," she told Virginia. Letha's letter to her continued:

> I thought of that challenge again over the weekend [dur-
> ing a Christian gathering on social justice] when I heard so
> much talk about identifying with and helping oppressed
> groups in general and one speaker said that Moses never
> wanted to be a liberator and kept resisting God at first.

Then one day [back at home] . . . I had what I suppose was
as close to a vision as I've ever had. Maybe not the kind
you've longed for, but God's presence seemed so real as I
looked up from my proofing and the sun was glowing
through the sycamore tree out front. There flashed through
my mind the challenge you had presented, the burden you
had shared, and I said, "But Lord, why should I? The costs
would be so great and what reward would I have?" Immediately, I heard in my heart, "Well done, thou good and
faithful servant; inasmuch as ye have done it unto one of
these the least of my brethren you have done it unto Me."
And then I said, "But what would people think?" And
immediately there flashed across my mind: "If this man
were a prophet, he would have known who and what sort
of woman this is who is touching him. . . . And Jesus said,
'Simon, I have something to say to you.'" And suddenly
I started to weep. What I felt at that moment—the concern
and compassion and call to help—seemed all the more confirmed when I read the new *Christianity Today* which had
an excellent article by Cheryl Forbes on Charles Williams
and his thoughts on "substitute love" or truly bearing one
another's burdens. One of the drawings showed a burdened-
down person carrying a huge skull on his back and, under it,
it said, "How can anyone else carry my fear?" I thought of
what a privilege it really is to be asked to help carry another
Christian's load. Another drawing illustrated Williams'
words, "We should die each other's life, live each other's
death." The words struck and moved me deeply.

And so, after exchanging with Virginia various ideas for content, Letha moved ahead with her chapter, only to have it grow so
long that Virginia telephoned her to say, "You don't have a *chapter* here; we have a book!" Virginia had plenty of ideas to flesh it
out and expand it with material of her own, including illustrations
from literature and history, after breaking the section headings
into book chapter divisions. And so we put aside the overall ethics
book project, and *Is the Homosexual My Neighbor?* came into
being.

In the years since then, we have both authored other books and continued our other writing and speaking ministries—often with different audiences than was once the case. Virginia's ever-expanding consciousness of God's love for her, just as she is—just as God made her in the beginning and delights in her now—emboldened her to declare her orientation openly, first at a church conference where negative statements about gay and lesbian people had been made, and later in print. She dedicated one of her books, *Sensuous Spirituality*, to her life partner, Debra Lynn Morrison, and together they have recently celebrated their fourteenth anniversary.

We send forth this edition of *Is the Homosexual My Neighbor?* as we sent forth the earlier edition, with the prayer that hearts and minds will be open to new ways of seeing, understanding, and caring in a world that is all too often characterized by neighbor-against-neighbor instead of loving our neighbor as ourselves. Readers of the first edition can be assured that, except where necessary deletions were made to update or correct, most of the original material remains. But each chapter is now longer, containing much new material gleaned from the latest research in biblical and theological studies and in the social and biological sciences. And an altogether new chapter has been added to this edition—chapter 10, in which we further address a myriad of current issues related to the topic of homosexuality.

LETHA DAWSON SCANZONI
AND VIRGINIA RAMEY MOLLENKOTT

Who Is My Neighbor?

NOT SO VERY long ago, the following statements were made to a national audience:

> Homosexuality is that mark of Cain, of a godless and soul-less culture which is sick to the core.

> The teaching of the youth to appreciate the value . . . of the community, derives its strongest inner power from the truths of Christianity. . . . For this reason it will always be my special duty to safeguard the right and free development of the Christian school and the Christian fundamentals of all education.[1]

The first statement comes from a Fascist pamphlet published in Nazi Germany; the second was made by Adolf Hitler in a 1933 edict on the education of German young people. In the name of Christ and moral purity, Hitler later had people who were suspected of homosexuality either shot without trial or exterminated in concentration-camp gas chambers.

Many homosexual people are aware of what happened to people like themselves during the Nazi period. They are also aware that during the Middle Ages, again in the name of Christ and moral purity, homosexuals were burned alive. So they are understandably concerned when they hear public cries to stamp out homosexuality. When, for instance, they hear news-media announcements that certain groups are working to rescind ordinances that guarantee the civil rights of lesbian and gay people, and doing so in the name of Christ and moral purity, they hear all that within the framework of centuries of persecution. It is frightening to know that some religious leaders have urged their followers to "stop the homosexuals once and for all," declaring that if homosexual men and women are "declared a legitimate minority group . . . the traditional family and basic morality and decency in America will be on their way to extinction!"[2] It is alarming to hear some who oppose homosexual civil rights using the rhetoric of warfare, claiming that the battle in which they are engaged is not their battle but "*God's* battle," and that "the Lord is on [their] side."[3] Or to read an official statement saying that "the Church has the responsibility to promote the public morality of the entire civil society on the basis of fundamental moral values" and find that the intent of the statement is to implore government to discriminate against homosexual people in order to "promote the traditional family and protect society."[4] To homosexual people, such pronouncements sound like a throwback to Fascism or even to the Inquisition. In the face of such threats, some gay and lesbian activists have grown defiant; but others, who want only to live their lives in peace, have simply grown afraid.

The anti-gay rhetoric that has found its way into certain religious and political arenas has spilled over onto numerous college campuses where hate-filled graffiti have sprouted up on the insides and outsides of buildings. Signs and scribblings have yielded unspeakably repugnant messages, such as "Heterosexuals fight back, hang a homosexual in effigy"; "Rape a lesbian, kill a queer"; "Kill a fag before he rapes your son"; and the initials K.A.G.O.S., which is said to stand for "Kill all gays on sight." Posters on one campus urged students to overcome boredom by joining a year-long crusade to "maliciously harass" homosexuals.[5] Harassment of gays has created an atmosphere of intimidation in many places. Ridicule, threats, and actual assaults against homosexual men and women have increased in recent years.[6] Yet in one study it was found that nearly three-fourths of survivors of gay-bashing incidents did not report the assaults. "Most said their reason was fear of encountering antigay treatment from police officers," reports social commentator Donna Minkowitz. She points out that "victims of gay-bashing often receive the same judicial treatment as rape victims; both sets of complainants are deemed to be 'asking for it.'"[7]

▼ THE MORE MODERATE MAJORITY

There is little doubt that much of the current discrimination against homosexual women and men is rooted in and fostered by the anti-gay sentiments voiced by certain religious leaders. Yet it is our opinion that many Christian people take a more moderate view of the issue than these leaders. Many would probably admit that they feel somewhat uninformed and puzzled about homosexuality. And although it is true that many people are deeply disturbed by the moral implications of extending social acceptance to avowed homosexual women and men, fearing that such acceptance would cause a rise in the incidence of homosexuality, many of these same people are also deeply disturbed at the thought of denying the civil rights of any person.[8] On some level, they know that when one group is deprived of its civil rights, the rights of other groups are placed in jeopardy as well.

In other words, we believe that most thinking and compassionate Christians would not approve of the abusive language employed in efforts to deny the basic civil rights and humanity of lesbian and gay people. But sincere people *are* feeling tremendous conflict about whether avowed homosexuals should be permitted to teach school or adopt children.[9] And the question of whether to ordain known homosexuals has forced mainline Christian churches to begin studying an issue that had formerly been discussed only in whispers. We can sense the profound distress, for instance, of the members of a Bible-study group from Indianapolis in their open letter to the Episcopal bishop Paul Moore criticizing his ordination of a lesbian, Ellen Marie Barrett: "The problem with your ordination of Ellen is that it seems to set a standard that homosexuality is spiritually and morally acceptable. We feel this is a wrong standard which, if universalized, would wrongly mold the Christian conscience."[10]

The letter goes on to note "a new organization of former homosexuals" whose members claim that when they were "born again" they ceased to be homosexuals. This might at first appear to be the ideal solution for concerned and compassionate Christians in their stance toward this hotly contested issue. If homosexuality is indeed a disorder that can be cured simply by acceptance of Christ as Savior, then obviously the churches need only preach the gospel to homosexuals and otherwise hold the line about church admittance and full social acceptance. Yet Sigmund Freud himself, the founder of psychoanalysis, did not believe that it is really feasible to change a person's homosexual orientation into a heterosexual one. "To undertake to convert a fully developed homosexual into a heterosexual," he wrote, "is not much more promising than to do the reverse."[11]

The matter of sexual orientation is, in fact, far more complex than many Christians realize. It is simplistic to presume that when homosexuals (erotically attracted to the same sex) become Christians, they automatically become heterosexuals (erotically attracted to the opposite sex). Some homosexual Christians may choose to become celibate and not act upon their homosexual desires, but this does not mean they have become heterosexual. Other Christians may be capable of responding to either sex to some degree (see our section on the Kinsey continuum in chapter 6) and may feel that as part of their commitment to Christ they should relinquish their past homosexual behavior and act only on their heterosexual inclinations. Still others are devoted followers of Christ and yet live in complete awareness that they are as fully homosexual now as before conversion, convinced that their homosexuality and Christian faith can be integrated according to Scripture-based ethical principles.

▼ HOW MANY ARE AFFECTED BY HOMOSEXUALITY?

There are also far more people touched by homosexuality than many Christians think. Unlike gender or skin color, homosexual orientation can be hidden indefinitely. For that reason it is hard to say how many homosexuals there actually are. But educated estimates range anywhere from 2 to 10 percent of the population, counting only those whose desire focuses predominantly and habitually on their own sex, not those who have had only one or two passing homosexual experiences. (See chapter 6 for further discussion of the incidence of homosexual orientation.) Assuming a 5 percent incidence, in a congregation of two hundred, as many as ten people have to sit through any mention of "the sin of homosexuality" outwardly pretending that it does not apply to them, but nevertheless feeling rejected and hurt inside.

In addition to the pain of these hidden homosexuals, there is the pain of their parents, many of whom either know of or strongly suspect the homosexuality of their children. (One homosexual Christian recently told us how his mother wept uncontrollably when their pastor preached that all homosexuals would be consigned to hellfire; she was heartbroken for her beloved son, and he was heartbroken for her suffering as well. Yet he had not *chosen* to be homosexual, and there was no formula by which he could relieve his mother's anguish.) So by counting the parents of lesbian and gay people, we see that in a congregation of two hundred, the number of individuals who may be directly affected by the issue of homosexuality now rises to at least thirty.

Since many homosexual people marry in order to avoid suspicion or in the hope of being "cured" by the union, we must also add the pain of their spouses, who know that something is wrong and who often blame themselves for not being attractive enough to their mates. Add to that number those uncles, aunts, brothers, sisters, children, and friends who may suspect the secret, and you have approximately one-quarter of the congregation.

At the other end of the spectrum of feeling on this issue, in a church of two hundred people there are probably at least a few who are filled with rage or disgust at the very mention of homosexuality. The stronger the feeling of revulsion, the stronger the possibility that the person harbors deep anxiety about his or her own sexuality. That could bring the number of directly concerned individuals up to approximately sixty in a congregation of two hundred.

But to one degree or another, *everybody* senses feelings of love for persons of the same sex, both within and outside the family unit. If fear and confusion about homosexuality are strong enough,

even common feelings familiar to all of us may cause anxiety,
furtiveness, and guilt. So here again is an illustration of how the
topic in some way touches our lives.

Thus there is no denying that, although lesbian and gay people
form a minority in society and a carefully hidden minority in most
churches, homosexuality is an issue that cannot be brushed aside.
In one way or another it directly concerns us all.

▼ A HOMOSEXUAL CHRISTIAN'S PAIN

Because many people are not aware that they know any homosexuals, and few Christians are aware that they are rubbing shoulders with homosexuals in their churches, it is worthwhile to quote
at length a letter to the editors of *The Other Side,* an evangelical
Christian magazine, written several years ago by a homosexual
Christian in response to an issue of the magazine on the theme of
torture:

> . . . I have never read in an evangelical magazine any ac-
> count of the kinds of psychological and sometimes physical
> suffering experienced by thousands of evangelical homosex-
> uals.
>
> The horrible pressures against these Christians causes
> incredible torture in countless lives today. Most Christian
> gays have opted to get married in order to avoid suspicion,
> but after years of marriage and children they still find them-
> selves homosexual. . . .
>
> I don't know why I'm homosexual, nor why neither
> prayer nor Bible reading, neither psychotherapy nor heal-
> ing lines have ever "cured" me. I wish I could "come out"
> openly and share what I know, but the time is too early.
>
> . . . I'm tired of seeing the gay bars filled with so many
> youths who once sincerely accepted Christ as Lord and
> Savior—only to find they hadn't become heterosexual and
> thus feel excluded from the body of Christ.
>
> Less than two months ago I was told by a sincere Christ-
> ian (!) counselor that it would be "better" to "repent and
> die," even if I had to kill myself, than to go on living and

relating to others as a homosexual. (A friend of mine, told something similar by a well-intentioned priest, did just that.)

All I can do is pray that somewhere, someday, someone with compassion will begin the long, slow process of uncovery, discovery, and reconciliation of all who know Jesus Christ as Lord and Savior—both gay and straight.[12]

The letter was signed, "An Accepted, Excepted One." Could that homosexual Christian be your neighbor?

If the homosexual is my neighbor, the Bible commands that I shall not bear false witness against that person (Exod. 20:16). Thus, it is necessary to find out the truth concerning homosexuality before saying anything about the topic, since in the absence of correct information anybody might, unwittingly, bear false witness. In an extreme example, some Christians have been echoing one anti-gay crusader's absurd claim that 80 percent of homosexuals consume fecal material as part of their sexual practices and are thus a serious health menace as food handlers and the like.[13] Other Christians have accepted unquestioningly the claims that homosexual people are dangerous to children and a threat to family values.

"They're not telling the truth about who I am," Eric Marcus, a gay man, wrote in a *Newsweek* article. Marcus, an author and a former associate producer for television's *Good Morning America*, attempted to set the record straight by telling how the family life he and his partner share is—like that of countless other homosexual couples—very much like the everyday lives of heterosexual families. He told of how they attended family weddings and funerals together, went to their nephews' and nieces' birthday parties, flew to the side of a parent who had suffered a heart attack, had relatives over to celebrate holidays in their home, and were asked by two heterosexual couples to be named as guardians of these couples' children in the event of the parents' deaths. Marcus spoke of the "full, happy, family-centered life" that has been his experience as a gay person in a loving partnership, and he decried the disinformation that is spread by those who malign homosexual women and men.[14] Christians who participate in the dissemination of hearsay based on ignorance and bigotry are violating the commandment "You shall not bear false witness against your neighbor."

In addition to speaking only the truth about our neighbors, we are given the responsibility of aiding our neighbors in their livelihood. This biblical teaching is illustrated by commandments given to ancient Israel to help one's neighbors if their animals were lost or overburdened (Exod. 23:4–5; Deut. 22:1–2). Since animals were a chief form of livelihood in that society, helping neighbors care for their animals meant assisting them in maintaining their daily sustenance. In the light of this enduring principle, if the homosexual is my neighbor, do I have any business supporting efforts to deprive him or her of the privilege of working for a living?

Zech. 8:17 specifies that none of us should allow ourselves to imagine evil in our hearts against our neighbor. Yet in the absence of accurate information about the homosexual condition, it is almost impossible to avoid distortions of our thinking. It is a universal human trait to fear what we don't understand. If the homosexual is my neighbor, I must do my best to understand what his or her life is really like, so that I will not be guilty of imagining that he or she intends evil toward me or my loved ones and therefore of harboring ill will in return.

▼ WHAT WE GIVE IS WHAT WE GET

The Bible has many other things to say about how we should treat our neighbor, but they are all summarized in the repeated injunction to "love your neighbor as yourself" (Lev. 19:18; Matt. 19:19, 22:39; Mark 12:31; Luke 10:27; Rom. 13:9; Gal. 5:14; James 2:8). The formula expressed in these passages is highly significant for our topic. We can love or accept our neighbor only to the degree that we are able to love and accept ourselves. True self-acceptance comes most readily through the realization that God loves and accepts us just as we are. When we begin to believe the wonderful truth that through atonement we are identified with Christ and clothed with Christ (Gal. 3:27), we can begin to look lovingly upon our neighbor. No longer tormented by inner guilt, we will no longer need scapegoats to project that guilt upon. Each time we look beyond our neighbor's fears and inadequacies and instead affirm the light that is in every person who ever came into the world (John 1:9), we reinforce our own recognition of the light that is within us.

But just as positive affirmation of others returns to bless the giver of the affirmation, so also negative judgment of others will boomerang painfully. The apostle Paul makes this point with force and clarity in Rom. 2:1: "Therefore you have no excuse, whoever you are, when you judge others; for in passing judgment on another you condemn yourself, because you, the judge, are doing the very same things." The passage immediately preceding this one (Rom. 1:18–32), ironically, has been widely used as a condemnation of homosexual love. But Paul's words about homosexual acts must be read within their context, as indeed every passage of Scripture must be read. Paul's *therefore* in the very next verse (Rom. 2:1, quoted above) bases his warning against condemning others precisely on the very passage that has been used to condemn homosexual people. Although interrupted by a chapter division, the flow of thought runs with tight logic from Rom. 1:18 through Rom. 2:16.

This passage explains why deeply homophobic people—that is, people who are enraged and feel revulsion toward homosexuality—need our help just as much as lesbian and gay people themselves. Because of human feelings of guilt and alienation, we have a tendency to latch on to certain passages of Scripture in order to condemn others, in an attempt to distance ourselves from our own guilty feelings. But by so doing, we only increase the sense of condemnation we are laboring under. As we'll be discussing in chapter 5, Rom. 1:18–32 is a passage primarily concerning idolatry, specifying that worship of the body and worship of things, indecent sexual acts, and such sins as envy, gossip, heartlessness, and slander all grow out of the stubborn refusal to recognize the invisible qualities of God through the visible creation. Paul is pointing out that *every* human being has been guilty to one degree or another of such alienation from God. It is one of the most dreadful ironies of Christendom that instead of responding to the utter universality of Paul's remarks in chapter 1 of Romans, many Christians have tried to evade confrontation with their own idolatrous ways by applying the whole passage only to homosexuals! By such scapegoating, these Christians have placed themselves directly under the self-condemnation described in Rom. 2:1: "In passing judgment on another you condemn yourself." Condemnation is, indeed, a boomerang. Fortunately, so is loving acceptance. Whatever we do to our neighbor, for good or evil, we do to ourselves.

▼ WHERE I FIND NEED, I FIND MY NEIGHBOR

But who is my neighbor? We must remind ourselves that when a certain expert in Jewish law was testing Christ and trying to justify himself, he asked Christ that very same question. In answer, Jesus told him the story of the man who was beaten by thieves and left for dead. A priest saw the man's plight, and later a Levite, but both chose to remain uninvolved. Finally, a Samaritan took pity on the man and, at great personal inconvenience and expense, helped him to safety. Jesus put it to the lawyer: which one of these was the neighbor to the unfortunate man? The lawyer naturally had no choice but to acknowledge that the Samaritan, who had shown mercy, was the real neighbor. Jesus said to the lawyer, "Go, and do as he did" (Luke 10:37, NEB).

It is interesting that Jesus did not define the concept of "neighbor" by geographical closeness, or by race, or by religion, but only by need. Anyone who crosses my path and needs my help is my neighbor. And I am neighbor to anyone to whom I give assistance. As Jesus said to the lawyer about loving God and neighbor with all his soul and strength and mind, *Do this, and you will live* (Luke 10:28). For when the sheep are separated from the goats in the day of judgment, and the puzzled righteous wonder *when* they performed the services for which they are being commended, "the king will answer them, 'Truly I tell you, just as you did it to one of the least of these who are members of my family, you did it to me'" (Matt. 25:40).

In the light of Christ's pronouncements on neighborliness, let us pause to ask ourselves some questions:

Do I care about the need of homosexuals who are without Christ and who cannot respond to an invitation based on the condition that they must either become heterosexual or live celibate forever after?

Do I care about the need of hidden homosexual Christians whose self-acceptance is impeded by the well-meaning remarks of those who have not taken the trouble to understand the homosexual condition?

Do I care about the need of self-affirming homosexual Christians who endure rejection from those who make them into scapegoats for their own inner alienation?

Do I care about the need of the parents of homosexuals who endure agonies of guilt and humiliation, wondering what they did wrong? Do I care about the need of the bewildered spouses and children of homosexuals who married out of a desire to hide, disprove, or "cure" their homosexuality?

Do I care about the need of those who must storm and rage against homosexuals because they have fears about their own sexuality?

Do I care about the need of Christian communities to build healthy, responsible attitudes toward human sexuality in all its tremendous variety?

Do I care enough to do something constructive about homosexuality, such as informing myself so that I can inform others?

If your answer to any of these questions is yes, then this book is written for you.

2

▽ ▼ ▽ ▽ ▽ ▽ ▽ ▽ ▽ ▽ ▽

The Risks and Challenges
of Moral Growth

IT IS NATURAL to feel a certain amount of fear when reopening questions that have seemed as closed as the topic of homosexuality has been to church people for many years. But the wider truth is that any questioning of familiar ethical standards on any topic, no matter how localized, can feel frightening to a person who sincerely wants to live a godly life.

The difference between moral maturity and moral childishness has nothing to do with puberty or chronological age. The morally mature person is one who has sorted through the standards learned in childhood, rejecting those that no longer apply and accepting and internalizing those that still do apply. He or she is also one who has developed the courage to obey God's voice in those highly unusual situations when long-accepted standards must for some reason be transcended. Rising above standards that have been ingrained from childhood may involve tremendous struggle and often real terror. But the refusal even to consider the possibility of such transcendence may well lead to moral rigor mortis. In order to deepen our grasp of the necessity for moral maturity, let's focus on two stories, one biblical and one extrabiblical, with a third story to follow later.

▼ THE AGONY OF OUTGROWING FAMILIAR PATTERNS

Our first narrative, recorded in Acts 10 and 11, involves Simon Peter, Jesus' most impetuous disciple. One day Peter went for prayer to the roof of the house where he was staying. After saying his prayers and while hungrily awaiting dinner, Peter experienced an extremely unsettling vision. He saw descend from heaven a great sheetlike container full of wild animals and other four-footed beasts, birds of the air, and creeping things. And he heard a voice say, "Get up, Peter. Kill and eat." Peter's flesh must have crawled at the very suggestion that he violate the dietary laws he had been taught from childhood: "All creatures that teem on the ground, crawl on their bellies . . . you shall not eat, because they are vermin which contaminate. . . . You shall make yourselves holy and keep yourselves holy, because I am holy. You shall not defile yourselves with any teeming creature that creeps on the ground" (Lev. 11:42–44, NEB).

Knowing that the voice he heard was that of the Lord, Peter must have quickly considered the available possibilities. Perhaps there were some animals in the sheet that chewed the cud and had divided hoofs and were therefore permissible for Jews to eat. Could he manage to separate one of those from the rest? But no, the presence of so many unclean creatures made his gorge rise. And there was no way on this rooftop to kill the animal or prepare the flesh in a kosher manner. Peter's answer was certain: "No, Lord, no; I have never eaten anything profane or unclean" (Acts 10:14, NEB).

Again that voice: "It is not for you to call profane what God counts clean." And then the whole sequence was repeated: the command to kill and eat, Peter's revulsion based on careful training in Jewish dietary laws, his refusal, and the Lord's correction of Peter's concept of cleanness. What could this mean? Certainly God had given the dietary laws to the Israelites (Leviticus 11, Deuteronomy 14). They were God's word. Yet this was God's own voice, giving instructions to transgress that general law in this specific case! A third time the whole sequence occurred. Again Peter refused to obey God's voice. He simply could not transcend rules he had followed for so long and with such care—not even in response to a special vision from God!

After the vision had passed, Peter sat thinking about it. Maybe he remembered a time when he'd been given three opportunities to show loyalty to Christ and had failed at each (Matt. 26:33–35, 69–75). While he was still rapt in thought, God's Spirit told him that some men were looking for him and that he should not fear to go with them because they had been sent by God. Peter must have wondered why God had bothered to tell him not to fear a couple of strangers. After all, he did not consider himself a coward. But when he heard where the men came from—the house of a prominent Gentile—he understood instantly. He normally would have recoiled from any association with such people, as he had been fully trained in Jewish laws that prohibited Jews from associating with Gentiles or visiting in their houses (Acts 10:28; Josh. 23:7). But this time, his *fourth* opportunity, Peter knew better than to disobey the voice of God. Without hesitation, he invited the men into the house and the next day went with them to preach the gospel to the Gentiles.

For Peter, such moral growth was not easy. It involved him in conflict with a strict party of Jewish Christians who believed Gentiles must first become Jews and observe Jewish rituals in order to become Christians (see Acts 15). In Jerusalem, members of this group, called "circumcised believers," at first could not understand why Peter had violated Jewish law (Acts 11). Later, Peter (also called Cephas) would give in to Jewish-Christian pressure and separate himself from the Gentiles to such a degree that Paul had to correct him in public (Gal. 2:11–16). But for now, because Peter had directly experienced the power of God's Spirit in his dealings with the Gentiles, he was able to explain his actions to the satisfaction of his fellow believers. Confronted with the evidence that God was working in new and unexpected ways, the Jewish Christians were "astounded that the gift of the Holy Spirit had been poured out even on the Gentiles" (Acts 10:45, 11:18). Even on Gentiles. It was mind-boggling. But the strength of Peter's vision and the overt manifestations of the Spirit forced the Judaizing Christians to develop a more mature understanding of the workings of God.

▼ God's Voice or Society's Voice?

Our second story comes from one of the most justly famous of American novels, Mark Twain's *Huckleberry Finn*. Huck, who has been raised to believe in the sacredness of private property (even if that property happens to be a human being), is appalled when he confronts the moral implications of helping his black friend, Jim, escape from slavery. At one point, when Jim has been captured and is imprisoned on the Phelps farm, Huck feels God is warning him to desist from such evil ways:

> It hit me all of a sudden that here was the plain hand of
> Providence slapping me in the face and letting me know
> my wickedness was being watched all the time up there in
> heaven, whilst I was stealing a poor old woman's nigger,
> that hadn't ever done me no harm, and now was showing
> me there's One that's always on the lookout, and ain't
> a-going to allow no such miserable doings to go only just
> so fur and no further, I most dropped in my tracks I was
> so scared.[1]

To Huck, as to every morally immature person, the voice of socialization seems to be the voice of God. Huck decides to pray; but his socially conditioned conscience tells him that God will not hear his prayer until he has written to Miss Watson, Jim's slave-owner, telling her how to recover her "property." He writes the note and at first feels "all washed clean of sin for the first time I had ever felt so in my life." He assumes that by upholding the laws of private property and returning a human being to slavery, he has saved himself from hell. But then he begins to think about Jim: "And got to thinking over our trip down the river, and I see Jim before me all the time in the day and in the night-time, sometimes moonlight, sometimes storms, and we a-floating along, talking and singing and laughing. But somehow I couldn't seem to strike no places to harden me against him, but only the other kind." Huck remembers Jim's humanity, his warmth, his kindness, and his grateful dependence on Huck as his only friend in the world. And suddenly, Huck tears up the note, saying, "All right, then, I'll go to hell,"[2] and resolves to steal Jim from the Phelps farm, regardless of the penalty.

Did Huck choose to serve humanity rather than God? Was his willingness to go to hell in order to free a friend from slavery simply a matter of blasphemous secularism? Before we jump to that conclusion, we might be wise to remind ourselves that the apostle Paul, thinking that some of his Jewish kinsmen were not among God's elect "children of promise," declared that he could wish himself accursed on their behalf (Rom. 9:3). In other words, Paul would have been willing to go to hell himself if that would have changed the destiny of his Jewish friends. Similarly, Huck was willing to take any risks necessary to help Jim. "No one has greater love than this, to lay down one's life for one's friends" (John 15:13).

IN BOTH of our stories we see a human being struggling for the courage to transcend what he believes to be a divinely ordained rule. Admittedly, there are some important distinctions between them. Peter had to contend with his knowledge of Jewish law as recorded in Holy Scripture. He had to have the courage to listen to the voice of God speaking to him directly, and had to obey that voice even when it ordered him to do something counter to the laws that the voice had earlier delivered to the children of Israel.

In Huck Finn's case, there was no question of an individual voice, recognizable as God's, directing him to disobey a more general God-given law. For Huck, it wasn't that clear-cut. Huck had been taught that private property was sacred, that to interfere with someone else's possession was to incur the wrath of God. Where Huck grew up, slavery was not considered immoral, but stealing was. Biblical injunctions against stealing were invoked frequently, since they protected the rich and powerful and helped to control the poor and needy. But nobody looked past the most literal sense of New Testament references to slavery. Nobody paid any attention to the liberating principles of passages like Gal. 3:28

and Col. 3:11. Since slavery had been part of first-century society, it was assumed that slavery was forever a part of God's plan for the human race. Huck had never questioned that this assumption was God's truth for his time and for all time. The only voice that encouraged him to help Jim was the still small voice of his own compassion. Because of his training, Huck assumed that his most decent human impulses were evil. But that did not *make* them evil. "Even if our conscience condemns us," says John, "God is greater than our conscience and knows all" (1 John 3:20, NEB).

▼ CAN WE EVADE STRUGGLE?

Each of our stories emphasizes an important point about moral and ethical choice. Peter's story indicates that there are times when human beings are directed to transcend general laws of God and society because of the specific work God has chosen them to do. Gone is the certainty of assuming that all we need to do is simply cling to the rules handed down to us by decent people. Gone, even, is the simplistic use of Scripture. Had Peter simply continued to obey the command of Josh. 23:7 that Jews should not associate with Gentiles, he would not have had the privilege of carrying the gospel to Cornelius and his household. Although the biblical rule had been a perfectly good one, intended to keep the Jews from slipping into idolatrous ways, Peter was made to recognize that in his situation it no longer applied, and that he should obey instead the directions given to him personally by God's voice. Attention to this story warns us that thoughtless obedience, even to a passage of Scripture, can be disastrous in its effects on our moral life.

Huck's story demonstrates how dangerously easy it is to confuse the voice of society with the voice of God. It warns us against the too-easy assumption that our consciences will always give us correct guidance. Having been brought up in a slave-owning society, Huck felt it natural to classify human beings as property if they had been paid for legally. It was easy to find moral justification for slavery in a few biblical passages if they were interpreted on the most literalistic level and without attention to context. Take, for instance, 1 Pet. 2:18: "Slaves, accept the authority of your masters with all deference." What could be clearer than that?

To help a slave escape was to violate the obvious, clear meaning of the Word of God. Anyone who said that a more careful exegesis would unearth the liberating principle of the One Body of Christ, with all Christians submitting to and caring for each other, and thus would do away with the concept of slavery, was accused of twisting Scripture in order to evade what was obviously there on the surface.[3] In such a society, poor Huckleberry was left with no choice except to think that his decent human concern was contrary to God's revealed will and therefore was an evil for which he would be punished in hell.

Thinking that he was violating the will of God, Huck chose human liberation. But what he was *really* violating were the standards of a corrupt society. Those standards had been programmed into his conscience, so that his heart condemned him even when God did not. His dilemma illustrates the fact that we sometimes feel very afraid to do what we sense to be right, not because we would actually be violating the will of God, but because we have been programmed in such a way that we think the voice of a corrupt society is the will of God. For instance, in recent years many married people have felt that, as human beings who are equally God's image bearers, they should rightfully relate to each other as equals. But all around them the voice of society says, as it has said for centuries, that it is proper for the woman to play only a secondary and supportive role. It has been only too easy for many churches to support society's sinful assumptions by latching on to a few verses of Scripture interpreted literalistically and without attention to context.

Anyone who tries to interpret the Bible contextually on this point, showing that mutual submission is everywhere applied to Christians married to each other and to all other Christians,[4] is accused of twisting the Scripture in order to evade what is obviously there on the surface. The result is that some Christian married couples have chosen to live in mutual submission of the husband to the wife and the wife to the husband, yet have staggered under the burden of feeling they were violating the will of God. In fact they were violating only the assumptions of a mistaken society as those assumptions have been rationalized by a superficial reading of the Bible. Other couples have struggled along in an unequal partnership, the woman oppressed by her subjection and the man oppressed by his role as oppressor, in the delusion that this was God's requirement for them both. It is as if Huck had chosen to save his own soul by allowing Jim to be returned to slavery; as if Peter had chosen to obey Jewish law by clinging to Josh. 23:7 and letting the Gentiles do without the gospel.

▼ THE SELF-EXAMINED LIFE

Both stories challenge us to study the Bible more closely. If we are to seek scriptural guidance concerning our moral and ethical attitudes, we must be extremely careful in our interpretations. When we assume that the Bible is perfectly clear on a moral issue—so clear that only a fool or a dishonest person could possibly differ from our view of what it says—that overconfidence should alert us to the possibility that our egos are clouding our interpretations. Self-suspicion is especially in order when our view happens to coincide with the prevailing view, whether of a particular church or of the secular society. If and when such a correlation is present, we cannot reasonably doubt that we need to open our minds to careful reconsideration.

Perhaps, after full and honest examination of all available evidence, we will still arrive at the same conclusions. Yet in the process, we will have internalized the issue and thus will have matured as far as that issue is concerned. On the other hand, perhaps we will be forced to move beyond the comfortable certainty of an old familiar rule. As G. C. Berkouwer says: "To confess Holy Scripture and its authority is to be aware of the command to understand and to interpret it. It always places us at the beginning of a road that we can travel in 'fear and trepidation.'"[5]

Those who stick to the thoughtless repetition of selected proof texts in order to rationalize a comfortable alliance with society's standards frequently fling accusations at those who want to probe the depth of the Bible. "By introducing such questions you will destroy the Bible's authority over humanity," they say. Or, "You will undermine belief in biblical infallibility." The painful irony here is that those who refuse to search the Scriptures concerning the assumptions of society are the ones who are refusing to submit social customs to the judgment of the Bible. By that refusal they are helping to erode biblical authority in contemporary society. Not the seekers, but those who fear to seek, are those who doubt biblical infallibility.

Here again we agree with Berkouwer, who comments that "those who, because of hesitancy and wariness, abandon new hermeneutical questions contribute to the relativising of scriptural authority. . . . In the history of the church it is evident that unrest can never be removed by ecclesiastical inattention to real questions."[6] We need the courage and faith to face the challenges posed by the questions of our day. And the Holy Spirit can supply the courage and faith we need, for, as Luther said, "the Holy Spirit is no skeptic."[7] We can probe, question, and study fearlessly, confident that the Bible is adequate to any honest dialogue.

▼ THE PERIL OF MISGUIDED CHOICE

But what of the personal risks involved in moving beyond thoughtless adherence to general laws and rules? Granted, Peter and Huck were ultimately right about their decisions. But doesn't their example give the perhaps misleading impression that simply listening to an inner voice is a safer moral guide than obeying the Bible's guidelines and society's well-established rules? And doesn't such an attitude contain perilous possibilities? It is bad enough to confuse the voice of society with the will of God. Isn't it even worse to confuse our own *subjective desires* with the will of God?

Here again, the Bible supplies us with an enlightening story— that of Samson recorded in Judges 13–16. Although Samson is listed among the great heroes of faith in Hebrews 11, the extreme violence of his personality causes great difficulty for many contemporary Christians. But we do not intend to focus our thinking on that aspect of the Samson story. Rather, we want to focus on Samson's method of finding the will of God for his life.

When Samson chose to marry the woman at Timnath, a Philistine, he made that decision not simply on the basis of his own desire but also on the basis of divine guidance. "The Lord was at work in this" (Judg. 14:4, NEB). Such guidance ran counter to the time-honored commandment given to Israel concerning idolatrous people: "Do not intermarry with them, giving your daughters to their sons or taking their daughters for your sons. For that would turn away your children from following me, to serve other gods" (Deut. 7:3–4). It was for this reason that Samson's father and mother pleaded with Samson to choose an Israelite woman rather than a Philistine (Judg. 14:3). But we are plainly told that it really was "of the Lord" that Samson should marry the woman at Timnath.

The problem that later developed was that Samson, having had such special guidance once, apparently *presumed* upon it and continued on his own to choose women from among the Gentiles: first the harlot at Gaza, and finally, Delilah. And as is commonly known, through his self-betrayal to Delilah, he found himself blinded and enslaved by the Philistines.

Samson's experience pinpoints the danger inherent in recognizing that in special circumstances the voice of God may direct us to transcend time-honored moral guidelines or laws. We may grow overconfident or arrogant, assuming that our own impulses are, without exception, sent from God. As in Samson's case, the result may be personal disaster.

Samson's story did not end, however, while he was "eyeless in Gaza at the mill with slaves."[8] The lords of the Philistines decided to celebrate their victory over Samson by holding a huge sacrifice and festival for their god Dagon. When they were in the full flush of rejoicing, they decided to crown the occasion by making the Hebrew champion of God, Samson, perform circus feats of strength. So they sent to the prison house to bring Samson to the festival for their entertainment.

Imagine the conflict in the imprisoned Samson's mind when he received their summons! His hair had begun to grow as soon as Delilah had shaved it from him, and with the return of his hair had come a gradual return of strength. It pained Samson enough that his strength, once dedicated to God, was serving God's enemies. But now they were ordering him to do the very thing that had landed him in such deadly trouble in the first place. He was being ordered by the Philistines to break a time-honored and frequently repeated commandment to Israel: "You shall not bow down to their gods, or worship them, or follow their practices, but

you shall utterly demolish them and break their pillars in pieces"
(Exod. 23:24). There could be no question that providing entertainment at a festival dedicated to Dagon constituted service to a
false god and therefore violated this commandment. Samson had
already experienced the consequences of violating general commandments on the basis of private impulse. Private impulse, he
had learned, could not be trusted as an unerring guide. And if he
was strong enough to perform feats of strength, he was strong
enough to put up effective resistance to appearing at the festival.
So Samson knew that his appearance would have to be his own responsibility. Because he had the strength to resist, he could not excuse himself by saying that he had no choice and was forced to
obey orders.

Samson chose to appear at that festival. And again, although he
violated one of the most fundamental Jewish commandments, his
choice was genuinely in keeping with the will of God. God
strengthened him to such a degree that he was able to tear down
the supporting pillars of the festival hall, killing more than three
thousand of the Philistine elite. He lost his own life in the process,
but he died with the satisfaction of knowing that he was once
again the champion of the Sovereign God.

▼ SECURE CERTAINTIES VERSUS COMPASSIONATE INVOLVEMENT

Samson's story is not a comfortable one for persons who are
concerned with ethical and moral certainty. It demonstrates the
tremendous risk we run of substituting our subjective impulses for
the voice of God prompting us from within. But it also demonstrates the equally great risk of playing it safe and sticking to the
tried-and-true rules of the past. Judging by Samson's story and
also by Huckleberry Finn's and the apostle Peter's, it appears that
nothing can safely relieve us of the complexities of moral responsibility concerning any social issue, including the issue of homosexuality.

Those who urge us to self-indulgently "do our own thing" commit the error of forgetting our responsibility to community, to society, to God-within-us-and-within-others-and-above-us-all. Those
who urge us to preserve our private reputations by separating our-

selves from human concerns make the same mistake, but for opposite reasons. In the context of Christ's story of the man fallen
among thieves (Luke 10:30–37), the "do your own thing" crowd
would encourage us to leave the poor man groaning in the ditch
because we don't feel like helping him and because there are more
pleasant ways to spend our time. The champions of private reputation would encourage us to leave the poor man groaning in the
ditch in order to avoid the appearance of evil and the guilt by association that might accrue to us if our robes were full of dirt and
blood. Either way, the result is the same: human pain is ignored
and unalleviated.

The issue of homosexuality involves an enormous amount of
human suffering. It is far easier to clutch our righteous robes
around us and pass by on the far side of the road than to become
actively involved in attempting to alleviate some of that suffering.
Many church groups have in the past chosen the path of self-right-
eous noninvolvement. So have many individuals. But Christ feels
the human pain of those whose needs we have rejected, and
Christ's voice reminds us from eternity, "Truly I tell you, just as
you did not do it to one of the least of these, you did not do it to
me" (Matt. 25:45).

▼ WHAT ABOUT THE "WEAKER BRETHREN"?

Those who advocate the preservation of a stainless reputation
as the top priority of the moral life frequently support their position by referring to Paul's remarks about the "weaker brethren."
The term is used in the King James version of the Bible to describe
Christians whose rudimentary understanding of the Christian
faith results in strict scruples that keep them from certain activities
that are regarded as matters of Christian liberty by more seasoned
Christians. Those who appeal to "weaker brethren" arguments
point out the teaching in 1 Cor. 8:7–13 that Christians must avoid
even the appearance of evil in order to keep from leading astray
the underdeveloped or unenlightened consciences of immature
Christians. The apostle Paul does indeed make a very persuasive
case in that passage, reminding us that we are Christians in community, not simply individualists doing our own thing. Eating

food consecrated to idols means nothing whatsoever to his own conscience, Paul says, because he knows that "'no idol in the world really exists' and that 'there is no God but one'" (1 Cor. 8:4). The mature Christian knows, continues Paul, that "there is one God . . . from whom are all things and for whom we exist, and one Lord, Jesus Christ, through whom are all things and through whom we exist" (1 Cor. 8:6). But the catch is that not every Christian is mature enough to be aware that idols are nothing and that God is all in all. And precisely because of our oneness in God from whom we all came and for whom we all exist, we cannot be callous toward those who are less enlightened than we are.

The principle is sterling. It cannot be ignored by any Christian worthy of the name. But there is a problem—and, as usual, the problem is one of implementation. Some Christians have gone so far in their interpretation of this passage that they have lived their whole lives trying never to do anything of which any other Christian might disapprove. One leader of a denomination where the "weaker brothers and sisters" looked down on theater attendance, for instance, sat in his London hotel room rather than accept a free ticket to a Shakespearean play at the famous theater in Stratford-upon-Avon. His reason: someone back in the United States might somehow find out that he had attended a theater, and might not be able to distinguish a play of Shakespeare's from the worst trash offered in the worst theater elsewhere. Such desperate concern for the opinions of others can bring about deafness to God's voice whenever that voice begins to direct toward new or unfamiliar practices within the Body of Christ. (The same gentleman who avoided theater for the sake of the "weaker brethren" frowned on missionary use of new technological devices like television and cassette tapes—yet he did not frown on the use of an airplane to get to the mission field!)

Had Peter thought only about the "weaker brethren" among the circumcised Christians, he would never have gone to a Gentile house to preach the gospel. What he actually did do suggests an alternative to Paul's conclusion in 1 Cor. 8:13. Instead of giving up whatever might be offensive to the "weaker brother or sister," it is possible to follow Peter's example and educate that person's conscience so that he or she will no longer be so easily offended.

That's what Peter did when he explained his reasons to the circumcised Christians in Jerusalem.

The unbreakable principle in 1 Corinthians 8 is that mature Christians cannot live their lives in blithe unconcern for those who may be less enlightened than they. But there are two ways of handling the unenlightened conscience: either defer to it by avoiding what would offend it so as not to lead the other person into spiritual difficulties; or *enlighten and educate* it, as Peter did. Obviously, what Huck Finn needed was for someone to come along and enlighten his conscience so that he could rejoice in what he was doing for his friend. But of course *Huckleberry Finn* is a comic novel, not a Christian treatise, and such enlightenment was outside the scope of Mark Twain's purpose.

▼ SOME APOSTOLIC EXAMPLES

To reassure ourselves that we are not violating the spirit of Paul's ideas in 1 Corinthians by suggesting a program of education for weaker consciences, we can look at several instances of Paul's own behavior toward those with less refined consciences than his own. As is implied in the story of Peter's vision and his subsequent preaching to the Gentiles, there was much turmoil in the early church concerning whether Gentiles who converted to Christianity should have to undergo circumcision and live according to Jewish customs. In Acts 16:3, we see Paul following his own principle of deferring to those of weaker conscience. He wanted to take Timothy with him on a missionary journey, but it was widely known that Timothy's father was Greek; so Paul "circumcised him out of consideration for the Jews who lived in those parts" (NEB). But on another occasion, Paul refused to circumcise another Gentile, Titus. And when Peter stopped socializing with his Gentile friends "because he was afraid of the advocates of circumcision," Paul accused him of hypocrisy and "opposed him to his face, because he was clearly in the wrong." Paul stood up in public and educated Peter's conscience (and, by extension, the consciences of those who were pressuring Peter for Jewish Christians to withdraw from uncircumcised Christians): "If you, a Jew born and bred, live like a Gentile, and not like a Jew, how can you insist that Gentiles must live like Jews?" (Gal. 2:3–14, NEB). We know from this example that educating "weaker brothers and sisters" is perfectly in order.

The sixteenth-century theologian John Calvin introduced another helpful distinction concerning Christian liberty and the "weaker brethren." He explains that we must distinguish between offense given and offense taken. If, for instance, certain Christians were to be rash or wanton in their public behavior (perhaps making thoughtless jokes about abortion or condom distribution in schools or some other topic on which some Christians are very sensitive), that would be offense given. But if certain Christians were to speak carefully and responsibly on a sensitive topic, and other people became offended because of malevolence or prejudice within themselves, that would be offense taken. According to Calvin's reasoning, those offended or hurt in the first case are the true "weaker brothers and sisters." Those offended in the second case are simply "ill-tempered and Pharisaical." Calvin suggests that although we are responsible for restraining ourselves in deference to the ignorance and lack of skill of the true "weaker brethren," we are not responsible for pleasing "the austerity of Pharisees."[9]

From the apostle Paul's behavior and from Calvin's distinction between offense given and offense taken, it is clear that even in reference to the "weaker brother or sister," there is no simplistic knee-jerk reaction that will relieve us from the responsibility of moral choice. Whether we like it or not, we are responsible for evaluating each situation in order to discover the most appropriate response. Through attention to the dialogue between the Bible and the best insights of human research, we stand the best chance of enlightening our own consciences so that we will have light to share with others. The quiet inner prompting of God's Spirit will take care of the rest.

The Homosexual as Samaritan

WHEN JESUS answered the question, Who is my neighbor? by telling the story of a Samaritan's compassion for a wounded traveler, many listeners were disturbed that Jesus should choose a Samaritan as the model of loving behavior. Taught to despise their neighbors in Samaria, they must have found it difficult even to *imagine* such an entity as a "good" Samaritan. Samaritans were considered people with whom one should not associate (John 4:9), people who deserved to have the fire of heaven called down upon their heads (Luke 9:54).

Don't you know that, Jesus? Couldn't you have used a better example to teach neighborly love? One of *us* could have been the model! Don't you realize, Jesus, that people prefer heroes like themselves—people they can identify with? Why did you ever speak so positively about somebody from a discreditable alien group? We'd like to keep them at as great a distance from us as possible! Such thoughts as these must have passed through the minds of many that day as Jesus tried to teach them what love is all about.

And it is likely that similar thoughts passed through the minds of some people nearly twenty centuries later with the discovery of the homosexual orientation of the Vietnam veteran whose quick thinking was credited with saving the life of President Gerald Ford in a 1975 San Francisco assassination attempt. A *homosexual*

hero? Impossible. (A good *Samaritan?* Preposterous!) Somehow it
didn't seem to fit the stereotypes, the familiar preconceptions
about "those people"—people we keep at a distance, people who
aren't "like us." It was rumored in the news media that government officials were somewhat embarrassed by the ex-marine's gay
activist associations. His heroic efforts were not rewarded with
quite the same fanfare that might otherwise have been the case.
(At the same time, reports indicated that the involuntary disclosure of his sexual orientation by the media caused great grief both
for him and his relatives and cost him his relationship with his
mother.)[1]

▼ MEMBERS OF A DIFFERENT SPECIES?

Most heterosexual people tend to think of homosexual people
as so different and so far removed from the norm that it's almost
as though they belong to a different species or come from another
planet. Or, if human at all, homosexuals are considered so strange
or depraved or sick or sinful that "respectable" people will be sure
to keep them at a distance. The Canadian social commentator
Pierre Berton has pointed his finger at Christians in this regard,
charging that although churches have a tendency to "cast out the
outcasts" in general, the homosexual person is more outcast than
anyone else. Berton writes, "A very good case can be made out
that the homosexual is the modern equivalent of the leper."[2] In
one midwestern city, for instance, some pastors and church members were so adamant in their fight against a city ordinance that
would guarantee homosexual civil rights that they purchased radio
time and newspaper space and collected thousands of signatures
on a petition urging Christians to "shun the Sodomites and their
supporters" and to purge the community of homosexual activity.
"I felt like somebody hated me, and I couldn't understand it," commented one lesbian woman. "I felt this must be a group of people
who knew nothing of homosexuals as people. They didn't want us
to be able to get jobs or have clothing or food or housing. That
must be hating."[3]

An attitude of disdain for homosexual people without consideration for them as human beings is, as we have already observed,

often evident in various Christian sermons and writings. Although we are frequently reminded that we should "love the sinner while hating the sin," the disgust and disdain felt usually obliterate this distinction. For instance, one radio preacher punctuated an entire sermon with some variation on the refrains "Sodom and Gomorrah were turned to ashes as an example of how God feels about being gay" and "God dropped an atomic bomb on Sodom and Gomorrah because they were perverts!" The minister emphasized that the ashes of these cities are the best witness concerning "how God feels about the gay community," and he reminded listeners that the Old Testament taught that homosexuals "ought to die by capital punishment." At the sermon's conclusion, the radio preacher's evangelistic appeal centered around the idea that Lot was a righteous man who chose God's way of escape rather than remaining in Sodom to die with such people. Listeners were admonished to think about how terrible it would be to be forced to associate with homosexuals in eternal hell. He urged his audience to accept God's gift of salvation—or else "go to hell with these people you can't stand."[4] By such sermonizing, this minister was doing something even more serious than increasing homophobia. He was increasing the insecurity and fearfulness of every man, woman, and child who was listening by reinforcing their sense of isolation and alienation from their deepest selves, where the human family is able to recognize its oneness.

A similar view of disdain for homosexual people comes through in statements by Tim and Beverly LaHaye, writers and lecturers in what has come to be known as the Religious Right. They have admonished Christians to keep in mind that "homosexuality seems to be the ultimate sin in the Bible that causes God to give men up." They have also written that "the children of Israel were commanded by God to stone to death homosexuals (Lev. 20:13), a severe treatment intended to keep them from becoming contagious."[5]

"These people you can't stand." These people whose sexual orientation is viewed as "contagious." If we accept such attitudes, it might seem that the world would be better off if it were rid of all homosexual people. Obviously, this was the belief of the Nazis, who sent tens of thousands of people suspected of homosexuality to concentration camps in Germany and Austria, where, like the Jews, they were made to wear an identifying emblem, in their case a lavender/pink triangle for men, a black triangle for women. Large numbers of homosexual people perished, some through torture, some through assignment to dangerous tasks, and some through Nazi "medical" experiments designed to find a "cure" for homosexuality.[6]

▼ HOMOSEXUAL CONTRIBUTIONS TO CIVILIZATION

We have expressed our opinion and our hope that most Christians today would not call for such drastic measures as internment and purges. The question, Would the world be better off without homosexuals? needs to be replaced with this one: Am I able to recognize the positive good that has come to the world through homosexual people?

Among the male "good Samaritans"—that is, homosexual men who have made important contributions to the good of humankind—we may number Erasmus (1466–1536), the greatest scholar of his age, a brilliant author, and the editor of an excellent Greek New Testament; Leonardo da Vinci (1452–1519), the great painter who gave us *The Last Supper,* with its moving portrait of Christ; Christopher Marlowe (1564–1593), the Elizabethan dramatist and poet best known for his great play *Dr. Faustus;* James I of England (1566–1625), who commissioned the translation of the Bible that bears his name; Sir Francis Bacon (1561–1626), an outstanding jurist, essayist, and scientific theorist; Thomas Gray (1716–1771), the author of the beloved "Elegy Written in a Country Churchyard"; Frederick the Great (1712–1786), who welcomed the persecuted Huguenots to Prussia and abolished press censorship and torture; Pyotr Ilich Tchaikovsky (1840–1893), the great composer whose *Pathétique* Symphony was dedicated to the nephew he loved; Vaslav Nijinsky (1890–1950), perhaps the greatest dancer who ever lived; Marcel Proust (1871–1922), the renowned author of *The Remembrance of Things Past*; A. E. Housman (1859–1936), the greatest Latin scholar of his day and an outstanding poet; T. E. Lawrence (1888–1935), best known as

Lawrence of Arabia; Walt Whitman (1819–1892), one of America's greatest poets; and Henry James (1843–1916), one of America's most outstanding novelists.[7]

Among the female "good Samaritans"—lesbian women who have made important contributions to humankind—are physician James Miranda Barry (1795–1865), the first British woman doctor, who successfully served the British government all her life disguised as a man; Willa Cather (1876–1947), an outstanding American novelist; Mary II (1662–1694), Queen of England, Scotland, and Ireland—the Mary of "William and Mary" (apparently William was also homosexual); Virginia Woolf (1882–1941), a distinguished novelist and the lover of Vita Sackville-West; Charlotte Cushman (1816–1876), a memorable actress, famous for her sensitive portrayals of Hamlet, Romeo, and other male leads; Rosa Bonheur (1822–1899), the great artist who gave us *The Horse Fair* and other magnificent paintings; Margaret Fuller (1810–1850), the brilliant transcendentalist author, editor, and poet; Mary Emma Woolley (d. 1947), president of Mount Holyoke College from 1900 to 1937 and one of the first American woman diplomats; Edith Hamilton (1867–1963), an outstanding classical scholar and the author of *The Greek Way, The Prophets of Israel,* and other books, who lived with Doris Reid for forty-seven years; and Carey Thomas (1857–1935), for many years the dean and president of Bryn Mawr College. (Profoundly spiritual and strongly influenced by her aunt Hannah Whittall Smith, Thomas lived with and loved Mary Garrett from 1904 until Garrett's death in 1915).[8]

We have prepared these lists for the sake of those who have previously been unaware that many homosexual people live responsible, productive lives and make impressive contributions to society. But now we would like to issue a warning. Sometimes, in an effort to create sympathy for gay men and lesbian women, some people attempt to enlist the names of famous persons without any definite evidence concerning their sexual orientation. For instance, the great American poet Emily Dickinson is sometimes identified as lesbian[9]—and it is hard to believe that the author of a poem like "Wild Nights" was without sexual experience:

Wild Nights—Wild Nights!
Were I with thee
Wild Nights should be
our luxury!

Futile the winds
To a heart in port—
Done with the compass—
Done with the chart!

Rowing in Eden—
Ah, the Sea!
Might I but moor—tonight—
In thee![10]

In Dickinson's correct Amherst society, such "wild nights" would have been well-nigh impossible to achieve with a man, without detection; but occasional overnights with a woman friend would not have aroused suspicion. There can be little doubt that Sue Gilbert (who later married Dickinson's brother) was the love of Dickinson's life, but evidence concerning Emily Dickinson's behavior is impossible to come by. So we will make no further claim beyond noticing that much of her imagery seems homoerotic, even transsexual.[11]

Shakespeare has frequently been labeled homosexual because he wrote sonnets to a "fair young man" whom he addressed as "the master-mistress of my passion." In the twentieth century, such an address might constitute reasonable proof, but not so during the Renaissance, when idealized friendship was frequently expressed in passionate terminology. The fact is that Shakespeare was enthusiastically heterosexual. He casually corroborated that fact when he wrote in the very same "master-mistress" sonnet that to Shakespeare's great regret, Nature had endowed his friend with "one thing to my purpose nothing." Punning as he loved to do, Shakespeare sighed that since Nature had "prick'd thee out for women's pleasure," Shakespeare could share the man's friendship but not his body. In other words, Shakespeare wished that a creature so beautiful had been made a woman, but he was not interested in a homosexual liaison.[12]

Because of her poem "Goblin Market," which exalts the love between sisters, Christina Rossetti has been claimed by lesbians as one of their own. Certainly she was a marvelous Christian poet who deserves a much wider audience in our time. But our research indicates that although she never married—she twice broke engagements, apparently for religious reasons—she may have rejected human love simply out of an all-consuming love for Christ. On the other hand, we do find it puzzling that so many of her love poems refer to the beloved as "she" rather than "he." At least one poem, "Annie," seems impossible to interpret apart from a lesbian context. When William Michael Rossetti prepared a collection of his sister's poetical works, he excluded her poems concerning Sappho and also excluded several love poems, including a "Song" beginning "I have loved you for long long years, Ellen."[13] In the absence of biographical corroboration, however, and because we do not think single people should be hounded about their sexuality, we will not make a definite assertion about Christina Rossetti.

To cite another example: some Christians have been trying to create sympathy for homosexuals by claiming that the great English poet John Milton, the author of *Paradise Lost,* was homosexual. They can be forgiven for their error, since a highly respected scholarly journal once carried an article asserting that Milton's youthful relationship with Charles Diodati was a homosexual one.[14] But the evidence seems shaky, at best. Furthermore, language loses its meaning if we assert homosexual orientation in a man who remarried after his first wife's death, remarried again after the death of his second wife, and lived with his third wife until his own death, and who showed every evidence in his poetic imagery of being attracted to female rather than to male beauty. It is true that Milton did not marry until he was thirty-four; and unlike other Cambridge undergraduates, he did not frequent prostitutes. But we would not want to fall into the stylish trap of assuming that either celibacy or close friendship automatically spells homosexuality.

In our list of homosexual men and women who have made outstanding contributions to society, we have included only those for whom strong evidence points toward lifelong homosexual orientation and/or activity. Our list is of course very sketchy and far from complete. Since most homosexual women and men married because of social pressure, many persons on our list were married; but letters, diaries, or other contemporary evidence indicates that the marriages were more or less in name only. We have omitted people who apparently were capable of *enjoying* sexual relations with both sexes, such as Madame de Staël and Lord Byron, because they were truly bisexuals, not homosexuals.

▼ HOMOSEXUAL CHRISTIANS

Some of the people on our list were obviously homosexual *Christians,* not just in a nominal sense, but in a very heartfelt one. The term *homosexual Christian* is a jarring one to those who claim it is impossible to be both Christian and homosexual. It can easily strike certain people in the way that the thought of a "good Samaritan" struck Christ's first-century audience. However, as Margaret Evening has written:

> It is often the case that the homosexual is a very loving and
> lovable person with a tremendous contribution to make. . . .
> If people wish to regard homosexuality as a freak of nature,
> and even if it is not the condition ordained by God when He
> said that it was not good for man to dwell alone, then we
> can only rejoice that God is, as ever, bringing good out of
> evil. We can thus accept with humility the special gifts medi-
> ated to us through those who are His homosexual children,
> our brothers and sisters whom we cannot and would not
> disown.[15]

Since some Christians may want to counter Margaret Evening's statement by asserting that God *has* no homosexual children, it may help to look more closely at several concrete examples.

First, let us take an imaginary journey to Rome and stand before Michelangelo's sculpture *The Pietà* to gaze in awe upon the Savior, his crucified body lying across the lap of his mourning mother. Touched by the beauty of the scene and the sensitivity of the artist, we are moved to worship God. Later, we marvel at Michelangelo's skill in bringing the biblical drama to life through the frescoes on the ceiling of the Sistine Chapel. At still another time, we are impressed by some of his sonnets of devotion to the Lord.

Then, in the midst of our journey, we find that Michelangelo was homosexual. What are we going to do with this information? Deny the authenticity of his Christianity? Deny the value of his contributions? Would we want to say that the world and the church would be better off had it been rid of *him?*

Such questions may continue to haunt us as we move on to other examples. We are impressed and challenged with the depth and insight of W. H. Auden's Christmas oratorio, *For the Time Being,* and we wonder how—if all the negative stereotypes are true—a self-identified homosexual could have put into the mouth of Simeon such words as these concerning the Incarnation:

> But here and now the word which is implicit in the Begin-
> ning and in the End is immediately explicit, and that which
> hitherto we could only passively fear as the incomprehensi-
> ble I AM, henceforth we may actively love with comprehen-
> sion that THOU ART. Wherefore, having seen Him, not in
> some prophetic vision of what might be, but with the eyes
> of our own weakness as to what actually is, we are bold to
> say that we have seen our salvation. . . . And because of His
> visitation, we may no longer desire God as if He were lack-
> ing; our redemption is no longer a question of pursuit but
> of surrender to Him who is always and everywhere present.
> Therefore at every moment we pray that, following Him,
> we may depart from our anxiety into His peace.[16]

Or we might think of the nineteenth-century priest Gerard Manley Hopkins. In a 1977 article in *Christianity Today,* Matthew Brown rightly assessed Hopkins as "a writer of 'exploding poetry' par excellence," who "did it to the glory of God." Brown called special attention to Hopkins's "The Wreck of the *Deutschland,*" correctly describing it as a poem "universally Christian," because "Christ is at its center and holds this chaotic world together, pro-viding hope."[17] Yet shortly before this conservative Christian pe-riodical printed Brown's article extolling the Christian life and message of Gerard Manley Hopkins, the *Hopkins Quarterly* had published an article on the homosexual orientation of Hopkins and its influence on his works.[18] Hopkins, a Jesuit, lived celibate, but his poetic images make clear that the beauty that tempted him was *male* beauty.

We would enjoy providing multitudes of examples of the poetic gift and the total Christian devotion of Gerard Manley Hopkins. But space limits us to just one example, and we have chosen the delightful poem entitled "Pied Beauty":

> Glory be to God for dappled things—
> For skies of couple-colour as a brinded cow;
> For rose-moles all in stipple upon trout that swim;
> Fresh-firecoal chestnut-falls; finches' wings;
> Landscape plotted and pierced—fold, fallow, and plough;
> And áll trádes, their gear and tackle and trim.
> All things counter, original, spare, strange;
> Whatever is fickle, freckled (who knows how?)
> With swift, slow, sweet, sour; adazzle, dim;
> He fathers-forth whose beauty is past change:
> Praise him.[19]

It should be obvious that Christianity would be impoverished by the loss of the contributions of Hopkins and Auden and Michelangelo—to mention only a few examples of homosexual Christians of the past.

▼ CONTEMPORARY HOMOSEXUAL PEOPLE IN THE CHURCH

Among our contemporaries, a number of lesbian and gay Christians have revealed their orientation publicly, while still trying to maintain their ties to the church and the Christian community as a whole. The Episcopal priest Ellen Marie Barrett has said that her relationship with her lesbian partner, a long-term and faithful one, is "what feeds the strength and compassion I bring to the ministry." Barrett commented privately to one of us that Christians seem willing enough to ordain into the ministry homosexual people who feel guilty, furtive, and ashamed of their homosexuality, but seem outraged at the prospect of ordaining those who fully accept their sexual orientation and live faithfully with their chosen partner. This has the effect, she said, of proclaiming that *neurotic* homosexuals make acceptable priests while *healthy* homosexuals do not. At Barrett's ordination ceremony, a priest named James Wattley said that her lesbianism rendered her ordination a "travesty and a scandal." But Bishop Paul Moore testified that Barrett was "highly qualified intellectually, morally, and spiritually to be a priest." Bishop Moore also noted that "many persons of homosexual tendencies are presently in the ordained ministry."[20]

Moore's observation in the 1970s was confirmed by many others. Indeed, the Archbishop of Canterbury startled the world with his public acknowledgment that a large number of homosexual people were to be found within the ranks of the Anglican clergy.[21] And in June 1972, a query in the *Baptist Times* asking for letters from Baptist ministers who are homosexual elicited a considerable response and revealed a profound need for contact with others of like mind.[22] It was becoming increasingly clear that homosexual people served in both clergy and lay capacities. Even so, as one observer has noted, "until the 1980s, most denominations handled the issue of gays in their congregations like a hot—but small—potato."[23] By the 1990s, the "potato" remained hot, but it was no longer small. There could be no denying that large numbers of homosexual men and women were to be found throughout organized religion.

One example is James D. Anderson, whose efforts on behalf of the church have included service as an elder in the Broadway Presbyterian Church of New York City, working as secretary of the presbytery's Committee on Mission, and serving on the Board of National Missions in Alaska. Elder Anderson now serves as communications secretary and newsletter editor for the Presbyterians for Lesbian and Gay Concerns. Says Anderson, who has lived in a covenantal gay relationship for over twenty-one years, "If the church is to fully do its job of reconciliation among people and between the human family and God, it must support gay people by helping them to accept their sexuality and to express it lovingly. Needless to say, the church cannot do this without full acceptance of gay people themselves as healthy and complete persons."[24]

Another such person must remain anonymous because she is in a fundamentalist environment from which she would be ostracized if her homosexuality became public knowledge. She formerly studied with Dr. Francis Schaeffer in L'Abri, Switzerland, her goal being a life of active Christian service. In an unpublished autobiographical sketch, she describes several years of her life in which she was associated with the lesbian feminist community, considered at the time to be an extremely radical segment of the larger women's movement.

> I went back and forth between the Christian community
> and the lesbian feminist community. I was never totally
> satisfied with either. The Christian community offered
> truth and some sense of direction. The lesbian feminist
> community offered support, love, and a deep caring for
> one another. . . . There is a deeper sense of community
> in the [secular] women's movement than there is in the
> church. . . . The Christian community seems to be more
> concerned with a respectable appearance than acting with
> compassion and responsibility. The church is not reaching
> out in love, it is erecting steel barricades.

Reading this, it is hard not to remember the priest and the Levite who kept their robes clean and their images respectable by walking on the far side of the road to avoid the man who had fallen among thieves!

Another homosexual Christian, Joyce Liechenstein, worked for many years in the Presbyterian Church in various capacities, including serving as director of Christian education. She comments: "I came to understand that God is a loving God; it makes no sense that God would reject me simply for being homosexual. The scriptures make it clear in Genesis that God's creation has unlimited variety, and we are part of that variety. God looked at his creation and saw that it was good."[25]

John McNeill, a Jesuit priest until the Vatican forced his expulsion from the order, has publicly affirmed his homosexual orientation. His ground-breaking book, *The Church and the Homosexual*, first published in 1976, remains a model of restraint, scholarship, and Christlike spirit. It is vital reading for anybody who wants to understand homosexual people from their own point of view and in a spiritual context.[26] So is *Taking a Chance on God*, McNeill's more recent book of "liberating theology for gays, lesbians, and their lovers, families, and friends."[27] In it, McNeill quotes the eminent Catholic theologian Edward Schillebeeckx concerning the political ramifications of experiencing Jesus as Lord:

> Christians may not be party to a political system in which structural or personal compulsion sacrifices the weaker, and injustice becomes a permanent state. Christianity is concerned with the progressive liberation of all humanity. In the light of the gospel, Christians must be partisans and advocates of the poor, those without rights, those who have no representatives anywhere.[28]

McNeill's placing of the homosexual Christian liberation movement into the context of seeking justice for all people is typical of the holistic emphasis of the movement in the nineties. Holism is evidenced every June at the annual Gay, Lesbian, and Christian event at Kirkridge, a retreat center in Bangor, Pennsylvania. Here, since 1976, Catholic and Protestant activists like John McNeill, Mary E. Hunt, John Boswell, William Smith, Virginia Mollenkott, John Fortunato, and Elizabeth Carl have been leading an always-packed house in the joyous experience of being God's church on the mountaintop. The holistic emphasis is present also in such homosexual Christian newspapers and journals as *Second Stone, Open Hands, Christus Omnibus*, and *CLOUTreach* (the quarterly newsletter of an organization called Christian Lesbians Out Together).[29]

Chris Glaser, who studied for the Presbyterian ministry but was refused ordination because he publicly acknowledged his homosexuality while a student at Yale Divinity School, continues to serve his church devotedly through leadership in Presbyterians for Lesbian and Gay Concerns. At the same time, he serves the entire Christian community by publishing collections of prayers, and by sharing his vision in such books as *Uncommon Calling: A Gay Man's Struggle to Serve the Church*[30] and *Come Home! Reclaiming Spirituality and Community as Gay Men and Lesbians*.[31]

In 1987 a United Methodist minister named Rose Mary Denman was tried by the church because, having discovered her lesbianism subsequent to ordination, and being in a covenanted union with a woman, Winnie Weir, she was no longer willing to hide her sexual identity. Denman has told her story in her 1990 book, *Let My People In: A Lesbian Minister Tells of Her Struggles to Live Openly and Maintain Her Ministry*.[32] Virginia Mollenkott, who was present at the Denman trial in an attempt to testify, witnessed the sorry spectacle of a United Methodist bishop's telling newspaper, radio, and TV reporters that he had no knowledge of the quality of Denman's ministry—in spite of the fact that he had privately sent a letter to Denman in which he had written, "We have shared together in many deep concerns, and you have been helpful to me and our family personally."[33] His letter praised precisely the pastoral skills that he now claimed publicly to know nothing about.

At the trial, Denman's defense counsel, the Reverend Dr. John McDougal, spoke of the Catch-22 the church has created by saying that marriage provides the only acceptable context for sexual activity of Christian ministers, yet on the other hand denying marriage to gay and lesbian people: "In my . . . career, so far, I have blessed motorcycles, packs of dogs, a time capsule, mobile homes . . . but were I to bless the union of two [gay or lesbian] Christian people, it would be an offense, chargeable before a trial such as this. . . . And so what sounds like a wonderful, fine moral standard is actually a trap for gay and lesbian people."[34]

Karen Thompson, a university professor, and Sharon Kowalski, a physical-education teacher, became lovers only after a profound friendship in which they studied the Bible together, Sharon seeking the spiritual strength she could see in Karen, who was a very active member of an evangelical Presbyterian church.[35] In 1983, just before their fourth anniversary, Sharon's car was struck by a drunk driver. The accident left her unable to move or communicate in traditional ways. Karen actively did all she could to help Sharon regain her basic life skills. But when the court awarded sole guardianship to Sharon's father, he placed her in a nursing home and lost no time in denying Karen all visitation rights because he disapproved of lesbianism. Thus began years of exhausting and expensive legal battles, during which Sharon's health care and best interests were neglected because her partner and all their friends had no access to her and were unable to provide her with needed emotional support. Nor could Karen continue the special physical therapy she had begun with her (including helping Sharon use a typewriter in order to communicate). It was critical that such therapy be provided within the first three years after the accident so that ground would not be lost and the degree of independence possible for Sharon could be maximized.

Yet not until December 1991 did the Minnesota Court of Appeals grant Karen guardianship over her partner, Sharon—a victory not only for lesbian and gay rights but for the rights of disabled people to make their own choices concerning who will care for them. (The Kowalski case highlights the need for gay and lesbian partners to hold durable power of attorney, and also points up the need for all unmarried people to make legal designation of the person they choose to authorize to make medical decisions in case they should become incapacitated.)

But where was the church during Karen Thompson's protracted legal battle on behalf of Sharon Kowalski? At first the associate pastor sought out Karen to offer his support and to assure Karen that, when it is properly interpreted, the Bible does not condemn same-sex love like hers for Sharon. But when a homophobic church member put pressure on that pastor, he told Karen never again to use his name in defense against attacks on her love for Sharon. Exhausted, feeling betrayed, and unable to face yet another emotional crisis, Karen felt she had no choice but to leave the church. Alas, nobody reached out to her. But letters and money did begin to arrive from people who had heard of her struggle through the newsletter of Presbyterians for Lesbian and Gay Concerns.[36] By now it should be clear why many churchgoing homosexuals keep their sexual identity deeply closeted.

Perhaps we can allow Malcolm Boyd—an Episcopal priest who, in August 1976, made public his homosexuality—to speak on behalf of all the homosexual Christians who must keep their sexual identity secret:

They stand inside your church, Lord, and know a wholeness
that can benefit it. Long ago they learned that they must regard the lilies of the field, putting their trust in you.

Pressured to hide their identities and gifts, they have
served you with an unyielding, fierce love inside the same
church that condemned them.

Taught that they must feel self-loathing, nevertheless they
learned integrity and dignity, and how to look into your
face and laugh with grateful joy, Lord.

Victims of a long and continuing torture, they asserted a
stubborn faith in the justice of your kingdom.

Negativism was drummed into them as thoroughly as if
they were sheet metal. They learned what it is to be hated.
Yet, despite real rejection, they insisted on attesting to the
fullness and beauty of all human creation, including theirs,
in your image.

They are alive and well and standing inside your church.
Bless them, Lord, to your service.[37]

Like it or not, we Christians can no longer avoid dealing, indi-
vidually and collectively, with the issue of homosexuality. No
doubt many of us may feel it distressing and unsettling to be told
about the many positive contributions homosexual people have
made and are making to the ongoing life of civilization and the
church. We may not be used to thinking of gay men and lesbian
women in such a positive light. No doubt some of us feel just the
way Jesus' first-century audience felt when he gave them a model
of loving-kindness in the shape of a despised Samaritan!

4

▼ ▼ ▼ ▼ **▼** ▼ ▼ ▼ ▼ ▼ ▼

Stigma and Stereotyping

BECAUSE CONSIDERING homosexuality in the abstract is quite different from confronting it personally, we have supplied some personal statements from homosexual Christians. Sometimes, though, the issue may unexpectedly come even closer to home, as it did in the following cases.

1. A minister's daughter came home to announce that she had been involved in a lesbian relationship that had just broken up, leaving her crushed. Her parents were shocked. The father was unable to face either her or the issue. The mother has been trying to be supportive.

2. A promising student at a church-related college sought psychological and religious counseling concerning his homosexuality. College officials told him they had no choice but to expel him.

3. A man and a woman met at a conservative Christian college. Drawn together by their mutual devotion to Christ and by their active participation together in Christian service, they looked forward to a life of continued ministry as husband and wife. The woman was impressed by the respect this man showed her: he didn't treat her like a sex object by pressing for physical involvement, as so many other men had seemed to do. After a few years of marriage and the birth of a child, however, his confession felt

like a knife passing through her entire being: he had been sexually involved with a number of men, beginning before their marriage, he said, and now felt so convinced of his homosexuality that he could no longer function as a husband. He said he loved his wife and child but needed to be released from the marriage.

4. He was an elder in a large, influential church and was known for his spiritual leadership. One day, after listening to a sermon in which brief mention was made of homosexuality as a sin, he could stand it no longer. He stood up and announced that he had been living in a committed homosexual union for four years; indeed, on that very day he and his partner were celebrating their fourth anniversary. He said he yearned for the day when the church could share their joy and welcome them as a couple. The congregation was stunned. Did this call for church discipline? Should he be relieved of his office? Or should he be given the loving Christian acceptance he had requested?

5. It is Sunday morning in another city. Two men singing in the choir are partners in a committed gay relationship. The pastor is convinced they should retain the privilege of serving Christ through music, but he does not feel free to grant their request for a public marriage ceremony. Some persons in the congregation accept these men as a couple; others object. Some minister-friends of the pastor tell him he is wrong to be so accepting of the relationship and should be preaching on its sinfulness.

6. The call came late at night. It was Greg, Marc's roommate from seminary days, now living in a distant state. "I've got to talk with you and Kathy," he said. "I can't go on any longer without telling somebody." Suddenly he blurted out, "Marc, you're my friend; I can trust you. Even so, I'm not sure how you'll take this. I—well, I might just as well say it. *I'm a homosexual.* No, wait. Don't say anything. Just let me finish. I've suspected it for a long time. Remember all my unloading on you about the problems I kept having with women? Well, now I know why. Yes, I *am* sure about it, and it probably sounds crazy but I feel sort of at peace about it—just admitting it to myself and you. Yet there are many

problems, too—like whether to continue thinking about the ministry. Maybe it's out of the question now."

7. They were devoted parents who felt as though their whole world was shattered when their only son, whose professional accomplishments had made them so proud, announced that he was gay and living with the man he loved. They wrote him long letters and sent him books and articles hoping he would see the error of his way and repent of his sin. They wanted their son to spend Christmas with them but told him to come alone—that his partner would not be welcome. And so the son chose not to come. Several years passed. Then one year, as Christmas approached, they realized they had not been showing Christ's love to their son and his partner. They bought gifts for both men and invited them for the holidays. Everyone had a wonderful time. They found their son's partner to be a delightful young man and a sincere Christian. The following year, a terrible tragedy occurred. Their son was killed in an automobile accident. The parents and the son's partner reached out their arms and hearts to one another and grieved together as a family. Now the partner has become like another son to the couple.

These are just a few contemporary examples from real life. Only the names and a few minor details have been changed; in fact, some of the stories are composites of several separate but amazingly similar experiences. That is why concerned Christians cannot continue to dodge the issue. We need to think it through.

▼ WHY CHRISTIANS FIND THIS TOPIC SO DIFFICULT

Over the years, Christians have tended to avoid thinking and talking about homosexuality in any depth for at least three reasons. There are, first, *social and psychological reasons,* including societal attitudes, anxieties about our own feelings or about what others might think of us if we show any interest in the subject, and more general fears about the entire topic. There are also *religious considerations,* including the matter of what the Bible does and doesn't say on the topic, questions of theology, and church traditions. Finally, there are *informational reasons;* that is, we may possess either inadequate knowledge or actual misinformation on the topic. In this and the following two chapters, we will consider these reasons for avoidance one at a time.

▼ SOCIAL AND PSYCHOLOGICAL STIGMATIZATION

In one of the less publicized sections of Jimmy Carter's controversial 1976 *Playboy* interview, the presidential candidate told the interviewers that "the issue of homosexuality always makes me nervous." He suggested that at least two factors might contribute to his sense of uneasiness: his lack of personal knowledge on the subject, and his Baptist faith. The interviewers wondered if his uneasiness was related to the political sensitivity of the issue. "No," replied Carter, "it's more complicated than that. It's political, it's moral, and it's strange territory for me."[1]

The area of homosexuality continues to be "strange territory" to many Christians, and the reasons are indeed complicated. Sociologist Paul Rock points out that "our ability to test information about objects in the social world diminishes as these objects become distant from us." Although we might question the validity of something we are told about a close acquaintance, "we have little opportunity to dispute contentions about those who are socially distant."[2] Furthermore, as other sociologists note, the more we keep people socially removed from us, the easier it is to think of them not as individuals but as "anonymous abstractions."[3] We can then think in terms of general characteristics that we apply to whole categories of people. The uniqueness of the individual is swallowed up in the impersonal and distorted stereotype.

The human tendency to create such anonymous abstractions explains why lesbian and gay people have often lodged justified complaints about the failure of many Christian leaders to recognize the shared humanity of all people regardless of sexual orientation. In the words of one gay activist: "There's such a tendency among Christians to lump all homosexuals together as a group of faceless, nameless 'perverts' and to make statements not rooted in fact. They don't see us as *people*."[4]

Because the social distance between most people and the homosexual community is signally wide, it becomes easy to make sweeping generalizations: "Male homosexuals are effeminate." "All lesbians are tough and masculine, and they hate men." "There's no such thing as a happy homosexual." "It's dangerous to let homosexuals work with children." "Lesbian mothers should not be permitted to have custody of their children." "Homosexuals are irresponsible workers." "Homosexuals are neurotic and immature." "All homosexuals ever think about is sex, sex, sex!" "Homosexuals are unable to sustain a relationship; they are by nature promiscuous." "Homosexuals know nothing about love, only lust." "Homosexuals are out to convert everybody to their life-style. Give them their so-called rights and they'll destroy the family and bring about the downfall of our nation."

It must be readily admitted that some gay activist leaders may at times seem to be their own worst enemies. Males wearing dresses and wigs or marching nearly nude and carrying whips and chains do nothing to calm the nervousness of the heterosexual majority. Wearing T-shirts that advertise obscenities, shouting rude remarks at hearings concerning gay civil-rights ordinances or AIDS research, or interrupting Mass at Roman Catholic cathedrals may indeed reinforce stereotypes and widen the gap between homosexuals and heterosexuals. Yet, as novelist Flannery O'Connor once said in a different context, when you are addressing people who cannot or will not hear, you *shout*. These acts are sometimes desperate attempts to capture attention for a worthwhile cause. It is also true that, in some cases, professional anti-gay agitators infiltrate protests in order to make the gay community appear less responsible and mature than it actually is.

It is also important to remember that the flamboyant attire and behavior of certain demonstrators is by no means representative of all homosexual people. Many lesbian and gay activists have attempted to bridge the gap between the heterosexual majority and the homosexual minority by tactics very different from those just mentioned. These tactics have often received less publicity than some of the more sensational expressions of anger and frustration. There have been quiet candlelight marches and vigils to mark incidents of gay-bashing or to commemorate people who have died of

AIDS. There have been organized efforts on college campuses to increase understanding, counter prejudice, and bring homosexual people and heterosexual people together in dialogue.[5] For example, when an organization for gay and lesbian academics at the University of Iowa sponsored a reception to begin the 1992–93 academic year, over a hundred people, including the college president, dropped in. Shortly before this event, the university's school of law had hired as faculty members an openly lesbian couple whose teaching skills, other scholarly endeavors, and exemplary lives (like those of other homosexual women and men excelling in various professions) serve to overturn the stereotypes many people hold about homosexual people.[6] In several states, gay and lesbian organizations have signed up for "Adopt-a-Highway" programs in which volunteer groups agree to pick up roadside litter along designated stretches of highway. Official signs announcing the group's adoption of the particular stretch of highway are put up by state departments of transportation, letting motorists know that they have a particular lesbian and gay coalition to thank for the clean roadside. As one spokesperson for a group engaged in such efforts expressed it, "We do take pride in ourselves and the community, and we want to be a visible part of the community we live in."[7]

Aware of the many injustices in the world, homosexual women and men have also worked for political and social change on the local, state, and national levels, using all the tools that are customarily used in such efforts—lobbying, petitioning, meeting with various officials, demonstrating before legislative bodies, providing accurate information to the public, and running for office. And it should be noted that, in addition to those whose energies are invested in effecting change in public policies, there are hundreds of thousands of homosexual people who choose not to participate in such highly visible activism, preferring instead to make their contributions to society in other ways. They ask only to be left alone in their quiet, private, apolitical lives.

Given the social stigma attached to homosexuality, however, and the dehumanized typifications of homosexual people, the social distance maintained, and the widespread support for certain generalizations ("Everybody knows that's what they're like"), it is

not surprising that most of us tend simply to accept the generalizations without question. For some reason, it doesn't occur to us
that the stereotypes, and the assumptions to which they give rise,
might be highly inaccurate. Nor does it occur to us that by repeat-
ing them we might be bearing false witness against our neighbor
and that we therefore owe it to ourselves to give some serious
study to the subject. And that may take a considerable amount of
courage. After all, we worry, what might it suggest about us if we
showed too much interest in obtaining more information? And
what might others think? Curiosity and a desire to learn all we can
about a topic are usually considered commendable, but somehow
we don't feel that way about this particular subject. It's set apart
and we fear it. Furthermore, there are the librarians and bookstore
clerks to think about. We feel timid and awkward about asking
them for books about homosexuality.

▼ SOME HELPFUL BOOKS

However, books are one of the most helpful ways of bridging
the social distance between the general population and the homosexual community—not only books that provide information
from a scientific standpoint, but also books that can help us understand the human element. Recent decades have witnessed the
appearance of several "classic" novels that especially underscore
this human element. *Patience and Sarah,* inspired by a true experience, is an engrossing love story about two nineteenth-century
women who spend a lifetime together in a lesbian union.[8] Another
absorbing novel in a more contemporary setting, *Consenting
Adult,* was written by Laura Z. Hobson (who years earlier had
taken on another controversial subject, anti-Semitism, in her criti-
cally acclaimed *Gentlemen's Agreement*).[9] *Consenting Adult* is the
story of a young man's confession of his homosexuality and the
struggle his parents go through in trying to come to terms with it.
Hobson herself was the mother of a homosexual son, and her
novel honestly and sensitively portrays the feelings of both the fic-
tional son and the parents.[10]

A third novel that helps readers enter into the lives of homosexual people movingly portrays the emergence of lesbian love between

two seventeen-year-olds and how the realization of their sexual orientation affects their lives and those of others. Entitled *Annie on My Mind,* the book was honored by the American Library Association as one of the Best of the Best Books for Young Adults, 1970–82.[11]

A nonfiction book specifically intended to acquaint heterosexual readers with the joys, fears, struggles, achievements, and everyday lives of homosexuals as "real people" much like themselves is *Familiar Faces, Hidden Lives* by the late Howard Brown, M.D. During John Lindsay's mayoral administration, Dr. Brown served as New York City's first health-services administrator. After a heart attack in 1972, at the age of forty-eight, this highly respected physician decided that, in what little time he had left, he would work "to free future generations of homosexuals from the agony of secrecy and the constant need to hide."[12] He announced publicly that he was a homosexual and began work on the book, which was published after his death. We also remind readers of the true stories of Christian gay men and lesbian women recounted in chapter 3.

From another viewpoint comes a book published by a conservative Christian press. Entitled *The Returns of Love* (a title adapted from a poem by the homosexual American writer Walt Whitman[13]), it consists of a series of letters describing the inner turmoil of a young man endeavoring to overcome his homosexual impulses and live a celibate life, which he believes is the only way to please Christ. His agony is evident as he speaks of his loneliness and bares his heart in candor:

> Peter, can you understand it? This is the impossibility of the situation—what I may have I don't want, and what I do want I may not have. I want a friend, but more than a friend; I want a wife. But I don't want a woman.[14]

Reading books such as these may be disturbing, and there may be much in them with which we disagree or find troublesome as Christians. But if we really want to understand and reach out in love to the homosexual person, loving him or her in the same unconditional way that God has loved us, these books can be a great step toward personal acquaintance with the human aspect of the question.

▼ WHAT IF A FRIEND OR RELATIVE IS GAY?

Those who wish to maintain the social gap between themselves and homosexuals (avoiding even the indirect acquaintanceship provided by books) find it especially difficult when confronted with homosexuality in a friend or relative. After all, we have been taught to regard homosexuality as deviancy—a violation of acceptable standards. Again to quote Paul Rock: "Instead of feeling that the moral and social gulf that separates us from deviancy is diminished when we make such a discovery, we frequently impose this gulf between ourselves and our redefined acquaintance."[15] We then reconstruct our image of that individual, replacing it with a stereotype so that we think we now know what the person is really like and "really was all along." And we tend to forget everything about the person that commanded our love and respect before the revelation.

The result is often ostracism. "We daily affirm our moralities and value structures by placing ourselves apart from others whom we regard as deviant," writes sociologist N. K. Denzin.[16] Such rejection then drives the shunned person even further from us, producing a cycle in which she or he is likely to stay away from us in order to avoid the pain of further rejection. We, in turn, then fail to reach out to the person we have hurt, because we view our rejection of that person as a statement of our superior moral values. At such times, it is easy to forget Scripture's harsh words to those who say, "Keep to yourself, do not come near me, for I am too holy for you" (Isa. 65:5).

The social distance thus maintained again facilitates thinking of the person in abstract, depersonalized terms ("he/she is a homosexual, you know; no need to bother with further information"). "I have a God-given right to say openly that I don't like homosexuals," said one letter writer to a newspaper. "I would not hire them nor do I wish to dine with them or go to church with them."[17] Psychiatrist Armand Nicholi II has called attention to the harm that can be done when such attitudes are found within churches: "The homosexual often encounters an insensitive ear and a closed door within the Christian community. Such a reaction intensifies the anguish, the pervasive loneliness, and utter despondency that haunt him and not infrequently lead to his suicide."[18]

Barbara Johnson, who ministers to evangelical and fundamentalist parents who have homosexual sons and daughters, frequently receives emergency phone calls and heartrending letters telling of both actual suicides and suicide attempts. In the short period between Christmas 1991 and the end of February 1992, she received fifteen letters telling of a loved one's suicide.[19] One woman asked how to reach out to a family in her church whose thirty-three-year-old son had recently hanged himself. She said that close friends "almost choke" when they mention that he was homosexual. His family hardly ever mentioned him to anyone, she said, adding that she herself had known the family for several years and had not known that they even had this son. "In our church," the letter writer explained, "the word homosexual is rarely used as though it does not exist in Christian families." Another woman wrote about her son's attempted suicide and said that, even though she and her husband were church members active as Sunday-school teachers, officers, and so on, very few friends from the church had contacted them after the attempt, not even their pastor.

Disclosure of an acquaintance's homosexuality doesn't always lead to rejection, of course. Instead of pushing the person as far away from us as the subject has always been, we may find ourselves bringing the subject as close to us as the person has been. When that happens, we examine the topic with new eyes. That's what happened to the mother in the novel *Consenting Adult*. Her love for her son led her, over a period of many years, to study and rethink homosexuality until finally she could accept him as he was. It is also what happened to a Christian mother who, while at first devastated over the revelation of her daughter's sexual orientation, was able later to say, "We have had to break down our 'walls of prejudice.' Homosexuals (lesbians) now have a 'face'—our daughter's."[20] Sociologist Erving Goffman has pointed out that passing through such a "heart-changing personal experience" is a common occurrence "before taking the standpoint of those with a particular stigma."[21]

▼ COGNITIVE DISSONANCE

Still, it is not likely to be easy. As we mentioned in chapter 2, the apostle Peter found it extremely difficult to accept the vision sent to teach him that God was ready to welcome the Gentiles. "No, Lord, no," he cried, feeling inner turmoil at the very idea of going against the principles of right and wrong as he had heard them all his life. Studies indicate that similar reasons lie behind the often-traumatic reaction parents have to the disclosure of a son's or daughter's homosexuality. First, the parents' misconceptions and lack of information about homosexuality result in their applying negative notions about the topic to their child's identity. "This creates for the parent a subjective perception that the child is suddenly a stranger," writes psychologist Erik Strommen.[22] Second, the parents (and often others in the family) no longer know where the homosexual person fits into the family. They tend to believe that the newly revealed identity negates the former roles he or she filled as a family member, and they feel unsure about how this new knowledge will affect their relationships with that person.

The psychological concept of *cognitive dissonance* is useful here.[23] In music, when two notes don't "fit together" to produce harmony, the resulting sound is called dissonance. Similarly, a clash occurs in our minds and emotions when two pieces of knowledge are hard to reconcile. For instance: (1) we learn that an acquaintance of ours, whom we consider a very "good" person, is homosexual; (2) we have been taught to think of homosexual people as "bad." These two facts clash, causing inner dissonance, which we may seek to resolve in some way or another. Perhaps we'll begin by changing our attitudes toward our friend (for example, cooling off the friendship). Perhaps we'll begin changing our ideas about homosexuality (like the mother in *Consenting Adult*).

Perhaps we'll try to change our friend (recommending, for example, psychiatric treatment or prayer for deliverance from homosexual desires). Or perhaps we'll try to quiet the inner tension by ignoring or denying what we know.

This last course was the one chosen by one of Michelangelo's contemporary admirers, Ascanio Condivi. Because he equated homosexuality with lewdness and shameful lust and could think of it in no other terms, Condivi found it impossible to believe that Michelangelo could be homosexual. He argued that only "the most honest of words" issued from Michelangelo's mouth and "no evil thoughts were born in him." How could a man be pure minded and profoundly Christian and yet be erotically drawn toward the same sex? Condivi could not deny Michelangelo's deeply Christian spirit, with which he had had personal contact. Therefore, it was the homosexuality that had to be denied, and this Condivi tried desperately to do.[24]

Sometimes the cognitive dissonance is felt in the homosexual person's own being. Dr. Howard Brown tells of the discovery of his own homosexual predilection at age eighteen:

> I had never met a homosexual man, or at least been aware
> that I had met one. But I knew what every other Midwest-
> erner knew in 1942: Homos were mysterious, evil people, to
> be avoided at all costs. And I was one. Often, when I thought
> of this, I would break out in a cold sweat. I couldn't be.
> I shoved the idea aside.[25]

Persons endeavoring to live as homosexual Christians find the problem particularly acute. Novelist Christopher Isherwood lived for years in a homosexual relationship with W. H. Auden. During the Modern Language Association meetings in New York in 1974, Isherwood told an audience that Auden suffered greatly all his life from the fact that he could not work out what he felt to be a satisfactory harmony between his Christianity and his homosexuality. Perhaps this is one reason Auden thought and wrote so much about guilt and the nature of sin.[26] Yet by the grace of God and despite the personal pain caused by many Christians, Auden was able to leave us such excellent poetry as this:

We belong to our kind,
Are judged as we judge . . .
Finite in fact yet refusing to be real,
Wanting our own way, unwilling to say Yes
To the Self-So which is the same at all times,
That Always-Opposite which is the whole subject
Of our not knowing, yet from no necessity
Condescended to exist and to suffer death
And, scorned on a scaffold, ensconced in His life
The human household. In our anguish we struggle
To elude Him, to lie to Him, yet His love observes
His appalling promise; His predilection
As we wander and weep is with us to the end.[27]

Auden's struggles bring us to what is without a doubt the single most important factor in the difficulties most Christians have with the topic of homosexuality: the Bible as it has traditionally been interpreted for centuries.

5

▼ ▼ ▼ ▼ ▼ ▼ ▼ ▼ ▼ ▼

What Does the Bible Say?

THE BIBLE does not have a great deal to say about homosexuality, and in the original languages the term itself is never used. Whenever sexual acts between persons of the same gender are mentioned in Scripture, the acts are always committed in a very negative context—in the context of, for example, adultery, promiscuity, violence, or idolatrous worship. The fact that this negative context is often ignored may explain why Christians have traditionally shown harsh, unloving, often cruel attitudes toward homosexual people.

The destruction of Sodom and Gomorrah, described in Genesis 19, is a case in point. As we noted earlier, this story has often been interpreted as showing God's abhorrence of homosexuality. Two angels in the form of men were sent to Sodom and were invited into the home of Lot, described in the New Testament as "a good man, shocked by the dissolute habits of the lawless society in which he lived" (2 Pet. 2:7–8, NEB). Lot showed the angels warm hospitality, as was the custom, but was stunned by the rude and violent behavior exhibited by his neighbors toward the guests. All the men of Sodom, both young and old, everyone down "to the last man," surrounded Lot's house and demanded to see his visitors. "Bring them out to us, so that we may know them," they shouted (Gen. 19:5). When Lot begged the men to leave his guests alone and take his two virgin daughters instead, the men angrily refused and stormed the door, only to be struck blind by the angels.

Lot and his family were warned to flee. According to Gen. 18:32, in response to Abraham's pleading *before* the angels had set out to examine conditions in Sodom, God had promised to spare the city if even as few as ten righteous persons could be found. But it was clear there weren't even ten. The sordid mob scene around Lot's house confirmed God's prior decision to destroy Sodom and showed that such judgment was fully justified.

It should be noted that some Bible scholars do not believe that the intent of the men of Sodom was sexual. They have pointed out that the Hebrew word translated "know" may here simply indicate the townspeople's desire to find out who these strangers were and examine their credentials (since Lot, considered an outsider himself according to Gen. 19:9, had apparently failed to get the permission of the town elders to entertain these strangers).[1] Whether the intent was sexual or not, however, the strangers were treated abominably and the sin of inhospitality was committed— one more instance of the city's wickedness that called forth God's righteous judgment.

There is no denying that, in the minds of most people, the incident has long been associated with homosexuality. Indeed, the word *sodomy* is derived from certain interpretations of this biblical passage. Laws against sodomy are notorious in their ambiguity. In England, the term is understood exclusively to refer to anal penetration by a penis—whether the parties involved are two men or a man and a woman.[2] American laws vary in their definitions, although most sodomy statutes forbid both oral-genital and anal-genital sexual contact, even if such contact occurs privately between two persons of the opposite sex, and even if they are married to each other.[3] Because of the prevalent notion that Sodom is somehow tied up with homosexuality and the belief that God's judgment on homosexual people and practices is epitomized in the destruction of the city, we need to consider the incident in detail.

▼ SODOMIZING AS HUMILIATION BY VIOLENCE

First, we must take note that the men of Sodom could not possibly have been exclusively homosexual in orientation in the sense
that the term is used today. Quite likely, they were primarily heterosexual, out for novelty, and seeking to humiliate the strangers.
For the city to have any continuing population at all, the group
must have included a substantial number of husbands and fathers,
since every last one of the city's males is said to have taken part in
this attempted gang rape! Sodom certainly was not a "gay community" in the sense described by the radio preacher mentioned
earlier in this book (p. 29).

Rape is not a sexual act so much as it is an act of violence. In
heterosexual rape, a man is showing his utter disdain for women.
The emphasis is on displaying force and demonstrating power over
someone who is perceived as weak and vulnerable.[4] Thus, among
some ancient peoples it was not unusual to flaunt one's triumph
over conquered enemies by treating them with the greatest possible
contempt. One way such contempt was demonstrated was by forcing captive men to "take the part of a woman" by being subjected
to anal penetration. Biblical scholar George R. Edwards applies
the term "phallic aggression" to this brutal practice.[5]

A similar pattern shows up in modern prisons. "We're going to
take your manhood" or "We're gonna make a girl out of you" are
common assertions in such sexual assaults. Evidence of this kind
of language showed up repeatedly in a 1968 study of the Philadelphia prison system. Researcher Alan J. Davis reports that "conquest and degradation" were the sexual aggressor's primary goals,
along with the goal of retaining membership in a sexually militant
group (thereby assuring protection in a conquer-or-be-conquered
situation and enjoying a sense of prestige, power, and peer approval). Gang rape is related to an emphasis on dominance
through the subjugation of others. Davis is careful to emphasize
that such incidents are totally different from incidents of *consensual* homosexuality—same-sex contact for the sake of sexual release or for the expression of love. Men who assaulted fellow
prisoners did not consider themselves homosexual, nor did they
even believe they had participated in homosexual acts. This denial

appears to be based on what Davis calls their "startlingly primitive view of sexual relationships, one that defines as male whichever partner is aggressive and as homosexual whichever partner is passive."[6]

If the men of Sodom had in mind a rationale for gang rape similar to what occurs in modern prisons, it is understandable that they did not accept Lot's offer of his virgin daughters. Women already had a low place in the society of Sodom. (The fact that Lot offered his daughters to the mob provides ample evidence of this.) The men were not looking for a sexual experience but rather wanted a chance to express their violent impulses and their desires to humiliate Lot's guests. Humiliating actual women would not have provided the sense of conquest they had anticipated in degrading the male strangers by "dragging them down" to the level of women.

In one parallel biblical case, however, a group of men *did* accept a female substitute, who was thrown out to them like a piece of meat to a pack of wolves (Judges 19). They sexually abused her all night long, and she died as a result, whereupon her husband cut her body up into twelve pieces and sent her parts to all the tribes of Israel. The story of rape and murder is hardly rendered any more palatable by the fact that the host, in whose home the traveling couple was staying, offered his virgin daughter in order to spare his male guest, and the guest handed over his own concubine wife to spare himself.[7] In the ancient Middle East, writes Roman Catholic scholar John McKenzie, "that the woman should be sacrificed to save the man was simply taken for granted."[8] No wonder that a man would dread the disgrace and punishment of being treated "like a woman," which is what male gang rape signified.

All of this is by way of saying that rather than concentrating on homosexuality, the Sodom story seems to be focusing on two specific evils: (1) violent gang rape, and (2) inhospitality to strangers. Surely, none of us would be prepared to say that if the men of Sodom had accepted the offer of Lot's daughters and abused them as did the men in chapter 19 of Judges, God would have withheld judgment because *heterosexual* acts had taken place! Violence—forcing sexual activity upon another—is the real point of this story. To put it another way: even if the angels had taken on the form of women for their earthly visitation, the desire of the men of Sodom to rape them would have been every bit as evil in the sight of God. And the rain of fire and brimstone would have been every bit as sure.

▼ HOW THE BIBLE INTERPRETS THE SIN OF SODOM

Concerning the inhospitality described in the Sodom story, John McNeill reminds Christians of the irony in the fact that although no group has been treated *less* hospitably by the church than the homosexual community, the biblical passage used to justify such treatment has been the very one that condemns uncharitable attitudes toward strangers. "In the name of a mistaken understanding of the crime of Sodom and Gomorrah, the true crime of Sodom and Gomorrah has been and continues to be repeated every day," argues McNeill.[9] To underscore the sin of inhospitality in Sodom, he reminds us of Jesus' words to his disciples in Luke 10:10–13: "Whenever you enter a town and they do not welcome you . . . I tell you, on that day it will be more tolerable for Sodom than for that town."

This brings us to a second factor to keep in mind while examining the story of Sodom: the Bible is its own best commentary on many issues. And the Bible provides explanations for Sodom's destruction that have nothing at all to do with homosexuality. In the first chapter of Isaiah, the nation of Judah is rebuked through a comparison with Sodom and Gomorrah. The specific sins mentioned are greed, rebellion against God, empty religious ritual without true devotion to God, failure to plead the cause of orphans and widows, failure to pursue justice, and failure to champion the oppressed. There is no mention of homosexuality.

In Ezek. 16:49–50 we read: "This was the guilt of your sister Sodom: she and her daughters had pride, excess of food, and prosperous ease, but did not aid the poor and needy. They were haughty, and did abominable things before me; therefore, I removed them when I saw it." Although it has been speculated that the "abominable things" mentioned are to be understood as references to homosexual acts, here again there is no specific mention of homosexuality. The specific charge is lack of concern for the poor.

Things that are considered detestable, repugnant, and disgusting in God's sight (in other words, abominable things) are not necessarily related in all cases to ancient Israel's sexual purity codes, as modern readers tend to assume. The book of Proverbs, for example, applies the label *abomination* to such behavior as dishonesty in business dealings (11:1, 20:23), speaking lies (12:22), and displaying arrogance (16:5). Prov. 6:16–19 speaks of "six things that the Lord hates, seven that are an abomination." The seven named are "haughty eyes, a lying tongue, hands that shed innocent blood, a heart that devises wicked plans, feet that hurry to run to evil, a lying witness who testifies falsely, and one who sows discord in a family." In Jer. 23:9–15, Jeremiah expresses dismay over the behavior of the prophets of Jerusalem and says that God considers these leaders to have "become like Sodom" and the inhabitants of Jerusalem "like Gomorrah" (verse 14). Again, nothing is mentioned about homosexuality. Instead, the focus is on adultery, lying, and cooperating with evildoers rather than urging people to turn away from wickedness.

In the New Testament, as we have seen, Jesus refers to Sodom not in the context of sexual acts, but in the context of inhospitality (Luke 10:10). Jude 7, however, does refer to the sexual sins of Sodom by saying that the people "indulged in sexual immorality and pursued unnatural lust." The words "sexual immorality" have sometimes been translated "fornication," with an emphasis on nonmarital heterosexual intercourse, and we have already seen in the Jeremiah passage that adultery was one of the sins mentioned when Jerusalem was compared with Sodom. But apparently Jude also had in mind some sort of conduct that is translated "unnatural lust," which, as biblical scholar L. William Countryman points out, "is not a translation at all and quite misleading in this case." He suggests that the King James expression "strange flesh" is a more accurate rendering of the text.[10] The original Greek reads in literal translation, "going after alien or other or strange flesh." Thus, the "unnatural lust" reported in the New Revised Standard Version translation of Jude 7 could, in this context, and in view of the apocryphal texts to which Jude made allusion, refer to a desire for sexual contact between human and heavenly beings.[11] The Jerusalem Bible footnote for Jude 7 reads, "They lusted not after human beings, but after the strangers who were angels" (Gen. 19:1–11). New Testament scholar George Edwards points out the logic in this interpretation in view of the verse that precedes Jude 7 and that refers to an incident in Gen. 6:1–4. There, the desire of disobedient angels for sexual contact with women of earth was a major factor in God's decision to bring judgment upon the world by means of the flood of Noah's time. Thus, says Edwards, "it is consistent with the context [of Jude 7] to say that Sodom's offense was likewise the violation of appointed status, although here it is mortals lusting after angels, the reverse of verse 6."[12]

Reference to the sins of Sodom and Gomorrah is also made in the second chapter of 2 Peter with its rebuke of false prophets and the people they lead astray. However, as New Testament scholar Robin Scroggs points out, "the author of 2 Peter, by speaking of adulterous lust (2:14), seems to give the whole attack a heterosexual direction." What Scroggs finds remarkable is that "whatever the sexual misconduct really was, both authors [the author of Jude and the author of 2 Peter] associate it with the agape meals of the Christian communities, as if the people attacked had turned these presumably religious meals into a secular banquet in which sexual encounters were sought."[13] Again these passages provide no evidence that same-sex encounters were the reason for God's wrath and Sodom's destruction. Nor is there any biblical support for referring to "the homosexuals of Sodom," as Paul Enns does in a popular 1991 book of daily readings in systematic theology.[14]

If, then, we decide to follow the time-honored principles of allowing the Bible to provide its own commentary and of interpreting cloudy passages in the light of clearer ones, we are forced to admit that the Sodom story says nothing at all about the homosexual condition. The only real application to lesbian and gay people would have to be a general one: homosexual people, like everybody else, should show hospitality to strangers, should deal justly with the poor and vulnerable, and should not force their sexual attentions upon those unwilling to receive them.

▼ ISRAEL'S HOLINESS CODE: THE LEVITICUS PASSAGES

In the fertility religions of Israel's neighbors, both male and female cult prostitutes were employed. It has long been assumed that the male cult prostitutes participated in same-sex erotic activity as part of their cultures' religious rites, the idea having been given wide dissemination through the King James version's use of the word *sodomite* in several passages discussing idolatrous practices (Deut. 23:17; 1 Kings 14:24, 15:12, 22:46; and 2 Kings 23:7). Pointing out that this idea arises from a mistranslation of a word meaning simply "cult prostitute," historian John Boswell states that "there is no reason to assume that such prostitutes serviced persons of their own sex." He points out that no such meaning can be found in the Hebrew word itself, "and there is so little evidence about practices of the time that inferences from history are moot." According to Boswell, "almost no theologians invoked these passages as condemnations of homosexual behavior until after the mistranslation of the words into English."[15]

At the same time, while basically agreeing with Boswell's point about the scarcity of evidence on ritual prostitution practices, biblical scholar George Edwards provides a number of reasons for not ruling out entirely the *possibility* that homosexual acts may have been included among the functions performed by male cult prostitutes. He bases his arguments on the male-centered nature of worship under patriarchy and the fact that, in the fertility religions, "intercourse with the deity was supposed to effect, in a magical way, the divine cosmic mystery of fructification, even among crops and animals." It was the *symbolic* union with a deity that mattered, not the fact that actual reproductive capabilities were lacking in the physical act (which some have argued would make sexual contact between two males seem strangely out of place in fertility rites). "The cultic act transcended the biological union of the parties engaged in the ritual event," writes Edwards.[16]

What we need to keep in mind, however, is that the warnings and condemnations in these various passages are centered around the *idolatrous practices* of the fertility religions, not whether the ceremonial sexual activity involved men with men or men with women. The people who loved and served the God of Israel were strictly forbidden to have anything to do with idolatry and commanded never to serve, nor to let their children serve, as temple prostitutes (Deut. 23:17–18).

Two Old Testament passages make explicit reference to homosexual acts. Lev. 18:22 commands, "You shall not lie with a male as with a woman; it is an abomination." And Lev. 20:13 warns: "If a man lies with a male as with a woman, both of them have committed an abomination; they shall be put to death; their blood is upon them." These verses are part of Israel's holiness code, which includes commandments not to eat meat with blood in it, not to wear garments made of two kinds of yarn, not to plant fields with two kinds of seed, and not to be tattooed, as well as specific instructions on sexual matters. Forbidden activities in Leviticus 18 and 20 include bestiality (sexual contact with animals), incest (sexual contact with relatives—children, parents, siblings, in-laws, and so on), male homosexual acts, adultery, and sexual intercourse with a woman during her menstrual period.

The reasons given for these proscriptions involve several factors: (1) separation from other nations and their customs (Lev. 18:1–5); (2) avoidance of idolatry and any practices associated with it (Lev. 20:1–7); and (3) ceremonial uncleanness. The prohibition of male homosexual acts in these passages may be partially understood in the light of the first two reasons, the context of the proscriptions in both chapters suggesting the association of such practices with the idolatrous neighboring nations. But the third reason—ceremonial uncleanness—may also be relevant.

Ritual purity was a way of showing Israel's distinctiveness as a people set apart for God. Avoiding those things that were defined specifically for Israel as "unclean"—and following precise instructions for purification and restoration to the worshiping community if defilement did occur—were understood in this sense. These ritual separation requirements were grounded in *ceremonial* law (with its emphasis on set-apartness, recognizing a distinction between the sacred and the profane, and honoring wholeness and right order) rather than in *moral and ethical* law (which is concerned with norms and principles of right and wrong behavior in a more general sense).[17] Rules surrounding both semen and blood—

fluids so crucial to the ongoing of human life—were important parts of the ceremonial law. For example, chapter 15 of Leviticus indicates that avoidance of ceremonial uncleanness was behind the prohibition of sexual intercourse during a woman's menstruation; and similarly, an emission of semen rendered men ceremonially unclean. This was true even in the case of an involuntary nocturnal emission (see Deut. 23:10). Thus, one could argue that a kind of "double uncleanness" might have been presumed when two males participated together in a sexual act. Martin Samuel Cohen, a rabbi and professor, suggests that the literal reading of the Hebrew ("You shall not have intercourse with a man of the type one generally has with women") seems to indicate that it is specifically homosexual *anal intercourse* that was prohibited here because such an act was considered a misuse of semen under the ritual purity standards. "It is the special quality of the semen itself that generates the reason for the prohibition," writes Cohen.[18] He further suggests that the word translated "offspring" in Lev. 18:21 can mean semen rather than actual children. ("You shall not give any of your offspring to sacrifice them [literally, to pass them over] to Molech.") According to Cohen, "perhaps we have reference here to some obscure pagan ritual in which semen itself was offered to the god."[19] In conclusion, Cohen writes: "Any attempt to describe the Scriptural prohibition of male homosexual intercourse as an instance of Biblical outrage against men of homosexual orientation or as a divine condemnation of love between men is based, I think, on a faulty understanding of the nature of Biblical context, nuance, and style."[20]

We must not forget that the ritual purity requirements were imparted to a specific people at a specific time for a specific purpose. Consistency and fairness would seem to dictate that if Christians insist on invoking the Israelite holiness code against twentieth-century homosexual people, they should likewise invoke it against such common practices as eating rare steak, wearing mixed fabrics, and having marital intercourse during the menstrual period. (See our discussion on pp. 132–34.)

It should be noticed that homosexual contact between women is not mentioned in the holiness code, even though women were certainly not ignored in the other sexual behaviors mentioned therein. Punishment is meted out to women and men alike for participating in adultery, incest, bestiality, and intercourse during menstruation. However, according to the Talmud, the only concern over sexual acts between women centered around whether or not such acts constituted a loss of virginity. If they did, the women would be disqualified from possible marriage to a priest. "Women that practice lewdness with one another are unfit for the priesthood," instructed one rabbi. Evidently, there was some disagreement over this point among the rabbis. Some argued that, while heterosexual intercourse would conclusively indicate a loss of virginity and thus rule out all possibility of marriage to a priest, the matter was less clear-cut if a woman had sexually related to another woman. In such a case, they said, "the action is regarded as mere obscenity." But in general, it appears that women who engaged in homosexual acts were classified by Jewish religious leaders as just one category among many categories from whom priests (especially the high priest) were not permitted to choose a wife: widows, divorcées, nonvirginal never-married women, proselytes, and emancipated slaves (Lev. 21:7, 13–14).[21]

▼ THE UNIVERSALITY OF ROMANS 1

Homosexual acts between women are mentioned only once in the Bible—which brings us to a discussion of the first chapter of Romans. In that chapter the apostle Paul, writing to both Jews and Gentiles, shows how sin has alienated all people from God. The Gentile world had turned from God to idols; the Jews had turned to smug self-righteousness, hypocrisy, and harsh judgments on others, in spite of their boasting in the law (Rom. 2:23). In other words, *all* of us have sinned and fallen short of the glory of God (Rom. 3:23). The point, then, of chapters 1 and 2 of Romans is not to set apart some category of people as the worst possible kind of sinners.

The association between idolatry and homosexual practices that we saw in Old Testament denunciations is also evident in Romans. After giving a detailed description of a world that "exchanged the truth of God for a lie and worshiped and served created things rather than the Creator," Paul continues:

Because of this, God gave them over to shameful lusts.
Even their women exchanged natural relations for unnatural ones. In the same way the men also abandoned natural
relations with women and were inflamed with lust for one
another. Men committed indecent acts with other men, and
received in themselves the due penalty for their perversion.
(Rom. 1:26–27, NIV)

The key thoughts seem to be lust, "unnaturalness," and, in
verse 28, a desire to avoid acknowledgment of God. But although
the censure fits the idolatrous people with whom Paul was concerned here, it does not fit the case of a sincere homosexual Christian. Such a person loves Jesus Christ and wants above all to
acknowledge God in all of life, yet for some unknown reason feels
drawn to someone of the same sex—*not* because of lust, but because of sincere, heartfelt love. Is it fair to describe that person as
lustful or desirous of forgetting God's existence?

We might think, for example, of an illustration presented by
Norman Pittenger, a Cambridge theologian. Two men who had
lived together devotedly and faithfully for ten years, and who were
known to be devout Christians, told him about their love relationship. Pittenger remarked that they had become so totally one that it
seemed impossible to think of their ever separating. But what may
seem shocking and even blasphemous to some Christians is that
they went on to tell Pittenger that they found great joy in sexually
celebrating their love on a Saturday night and then kneeling side by
side the next morning to take Holy Communion together.[22] Because
of the training most of us have received, such a story probably sets
up waves of cognitive dissonance once again. Pittenger's comment
was that what these men told him was "both beautiful and right."

Possibly Pittenger's reasoning was similar to that of former Jesuit priest John McNeill, who has criticized the traditional Catholic attitude for unwittingly encouraging promiscuity:

A Catholic homosexual who confessed occasional promiscuity could receive absolution and be allowed to receive
communion in good conscience. If, however, that person
had entered into a genuine permanent love relationship, he

or she would be judged in a "state of sin," and unless the
person expressed a willingness to break off that relationship
he or she would be denied absolution.

McNeill goes on to say that the Church's attitude "tended to undermine the development of healthy interpersonal relationships
among homosexuals and gave the appearance that the Church disapproved more of the love between homosexuals than it did of
their sexual activity as such."[23]

▼ NATURAL VERSUS UNNATURAL IN ROMANS

The passage in Romans quoted earlier says nothing about homosexual *love*. The emphasis is entirely on sexual activity in a
context of lust and idolatry. But what about the third point in this
passage—doing that which, in the traditional King James wording, is "against nature"?

What seems "natural" in any culture is often simply a matter of
accepted social custom; and sometimes Paul spoke of nature in
that way. For example, in 1 Cor. 11:14–15, Paul raises a question:
"Does not nature itself teach you that if a man wears long hair, it
is degrading to him, but if a woman has long hair, it is her glory?"
Obviously, nature has not designed male heads in a way that pre-
vents men's hair from growing long! But social custom in various
times and places has dictated shorter hairstyles for men. When
such customs are challenged (as when women had their hair
"bobbed" in the 1920s or when men grew their hair longer in the
1960s and 1970s), there is often a public outcry. Later, as social
customs change, what was once vigorously opposed as a sign of
moral decay often becomes acceptable and commonplace.

In the Greek and Roman culture of the time in which Paul
wrote, however, homosexual conduct was to some extent an accepted social custom, and it no doubt seemed neither "against nature" nor "against custom" to some people. Thus, it would have
made little sense to speak of nature in the sense of generally
agreed-upon social convention, unless Paul was referring to a violation of Jewish custom and law.

This possibility should not be ruled out in the light of a decree from later Judaism. Then, according to Morton Scott Enslin, the forbidden activites of Leviticus comprised the third of three categories that were considered "cardinal sins."[24] Even in times of persecution, the requirements of the Torah were to be strictly observed, and such faithful observances were often difficult. As the Romans squelched various Jewish uprisings over the years, destroying the temple at Jerusalem and forcing upon the Jews imperial rule, the Jews were concerned about living as a special people who could clearly demonstrate their distinctiveness even in the most trying circumstances. They resented the altar to Jupiter that had been set up at the site of their destroyed temple. They resented Roman disregard for their religious customs and traditions. The emperor Hadrian, for example, considered circumcision inhumane and prohibited its practice. In his suppression of the rebellion that erupted under his rule, Hadrian's armies came close to exterminating the Jewish population of Judea.[25] During this time, a conference of rabbis met to form a policy on observance of Jewish law. These religious leaders decided that, because of the persecutions taking place and the possibility of execution, a Jew would be permitted to set aside temporarily any of the demands of the Torah except three: one, a Jew must not give recognition to heathenism; two, a Jew must not shed blood; and three, a Jew must not yield to the sexual practices outlined in Leviticus 18, including incest and one male's lying with another male "as with a woman." Even though the rabbis' threefold list was drawn up many years after Paul had written his letter to the Romans, it helps us understand in general "the abhorrence the Jew felt at such irregularities" and, says Enslin, "goes far toward explaining Paul's attitude."[26]

A number of scholars have pointed out that the material in Rom. 1:18–32 reflects a commonly accepted Hellenistic-Jewish listing of Gentile failings that would have been familiar to many of Paul's readers.[27] Chapters 13 and 14 of the apocryphal Wisdom of Solomon contain many similar ideas about Gentile wrongdoing, and Paul may have been drawing upon this description. Thus, as a rhetorical device in his letter to the church at Rome, Paul began his argument with this accepted catalog of Gentile vices, the intent being to win over the sympathies of Jewish Christians in his audience.[28] Having laid that groundwork, he next focused on the error of self-righteousness characteristic of all people who boast of their own goodness (feeling superior to the ceremonially "unclean" Gentiles, for example) while condemning others for actions and attitudes of which they themselves are guilty.

L. William Countryman suggests that homosexual practices were singled out in this passage as one striking illustration of the ritual impurity differentiating Gentiles from Jews. Such violations of the ceremonial purity code were therefore viewed with special revulsion by many in Paul's audience,[29] and abstaining from such conduct was something in which they could take pride. As we have already seen, in Israel's earlier history, the avoidance of such practices had been only one of the many ways Israel had shown that it was unlike surrounding nations—a way of demonstrating "an ideal of holiness as wholeness and distinctness." Thus, the prohibition against homosexual acts traditionally had served "the basic function of all purity law—that of setting a boundary between one group of people and another."[30]

But now there was a new challenge to be faced by the many Jews who were scattered throughout the Greek-speaking cities of the Roman Empire. Countryman writes:

> Jews of the Hellenistic Diaspora . . . found themselves living in the day-to-day context of a culture which accepted homosexual relationships, usually of a pederastic type [adult males having sexual relations with youths], as quite usual. From being a largely theoretical dimension of the purity code, disapproval of homosexual acts thus became a day-to-day defining characteristic of Jewish culture.

Countryman goes on to say that this "ethnic distinctiveness" was in one sense a problem, making the Jews "seem odd," but in another sense it provided an opportunity "because they could claim it as a point of ethical superiority in terms that at least some Gentiles would acknowledge as valid." Hellenistic Jewish authors therefore "made homosexual acts a perennial theme of their ethical discourse and borrowed motifs from those streams of Greek philosophical thought which had come to be critical of homosexual relations."[31]

One of these motifs was that of "nature"—the idea that homosexuality violated nature's law for males and females. Countryman points out that, according to Stoic teachings at that time, procreation was the sole purpose of sexual intercourse. "Since the Stoics often described what is morally right as 'according to nature,'" Countryman writes, "Jewish authors could appeal to 'nature,' however defined, as a universal criterion which would justify their culture's traditional antagonism toward homosexual acts."[32]

Thus, building upon teachings familiar to many in the church at Rome, Paul may have been referring in Rom. 1:26–27 to the "natural" complementary design of male and female bodies—specifically, their ability to fit together sexually in such a way as to produce children. Throughout church history, such so-called natural-law arguments have played an important role in shaping attitudes toward human sexuality. The question arises, Are certain acts in and of themselves unnatural? Many heterosexual couples include in their lovemaking a variety of sexual expressions in addition to coitus (penis in the vagina). Modern marriage manuals, for example, often recommend oral-genital sex. Margaret Evening hints at a certain inconsistency in the common view held by many Christians who feel that homosexual *acts* are sinful even though the *condition* of being homosexual is not sinful in itself. She points out that such individuals are disgusted and revolted by acts of tenderness and intimacy between homosexual people even though they themselves engage "in almost exactly the same love play" in their own heterosexual relationships.[33]

There are other problems with the "crimes against nature" view as it is commonly held in law and theology. Enslin assumes that in order to stress the degradation to which idolatry led, Paul is saying that the heathen had sunk to the point of exchanging the "normal intercourse that animals indulge in for that actually contrary to nature."[34] A prominent evangelist has reflected the same assumption by claiming that "homosexuality is a sin so rotten, so low, so dirty, that even cats and dogs don't practice it."[35] Yet modern research has shown that homosexual contact is not at all "unnatural" if we are going to use practices in the animal world as our criteria. Not only do many animals engage in same-sex relations (including mounting),[36] but among some primates the elements of same-sex affection and loyalty have also been observed.[37] Researchers have even discovered "lesbian" seagulls. In a study of seagull nesting habits, scientists were surprised to discover that some of the couples consisted of two females that had simply set up housekeeping together in the manner customary for male and female. They had eggs in their nests—but the eggs were usually infertile. However, there were a few cases of "bisexuality," in which a female seagull would get together with a male and produce fertile eggs, yet continue to nest with another female.[38]

▼ THE SOCIAL CONTEXT OF ROMANS 1

Just as we have kept in mind that the Sodom story must be studied in the context of the reprehensibleness of *inhospitality* and *gang rape,* we must keep in mind that the context in chapter 1 of Romans is that of *idolatry* and *lust.* No reference is made to persons whose own "nature" (or primary orientation) is homosexual, as that word is understood today by behavioral scientists. Speaking in terms his audience would understand, Paul is basing his comments on the commonplace assumption that all persons are inherently 100 percent heterosexual, without any room for variance. Thus, the lustful behavior being participated in by those described in Rom. 1:24–27 was viewed as an example of "foolish exchanges" being made. Exchanging the true God for a false one was akin to exchanging one's "natural" heterosexual inclination for something assumed to be unnatural for all persons. The portrayal is one of people so controlled by insatiable sexual appetites that no sexual adventure was considered out of bounds. Relationships of loving commitment were not even under discussion. The pattern was one of debauchery, promiscuity, and wantonness.

As various New Testament scholars have pointed out, many of the points emphasized in Romans 1 correspond to the thirteenth and fourteenth chapters of the Wisdom of Solomon.[39] In the strong denunciation of idolatry in that passage, it is asserted that sexual immorality of every kind springs from idolatry. "For the idea of making idols was the beginning of fornication" (Wisd. of Sol. 14:12). Those who "err about the knowledge of God" are said to "no longer keep either their lives or their marriages pure, but they either treacherously kill one another, or grieve one another by adultery" (Wisd. of Sol. 14:22, 24). The passage goes on to say that such people are characterized by, among other things, "confusion over what is good, forgetfulness of favors, defiling of souls, sexual perversion, disorder in marriages, adultery, and debauchery. For the worship of idols . . . is the beginning and cause and end of every evil" (Wisd. of Sol. 14:26–27).

The homosexual practices known to Paul usually involved adultery. In Greece, it was common for a man to have a wife and also a young male lover on the side. According to James Graham-Murray, such an arrangement was regarded "as a supplement to marriage recognized by the state." Male prostitution was a flourishing business on the Athens streets and in brothels, where slave boys serviced clients, angering the city's female prostitutes, who complained about the competition.[40]

David Halperin, a professor at the Massachusetts Institute of Technology, leaves no doubt about the nature of erotic experience in classical Athens: "sexual partners came in two kinds—not male and female but active and passive, dominant and submissive." An adult male citizen of Athens could choose legitimate sexual partners only among his inferiors in social and political status: women, boys, foreigners, or slaves. The sexual activity between them was not meant to express commonality and certainly not oneness, but rather served to "articulate the social difference between [the partners]."[41] No student of the Bible could expect its authors to express approval of that misuse of sex. The issue here is not heterosexuality or homosexuality, but an abusive understanding of society, sex, and power.

As for Roman society, Paul was by no means the only one to express alarm over the emphasis on sensuality and luxury. About two centuries before Paul wrote his letter to the Romans, the Greek historian Polybius had written a massive account of the changing world during the rise of the Roman Empire. He complained of the "widespread depravity" of young Romans:

Some of them had abandoned themselves to affairs with
boys, others to the favors of courtesans, and many others to
licentious music, to drinking, and to the extravagance that
accompanies these pursuits, since they had quickly acquired,
in the war with Perseus, the moral laxity of the Greeks with
regard to this kind of life.

It was a sad state of affairs, he said, when young men were willing
to pay "a talent for a young male lover or 300 drachmae for a jar
of smoked fish from the Black Sea," and he referred to Cato's assertion that "the degeneration of the state could be seen most
clearly when alluring boys were found commanding a higher price
than farms, and jars of fish were worth more than plowmen."[42]

New Testament scholar Victor Paul Furnish calls attention to
some useful insights into the conditions of Paul's day provided by
various first-century Greek and Roman social critics. According to
Furnish, these writers shared three basic beliefs about homosexual
behavior: (1) they had no conception of homosexuality as an orientation but considered same-sex physical acts to be simply another avenue of lust (comparable to lust for women) that was
open to any man; (2) they associated such physical acts with "insatiable lust and avarice" and considered them a "rich man's
sport"; and (3) they were convinced that the homosexual behavior
they saw around them during this period "necessarily involved
one person's exploitation of another." Furnish writes, "By Paul's
day the old Platonic ideal of the pure, disinterested love between a
man and a boy was coming to ruin on the hard realities of Roman
decadence."[43] (The emphasis was clearly on male homosexuality.
Of the scarcity of references to lesbianism during that time, Scroggs
writes, "Perhaps from the claimed pedestal of male beauty the
male society did not think female homosexuality important or interesting enough to worry about."[44])

▼ TWO PROBLEMATIC GREEK WORDS

In this atmosphere of lust, avarice, and exploitation, the harsh
judgments of the remaining two Bible passages that apparently
deal with some type of homosexual activity are understandable:

Know ye not that the unrighteous shall not inherit the kingdom of God? Be not deceived: neither fornicators, nor idolaters, nor adulterers, nor effeminate, nor abusers of themselves with mankind, nor thieves, nor covetous, nor drunkards, nor revilers, nor extortioners, shall inherit the kingdom of God. (1 Cor. 6:9–10, KJV)

Knowing this, that the law is not made for a righteous man, but for the lawless and disobedient, for the ungodly and for sinners, for unholy and profane, for murderers of fathers and murderers of mothers, for manslayers, for whoremongers, for them that defile themselves with mankind, for menstealers, for liars, for perjured persons, and if there be any other thing that is contrary to sound doctrine. (1 Tim. 1:9–10, KJV)

Interpretations of these passages depend on two Greek words that have presented a problem for translators. In the King James version of 1 Cor. 6:9, one of these words (*malakoi*) is translated "effeminate," and the other (*arsenokoitai*) is translated "abusers of themselves with mankind." In the Revised Standard Version of 1946 and 1952, the two words were arbitrarily combined and rendered simply "homosexuals," giving the unfortunate impression that all persons whose erotic interests were oriented toward the same sex were by that very fact excluded from membership in God's family—even if they lived celibately. The original language, however, made no reference whatsoever to sexual orientation. The intent seems to have been to single out specific *kinds* of sexual practices that were considered deplorable. Thus, in a second edition (1971), the translators of the Revised Standard Version attempted to correct their inaccurate rendering. But once again, they merged the two Greek words, overlooking their distinctly different meanings. This time "homosexuals" was changed to "sexual perverts"—hardly an improvement from the standpoint of erasing prejudice (since in many people's minds the two terms are considered synonymous). Conscious of the problem, the committee that worked on the New Revised Standard Version (1989) saw the need to translate each Greek word separately rather than attempting to combine them. The final working draft rendered the words as "boy prostitutes" and "practicing homosexuals" (thereby reflecting current attitudes of many Christians who believe that it is acceptable for someone to *be* homosexual in orientation but not acceptable for him or her to express love physically in a homosexual relationship). But at the last minute the committee shifted to the translation that has been published: "male prostitutes" and "sodomites."[45]

The translators of the New International Version attempted to capture the intent of the two Greek words by employing the terms "male prostitutes" and "homosexual offenders." Similarly, the Jerusalem Bible uses the terms "catamites" and "sodomites." Catamites were youths who provided sexual gratification for adult males. They often were able to extort huge sums of money from the older men who were interested in them. The English expression "call-boy" is employed by Scroggs, who suggests that *malakos* may have referred to "the youth who consciously imitated feminine styles and ways and who walked the thin line between passive homosexual activity for pleasure and that for pay."[46]

The second Greek word from 1 Cor. 6:9 is also found in 1 Tim. 1:10, where, in the King James Version, it was translated "them that defile themselves with mankind." The word could mean "obsessive corruptor of boys"; or it could refer to male prostitution.[47] Based upon his study of language usage and social customs at the time Paul wrote, Yale historian John Boswell argues that the apostle is speaking here of "male prostitutes capable of the active role with either men or women."[48] Clearly 1 Cor. 6:9–10 and 1 Tim. 1:9–10 do not contain a blanket condemnation of the homosexual orientation or homosexual love. Specific kinds of sexual abuse are under discussion in these passages.

By using the two Greek words just discussed, could Paul have had in mind sexual exploitation of the kind mentioned, for example, in the first-century manuscript *The Satyricon*? In one incident recounted there, a man was staying in a private home while on a business trip. Attracted to the beauty of the family's young son, he found a way to become the boy's constant companion, protector, guide, and tutor. The tutor boasted to friends that he had conned the parents into believing he was a paragon of virtue who was scandalized by the very mention of pederasty. He pretended to consider man-boy sexual contact to be an evil of the worst sort and offered to chaperone the boy constantly so that no seducers could possibly get near him. All the while, his intent was to violate the parents' trust. He gradually persuaded the young boy to grant him sexual favors by promising gifts of increasing value—first some doves, then a rooster, then a stallion that he was unable to deliver.[49] Petronius, the author of *The Satyricon,* was the director of court entertainment under the emperor Nero. His manuscript gives us a vivid and extremely realistic picture of the luxuries and vices of the Imperial Age. Nero himself deserved the title "corruptor of boys." Another first-century writer, Suetonius, who delighted in revealing gossip about the Roman rulers, had this to say about one of Nero's affairs:

> Having tried to turn the boy Sporus into a girl by castration, he went through a wedding ceremony with him—dowry, bridal veil and all—which the whole Court attended; then brought him home, and treated him as a wife. . . . A rather amusing joke is still going the rounds: the world would have been a happier place had Nero's father Domitius married that sort of wife.[50]

Apparently, it was not unusual for young slaves to be forced into sexual servitude by their masters, some youths having been kidnapped for that very purpose. Scroggs suggests that the particular sequence of words translated "fornicators, sodomites, and slave traders" in 1 Tim. 1:10 could be rendered "male prostitutes, males who lie [with them], and slave dealers [who procure them]."[51] Scroggs reports that some of theses slave boys were castrated to preserve their youthful appearance (as in the case of Sporus, just described).

In other situations, young boys *voluntarily* entered into arrangements in which they permitted adult males to use their bodies for sexual gratification. Scroggs emphasizes that, even though relationships in this category were voluntary, they too were permeated with destructive elements—namely, built-in inequality due to age and power differences, impermanency because the adult males tended to move from boy to boy, and the potential for humiliation and abuse. Then there was the third category of youths participating in man-boy sexual liaisons, those Scroggs labels "call-boys," who sold their sexual services to adult males for pay.[52]

Although some translators have used the English word *catamite* to capture the meaning of the first of the two Greek words usually associated with homosexual practices in 1 Cor. 6:9, the Greek word *malakos* literally means "soft," and is used elsewhere in the New Testament in ways that have nothing whatsoever to do with sex (for instance, in Luke 7:25 and Matt. 11:8, "What then did you go out to see? Someone dressed in soft robes?").[53] Enslin tells us that "the uncertainty of the exact meaning of the term is as old as Dionysius of Halicarnassus (30 B.C.E.), who said that the tyrant Aristodemus had received the epithet either because of his effeminate practices or else because of his gentle disposition."[54]

Countryman points out that it is a mistake to equate "the ancient notion of 'softness'" with "effeminacy," as we usually think of that term today. Rather, "softness" had to do with "indolence and a propensity toward sensuality."[55] He reports that the Greek word *malakos* was applied to any male who was not considered to be upstanding in character and goes on to say that Philo, an Alexandrian Jewish philosopher and theologian, even applied this Greek word to a man who remarries a former wife[56]—such remarriage being a violation of Deut. 24:1–4 and considered an abomination under the Jewish purity laws.

Poet and theologian John Milton may have caught the biblical meaning behind the translation of the word *soft* or *effeminate* when he applied the expression *effeminate* to males who can think about nothing but running after women, giving sexual conquest so much importance that they ignore God's will for them and thus contribute nothing to the good of humanity.[57] Since the word *effeminate* usually meant "self-indulgent" or "voluptuous" in the seventeenth century,[58] it seems probable that the King James translators meant it to convey that meaning (rather than homosexuality) in 1 Cor. 6:9. But since self-indulgence is far more widespread than homosexuality, it has perhaps been convenient to narrow the meaning of the passage so that it applies to only a scapegoat minority of the population.

▼ LAW VERSUS GRACE

Whatever specific same-sex abuses are referred to in 1 Cor. 6:9 and 1 Tim. 1:10, an important point needs emphasis. First Cor. 6:9–10 (KJV) says that not only "effeminate" persons and "abusers of themselves with mankind" will be excluded from God's kingdom, but also "idolaters" and "covetous" persons and "revilers" and "extortioners" and several other categories of people as well. Can any member of any Christian church honestly claim that he or she is completely guiltless of idolatry? To make that claim, we would have to be living in total selflessness, without the preoccupation with the private ego (the "old nature") with which the apostle Paul wrestled all his life and with which all the rest of us must constantly wrestle as well. Repeatedly the ego usurps God's place in our minds, and repeatedly we have to turn from that idol to serve the living God. So we are all, repeatedly, idolaters.

And can any of us claim that we are not frequently guilty of covetousness, of having a craving for something we do not currently possess? And do we never revile other people (that is, use abusive language toward them)? And how often are the corporate executives and other businesspeople in our churches reminded that to grossly overprice their products (that is, to be extortioners) will exclude them from heaven? Like the first chapter of Romans, 1 Cor. 6:9–11 applies to us all.

In general terms, 1 Cor. 6:9 (KJV) tells us that the "unrighteous shall not inherit the kingdom of God." And that generalization surely includes *all* of us, unless and until by the grace of God we are washed and sanctified and justified (verse 11). To be washed and sanctified and justified permits us to participate in the all-inclusive realm of God. (Although the term *kingdom* is usually applied to that realm, we prefer to drop the *g* and speak of God's *kin-dom* in order to emphasize the nonsexist, nonclassist nature of that realm and to underscore our common kinship with God and one another.[59]) The point of 1 Cor. 6:9–11 is that no unrighteous person will enter the kin-dom, no matter what his or her particular brand of unrighteousness may be. But some in Paul's audience, formerly unrighteous but now washed, sanctified, and justified, had become heirs of the kin-dom. The contrast here, in other

words, is the one so often present in Paul's writings: we are unrighteous and cannot please God in our old natures, but through
the acceptance of a new nature in Christ Jesus we are made fit for
the kin-dom. Similarly, in 1 Tim. 1:8–11 there is a contrast between condemnation of various sins under the law and the "glorious gospel of the blessed God."

When Paul says in 1 Cor. 6:11, after presenting his list of sinners, that "such *were* some of you," he cannot mean that only
some of his readers used to be unrighteous, for Paul is very clear
about the fact that "there is no one who is righteous, not even
one" (Rom. 3:10). He must therefore mean that only some have
been washed, sanctified, and justified, while others remain in their
unregenerate state. Or perhaps he means that some of his listeners
had in the past been guilty of the specific *kinds* of unrighteousness
included in the list. But by no means can the definition of unrighteousness (and the need for grace) be limited to the specific sins
mentioned. *All* of us must see ourselves included here, for we cannot doubt that we all need to be washed, sanctified, and justified
in order to enter God's kin-dom.

Since the Greek words concerning same-sex abuses refer to specific kinds of acts rather than to the condition of being homosexual, it is improper to use 1 Cor. 6:11 as proof that conversion to
Christ changes a homosexual orientation into a heterosexual one,
as some groups have tried to claim. And to tell homosexual men
and women on the basis of this passage that to belong to the family of God they must cease to be homosexual, or at least cease to
express their sexuality, is to place them under the law rather than
under grace. Homosexual people cannot earn salvation by the sacrifice of their sexuality any more than heterosexuals can. According to the apostle Paul, only Christ's sacrifice is sufficient to put
away sin. After conversion, just as the heterosexual has the old
ego nature to contend with, so does the homosexual convert retain
the old ego nature. Therefore, homosexual people must certainly
learn to cease from unloving abuses of sexuality, as heterosexuals
must; and all of us must struggle against idolatry and other manifestations of the ego nature. But Paul *is* telling us that *all* unrighteousness or wickedness or ego-centeredness separates us from

God's presence, and that inclusion in the kin-dom comes only through acceptance of God's grace, "by the Spirit of our God."

▼ But What About Genesis?

An elder statesman of evangelicalism, John Stott of London, has in recent years argued that it is no longer useful for evangelical Christians to emphasize the passages we have just discussed, because "the gay lobby is very clever" in arguing that "the prohibitions in Leviticus and in the Sodom and Pauline passages" are all "special cases." Instead, Stott says, the church should focus on Gen. 2:24 and Matt. 19:4–6, arguing "that Creation establishes heterosexual monogamy as the norm" and therefore the only context in which sexual expression is approved by God.[60]

The major problem with Stott's advice is that it violates the time-honored hermeneutical principle that one must pay attention to context, which includes the genre or literary type of the passage in question. The first two chapters of Genesis are creation stories; as such, their purpose is to describe how the world was created and how the human race got here. In order to fulfill the second purpose, it was necessary for the first couple to be both heterosexual and fertile. But the narrative in no way indicates that this first couple was to be considered normative for all sexual experience forever after. (If that were true, all childless marriages would have to be relegated to sinful status or, at best, to a status of sickness.)

To argue that Genesis mandates only heterosexual marriage is to turn the Genesis creation stories into scientific textbooks. That mistake was already made by forcing Genesis 1 to bear a scientific burden it was never intended to carry in an attempt to discredit all evolutionary theories. But today many Christians and Jews accept some form of theistic evolution, arguing that Genesis insists *that* God created, without specifying precisely *how* God created. Must the church work through the same dishonest attempt to turn Genesis 2 into a scientific textbook concerning human sexuality? As our next chapter, on science, makes clear, the subject of sexuality is vast and complex. To address that topic is not the purpose of the Genesis creation stories. The point of Genesis is well expressed by Isaac Bashevis Singer: "No matter how the human brain might grow, it will always come back to the idea that God has created heaven and earth, [humankind], and animals, with a will and a plan, and that, despite all the evil life undergoes, there is a purpose in Creation and eternal wisdom."[61] Let us not dishonor Genesis and dishonor our own hermeneutical principles by asking the creation stories to become either scientific prescriptions or moral legislation.

John Stott argues that Jesus' words in Matt. 19:4–6 constitute his endorsement of heterosexual marriage as the only proper avenue of sexual expression. But here again, Stott is guilty of violating the context. The Pharisees had asked Jesus a question about the lawfulness of divorce laws under which Jewish men could easily divorce their wives but women had no way to get out of a painful marriage. Jesus strongly opposes this double standard by referring to "the beginning" and then quoting Gen. 2:24 before asserting that "what God has joined together, let no one separate." Jesus' male disciples fully understood that his intention was to demolish the double standard, because they said, "If such is the case of a man with his wife, it is better not to marry" (Matt. 19:10).

Since this entire dialogue takes place within the context of divorce laws, and therefore must of necessity concern itself only with heterosexual marriage, it is dishonoring to the Scriptures to claim that Jesus' purpose here was to affirm marriage as the only approved avenue for human sexual experience.

In neither Matthew nor Genesis is an attempt made to cover the topic of human sexuality in a scientific fashion. Thus, by attempting to make Matt. 19:5 a scientific prescription, Stott has once again violated the generic integrity of the text. Furthermore, if this quotation of Gen. 2:24 is to be taken as the church's norm for all sexual experience, does that mean that the church will now require a return to matrilocal marriage, where the husband must move to become part of the wife's family? In patriarchal society, it is usually the woman who is expected to relocate in order to accommodate her husband, but Genesis mandates that it is the male who must always leave father and mother, the male who must be the one to relocate. Should evangelical churches attempt to follow Stott's advice by making Matt. 19:5 the norm for all human sexuality, some interesting changes will have to take place in heterosexual marriages! But of course that is not the intention of the passage when it is read in context, as all passages deserve to be. (See our chapter 9 for a further discussion of the creation accounts.)

▼ QUESTIONS LEFT UNANSWERED IN THE BIBLE

A careful examination of what the Bible says about issues relating to homosexuality still leaves us with many unanswered questions. For one thing, the idea of a lifelong homosexual orientation or "condition" is never mentioned in the Bible. An evangelical pastor in the Netherlands, J. Rinzema, explains that "the confirmed homosexual was not recognized until roughly 1890. The Bible writers assumed that everyone was heterosexual and that in times of moral decay, some heterosexual people did some strange and unnatural things with each other."[62] Since the Bible is silent about the homosexual condition, those who want to understand it must rely on the findings of modern behavioral-science research and on the testimony of those people who are themselves homosexual.

The Bible, furthermore, does not mention the possibility of a permanent, committed relationship of love between homosexual people that is analogous to heterosexual marriage. Surely such a union is to be distinguished from the contexts we have looked at—contexts of violence, idolatry, lust, and exploitation. But would such a loving, committed relationship be permissible according to biblical standards? Or do theological considerations such as God's plan in creating male and female and bringing them together to be "one flesh" rule out homosexual unions entirely?

These questions, about which the Bible is silent, are stimulating a great deal of rethinking and renewed study among Christians today. A continuum of views concerning homosexuality has gradually developed. But in order to understand homosexuality fully, we need first to give attention to information provided by behavioral scientists. Then, relating that knowledge to biblical and theological considerations, we will be able to turn more intelligently to the issues confronting the age in which we live.

What Does Science Say?

TO UNDERSTAND homosexuality, we must first know what it is. Finding an answer may be more difficult than we think! The very complexity of the topic provides good reason for Christians to refrain from hasty generalizations, labeling, and hysteria.

Some of the most noteworthy efforts toward solving the puzzle have been made by the Kinsey Institute for Research in Sex, Gender, and Reproduction at Indiana University. Paul Gebhard, a former director of the institute, has emphasized that no scientific investigation can take place without a workable definition of the phenomenon being studied. His own definition of homosexual behavior is simple, pragmatic, and applicable cross-culturally. Here it is:

> We have found the most practical definition of homosexual behavior to be: physical contact between two individuals of the same gender which both recognize as being sexual in nature and which ordinarily results in sexual arousal. Psychological homosexual response may be defined as sexual arousal from thinking of or seeing persons of the same gender.[1]

▼ DEGREES OF HOMOSEXUALITY AND HETEROSEXUALITY

Studies conducted by the Kinsey Institute have shown homosexuality to be a matter of degree—both in terms of *overt behav-*

ior and in terms of *orientation,* or psychological response. Researchers have devised a scale from zero to six to locate persons on a continuum between *exclusive heterosexuality* (zero) and *exclusive homosexuality* (six). Varying degrees of heterosexuality and homosexuality characterize persons in between. For example, a person who is predominantly heterosexual but who has an incidental homosexual history would be rated one on the scale. Conversely, someone mainly homosexual but with an incidental response toward, or experience with, the opposite sex would be rated five. Midway on the continuum (rated three) are those persons whose erotic arousal and/or overt experience are equally heterosexual and homosexual.

Such ratings can be used to describe an entire life span, or they can be used in reference only to particular periods in a person's life. Transitory homosexual experience around the time of puberty, for instance, does not necessarily mean a person is "a homosexual" or that homosexual behavior will continue into adulthood. "In terms of social and psychological significance," Gebhard stresses, such experimental behavior "is quite different from activity engaged in as an adult." Therefore, "it is not only useless, but confusing to learn that X percent of a group has had homosexual experience at some time in life—one does not know how much was confined to childhood and how much was in adult life."[2]

In other words, simple "never-ever" surveys tell us little about the incidence and meaning of homosexual experiences in people's lives.[3] Furthermore, the simple heterosexual-homosexual dichotomy becomes even more of a problem. If *any* overt homosexual experience at *any* point in life becomes the deciding factor that places an individual in the "homosexual" category, many people would be labeled homosexual who do not fit that classification at all by any reasonable criteria. For if a person's present erotic responses and experiences are entirely heterosexual and he or she has long forgotten a few homosexual experiences at the time of approaching puberty, what sense does it make to call the person homosexual?

Suppose, however, we limit ourselves only to people who have had overt sexual experience (not just psychological response) with persons of the same sex. We will also limit ourselves to those who have had that experience *since puberty,* because postpubertal activity is somewhat more significant than childhood activity. According to studies conducted by the Kinsey Institute, between one-fourth and one-third of adult males and slightly more than one-tenth of adult females in the United States have had such experiences. But again, it would be erroneous to apply the label "homosexual" to all such people, because many, mainly males, have had only incidental experience, which occurred chiefly between puberty and age sixteen.[4] After such transitory adolescent experimentation, many of these people go on to lead quite conventional heterosexual lives that include getting married and having children. It should be clear by now why we speak of the homosexual issue as *complex.*

▼ ORIENTATION VERSUS OVERT EXPERIENCE

Psychologist Braden R. Berkey and his colleagues observe that "the confusion surrounding sexual orientation is further complicated when genital sexual activity is used as the sole deciding factor in identifying a person's sexual orientation while completely ignoring factors such as affection, attraction, affiliation, emotional preference, and fantasy." By failing to take such factors into consideration, say these scholars, "an entire aspect of human sexuality is overlooked."[5] The Kinsey researchers combined both experience and psychological response in their continuum ratings, because, as Gebhard has pointed out, "most persons have the same numeral for both their psychic and overt." However, because this is not *always* the case, Gebhard now advocates a combined scoring system that can show discrepancies. For example, a rating of zero/one would tell us that a person has no conscious interest in homosexuality (a rating of zero on psychological response) but is currently engaged in a small amount of homosexual activity (a rating of one on behavior). Although such a case may not indicate any personality problems, "a discrepancy of two or more points indicates stress and/or emotional or social disturbance."[6]

Research psychologist Alan Bell points out that it would be theoretically possible for someone to be exclusively heterosexual in activity while exclusively homosexual in feeling. (A case of psychological lesbianism illustrates the point—that is, a woman who, during sexual relations with her husband, habitually fantasizes being with a woman.) While many homosexual people of both sexes are able to perform heterosexually, Bell explains that "it is a performance frequently bereft of either deep emotional satisfactions or intense sexual arousal." He cites the conviction of many social and behavioral scientists that a person's past or present sexual *behavior* is a "poor indicator of his or her true sexual orientation." A detailed history of an individual's sexual *feelings* can tell us much more.[7] In a large-scale research project conducted by Bell himself, along with his colleagues Martin Weinberg and Sue Kiefer Hammersmith, most gay and lesbian people reported that their homosexual feelings were present long before they participated in any homosexual activity.[8] Many recalled having first become aware of their same-sex attraction and arousal sometime during childhood or in the early years of adolescence.

On a similar note, after an extensive review of the research literature, sociologist Joseph Harry concluded that "sexual orientation is immensely resistant to change, that it is established early in life, and that most of the evidence suggesting flexibility pertains only to sexual behavior."[9] He too emphasizes that it is erotic attraction rather than sexual activity that is central in defining sexual orientation.

Persons rated four or five on the Kinsey scale are considered by researchers at the Kinsey Institute to be "predominantly homosexual." These are people whose erotic arousal and/or overt behavior are directed more toward the same sex than toward the other sex. If we combine the predominantly homosexual with the exclusively homosexual—people who respond *only* to the same sex (rated six on the scale)—we are able to gain some idea of the percentage of homosexuals in the United States. After taking into account the sampling problems in the original Kinsey research and also incorporating some later research and tabulations, the institute has estimated that 4 to 5 percent of adult American males may be considered homosexual (most of this percentage is in the "exclusive" category). Among adult females, about 1 to 2 percent are predominantly or exclusively homosexual (four through six on the scale).[10] These findings, it is interesting to note, correspond with various European studies.[11] Gebhard reminds us that these figures refer only to people whose homosexuality is overt, and do not include people who may be "psychologically predominantly gay" but who have seldom if ever acted upon their feelings.[12] William Paul and James Weinrich, two other authorities on the topic, have pointed out that, given societal disapproval of homosexuality, the risk of self-disclosure can also affect statistics on homosexuality—especially if anonymity is not guaranteed. They voice the opinion that it is possible—even likely—"that these recurrent 2–5 percent figures represent those people who live gay lifestyles within tolerant or cosmopolitan communities."[13]

In recent years, similar figures have shown up again when a few questions on both heterosexual and homosexual sexual behavior were added to the General Social Survey, which is based on a full-probability sample of the U.S. adult household population and regularly conducted on a wide variety of topics by the National Opinion Research Center based at the University of Chicago. After in-person interviews on other topics of public interest, respondents were asked to fill out a brief, self-administered questionnaire about their sexual experience and then return the questionnaire in a sealed envelope to ensure confidentiality. It was found that, during the year preceding the survey, about 2 percent of sexually active adults had engaged in exclusively homosexual or bisexual activity. Between 5 and 6 percent reported that, since age eighteen, they had engaged in bisexual activity or homosexual activity exclusively.[14] Again, these figures refer only to sexual activity and tell us nothing about erotic or romantic *feelings*. In other words, they don't measure orientation, including the orientation of the 3 percent of American adults over age eighteen who have never been sexually active.

There are social and political reasons for the dearth of scientific data on human sexuality. In the late 1980s, for example, the dean of the Division of Social Sciences at the University of Chicago, Edward Laumann, was awarded a contract by the National Institute of Child Health and Development (a branch of the National Institutes of Health) to design a national longitudinal survey of teenagers' sexual practices over several years. The goal was to obtain information relating to contraception, fertility, and the prevention of sexually transmitted diseases. It would also have updated much of the information from the original Kinsey studies of the 1940s and 1950s. Great care would be taken to avoid violating the privacy of the respondents. However, just before Laumann's study was to be launched, conservative members of the House of Representatives and Senate took steps to stop it by withdrawing the project's funding. When in 1991 Laumann again tried to obtain funding for a smaller adult study (the scientific merits of which were applauded by peer review), his project was again halted. The leaders of the opposition, Congressman William Dannemeyer of California and Senator Jesse Helms of North Carolina, charged that such surveys were part of a homosexual conspiracy. Claiming he was "sick and tired of pandering to the homosexuals in this country," Helms asserted that the purpose of such studies is not to stop AIDS from spreading. "The real purpose," he told the Senate, "is to compile supposedly scientific facts to support the left-wing liberal argument that homosexuality is a normal, acceptable life-style."[15]

Interestingly, however, people who take a negative stance toward homosexuality are often quick to quote social scientific findings if they believe such findings support their own viewpoint. For example, some Christian leaders have gleefully seized upon the National Opinion Research Center's data (cited above) to argue that gay and lesbian people are fewer than has generally been claimed in the media. Apparently, these leaders think that if only a small percentage of people are homosexually oriented, it is not important to acknowledge their civil rights and respect their human dignity. But what do numbers have to do with Christian compassion? If even one sparrow falls, God cares. Besides, a small *percentage* can mean a large *number* of people. If even 5 percent of adults over age eighteen have had homosexual experience (either exclusively or in combination with heterosexual experience), that translates into over 9 million people in the United States alone.[16] And this does not take into account people under age eighteen who may be discovering their romantic attraction to the same sex, as well as older people who have not acted upon their feelings but who are conscious of their homosexual orientation.

▼ AN ANALOGY BETWEEN HOMOSEXUALITY AND LEFT-HANDEDNESS

For Christians who are concerned about biblical ethics, the real problems center on sexual orientation, because nothing in the Bible deals with it. We saw that there were prohibitions about homosexual behavior in various contexts, such as idolatry, gang rape, promiscuity, defilement under ritual purity laws, and as a violation of what was assumed to be a universally heterosexual nature in human beings. But no provision was made for people whose "nature" itself appears to be homosexual—that small percentage of people whose erotic response is directed toward the same sex, regardless of whether they ever act on that response.

A British group of Quakers saw the issue clearly when they wrote in 1963: "The word 'homosexuality' does not denote a course of conduct, but a state of affairs, the state of loving one's own, not the opposite sex; it is a state of affairs in nature. One should no more deplore 'homosexuality' than left-handedness."[17] And in Holland, as long ago as 1949, it was suggested that the word *homophilia* (from the Greek for "same" and "loving") be used to refer to the orientation, because the term homo*sexuality* "so strongly implies the sexual act."[18]

The British group's comparison of homosexuality with left-handedness suggests that homosexuality is simply a variant of sexual expression rather than a matter of morality. Homosexuality can certainly *become* a moral matter, depending on how it is expressed. And the same is true for the heterosexual orientation. Handedness, as a human variation, can become a matter of morality, too. In general, it doesn't matter whether we are naturally right-handed or left-handed; but what we *do* with our hands does matter. A hand can be used to soothe a crying baby, brush away a tear, perform surgery, prepare a meal, assist a homeless person, write an outstanding novel, play a musical instrument, drive an ambulance, or repair a broken water pipe. Or it can be used to beat a child, shoplift, scribble hate-filled graffiti on a public building, forge a check, point a gun at a convenience-store clerk, mug an elderly pedestrian, or build explosives for terrorist acts against a minority group. Obviously, the moral question doesn't lie in the fact of being left- or right-handed but in the use to which the hand is put. (In the final chapter of this book, we'll be discussing the analogy between handedness and sexual orientation further.)

Psychology professor John Money, a leading authority on psychosexual development, points out that "the disposition toward one sexual orientation or the other does appear to be inborn," and suggests that this disposition is "the result of the influence of sex hormones on the development of sexual pathways in the brain." He, too, uses the analogy of a person's being left-handed, ambidextrous, or right-handed. "The cause [of handedness] is not fully explainable, though there does appear to be an innate plus a learned component," he writes. "The same applies to homosexuality, bisexuality, and heterosexuality." Yet, just as schoolteachers and parents at one time punished left-handed children in efforts to force them to become right-handed (including tying their left hands behind their backs), society in effect punishes homosexual people today through discriminatory practices and laws. Money calls such punishment "ineffectual" and argues that its aim is unrealistic, since forcing homosexuals to become heterosexuals is not possible, "any more than it is possible to force a heterosexual person into becoming a homosexual."[19]

A great deal of controversy has arisen among adherents of the three major viewpoints on homosexuality, with one school of thought considering homosexuality to be a matter of morality, another viewing it as a mental illness, and still another persuaded it is nothing more than a natural variant (as in the comparison with left-handedness). Those who see homosexuality as nothing less than *sin* appeal to the biblical passages we have already examined. Those who see homosexuality as *sickness* appeal to a long tradition within the psychoanalytic school of thought.

▼ CONTRADICTORY PSYCHOANALYTIC THEORIES

From a psychoanalytic standpoint, homosexuality is viewed by some as an arrested state of development—a failure to pass beyond a normal "homosexual stage" of life and to go on to more "mature" sexual feelings and relationships. Others argue that it is the result of an incestuous attachment to the parent of the opposite sex, which creates a sense of "forbidden attraction" with regard to that sex. Conversely, some have postulated an attachment to the *same*-sex parent, with the other parent being seen as a rival, along with all other people of the "rival's" sex. Still others suggest that the problem lies in a failure to identify with the same-sex parent. Some psychoanalytic theories relate homosexuality to castration anxieties among males; others relate it to feelings of hostility toward, or fear of, the other sex—feelings stemming from disturbed parent-child relations. According to still other theories, the choice of a same-sex love object indicates a narcissistic quest for a symbol of one's own self. Thus Wilhelm Stekel, a Viennese psychiatrist who was a friend of and assistant to Sigmund Freud, argued: "I believe I have proven successfully that the homosexual is a neurotic. . . . But we must not think that, like the average neurotic, the homosexual is incapable of love. Only, all his love is a love centered exclusively on self. . . . Since the homosexual loves only himself he seeks only himself in others."[20]

Many of these theories and the studies cited to support them are internally inconsistent and contradictory to one another. All are based on what has come to be called the "medical" or "illness" model of homosexuality—the assumption that homosexuality is pathological, a sickness in need of treatment. Sociologists Martin Weinberg and Colin Williams argue that "the emphasis on cure has often inhibited theoretical progress and a better understanding of homosexuality and the homosexual." Furthermore, many of the studies related to these theories use faulty methods "which do not measure up to minimal canons of scientific research."[21] Many psychologists and psychiatrists have tended to base their conclusions upon small samples from among their own patients. For instance, how could Stekel honestly claim to have *proven* that "the homosexual is neurotic" when the only homosexual people he had studied were the subjects of clinical case studies? All of his evidence was drawn from people who felt they had serious enough problems to search out psychiatric help! This bias was already pointed out in the late nineteenth century by Edward Carpenter, who took issue with the prevailing medical opinion of that time. He argued:

It must never be forgotten that the medico-scientific en-
quirer is bound on the whole to meet with those cases [of
homosexuality] that *are* of a morbid character, rather than
with those that are healthy in their manifestation, since indeed it is the former that he lays himself out for.[22]

Weinberg and Williams point out that instead of claiming "by
fiat" that homosexuals are maladjusted, anyone interested in
learning about the topic must study homosexual people in comparison with adequate heterosexual control groups.

▼ INADEQUATE RESEARCH METHODS

Some theories that have emerged from clinical case studies have
provided the basis for sweeping assertions about homosexuality
that have caused much pain and grief—not only for gay and lesbian people themselves, but for their parents as well. In the psychoanalytic tradition, fathers of homosexual people have been
described as cold and rejecting. Mothers have been portrayed as
dominant, strong, and controlling—or, in some cases, extremely
close-binding even if not necessarily dominant. In still other writings, mothers of homosexual people have been characterized as
hostile and rejecting. As behavioral scientist David Lester has
noted, "It is remarkable that despite the fact that the evidence on
these points is inconsistent, the description of the parents of the
homosexual has become standardized and appears with great frequency in textbooks."[23] Lester considers this practice both remarkable and worrisome, since certain careful researchers have
demonstrated that when different controls are introduced into the
research methodology, *no differences have been found* between
parents of homosexuals and parents of heterosexuals!

Lester is also critical of the fact that almost all studies have
been based on retrospection—on how homosexual adults remember the past, including their perceptions of how their parents be-
haved toward them many years ago. The parents themselves have
not usually been studied, nor have other people who might be able

to provide further information on the home situation. Although Lester calls such oversights inexcusable, they are certainly understandable in that it would be difficult if not impossible to find a research sample of parents who are aware in advance that their children will grow up to affirm a homosexual identity. The best that could be hoped for would be longitudinal studies that would trace a representative sample of *all* families over the child-rearing years and look for similarities and differences among those whose children approach adulthood with homosexual, heterosexual, or bisexual identities.

For the present, however, retrospective studies (both from parents' and childrens' perspectives) can be quite useful. In a Kinsey Institute–sponsored study, after interviewing close to one thousand homosexual men and women and a comparison group of nearly five hundred heterosexual men and women in the San Francisco Bay area, researchers Alan Bell, Martin Weinberg, and Sue Kiefer Hammersmith concluded, "No particular phenomenon of family life can be singled out, on the basis of our findings, as especially consequential for either homosexual or heterosexual development. . . . In short, to concerned parents we cannot recommend anything beyond the care, sympathy, and devotion that good parents presumably lavish on all their children anyway."[24] In another study, a national sample of lesbian women and gay men was drawn from chapters of Dignity, an organization originally formed for Roman Catholic homosexual people but that includes people from other religious perspectives—and even no religious preference—as well. In looking back over their childhoods, nearly two-thirds of these gay men and lesbian women reported having had satisfactory or extremely satisfactory relationships with their fathers, and 82 percent reported having had satisfactory or extremely satisfactory relationships with their mothers.[25]

In still another study, three professors who specialize in child and family development focused their research on parents themselves to find out how *they* felt about the homosexuality of their offspring.[26] Confusion, regret, and denial were common reactions reported in this research sample, which was drawn from across the United States. Participants were recruited through chapters of two organizations, the Federation of Parents, Families, and Friends of

Lesbians and Gays (P-FLAG) and the National Federation of Parents and Friends of Gays (P-FOG). Almost two-thirds of the fathers and mothers reported having experienced a five-stage grief process in coming to terms with their offspring's sexual orientation. Over a period of time, these parents went through shock, denial, guilt, and anger before coming to a point of acceptance. (Of course, this tells us nothing about parents who do not seek out support groups such as P-FLAG and P-FOG. The researchers themselves were aware of that fact in their reporting of the high level of acceptance by the parents in this particular study.) Of particular relevance here is the fact that the vast majority of these parents (87 percent) believed their child had been born homosexual and that neither parent was responsible. In looking back over the child-rearing years, they did not feel that their relationships with their children had been deficient.

Many parents of homosexual people, however, suffer great anguish because they have been led to believe they are somehow responsible for their children's homosexual orientation. They may even come up with evidence from the past that seems to support certain theories they have heard, even though the evidence is questionable and would have been considered insignificant under other circumstances. "I must have done *something* wrong," they reason. "If I think long and hard enough, maybe I can figure out what it was."

A parallel case illustrates the problems researchers face because of such parental guilt. In 1958, a study was published showing that mothers of children born with Down syndrome (then called mongolism) had experienced more shocks during pregnancy than had other mothers. These results were assumed to indicate that a pregnant woman's emotional state influenced the development of this condition in her unborn child. However, an important scientific breakthrough occurred shortly after that study was published. Researchers found that Down syndrome is associated with a chromosomal abnormality and that the earlier inference about emotional factors was wrong. As sociologist George W. Brown has explained, the findings of the original study quite likely stemmed from the attempts of the mothers to find reasons that their infants had been born with Down syndrome, an occurrence that was considered a terrible tragedy. They therefore "were likely to recall shocks or to define quite ordinary events as shocks where mothers of normal children would not. In other words, they assigned a meaning to what happened during pregnancy, *after* the birth of their child, which they would not necessarily have considered noteworthy *prior* to its birth." Brown goes on to warn that "such reworking of the past can obviously play havoc with aetiological studies and the example is representative of a number of problems that have to be faced."[27] (In citing this illustration, we are most certainly *not* suggesting that homosexuality is a mental or physical impairment to be compared with Down syndrome, but simply that there may be parallel problems associated with research on homosexuality.)

An additional point made by David Lester may also be appropriate in critiquing the traditional psychoanalytic approach that considers parents to be responsible for a son or daughter's homosexuality. He asserts that "we fall too easily into the error of assuming that the parent causes the child's behavior" and ignore those studies that show how children's behavior can affect parents.[28] Psychiatry professor Richard Green provides the example of a sports-minded father who tries long and hard to persuade his young son to join him in rough-and-tumble games, only to find the son not interested in and "temperamentally unsuited" to athletics. The father, after repeatedly meeting with reluctance on the part of the boy, may begin withdrawing his efforts to participate in activities with his son. Their interests are too different, and both may feel rejection. "Here, however," argues Green, "the emotional distance seems to have been activated more by the child than by the parent. Regrettably, such distinctions are frequently lost in the study of adults who recall an alienated relationship with their fathers and an intimate one with their mothers."[29]

▼ WEAKENING OF THE THEORY THAT HOMOSEXUALITY IS AN ILLNESS

Not only has the methodology of various studies come under attack in recent years; the medical model itself has become much less widely accepted. Investigations by anthropologists and sociologists have provided data that call into question certain long-held assumptions of psychotherapy.[30] Psychologists and psychiatrists themselves have done a great deal of rethinking on the subject as new knowledge has been gained. One of the outstanding examples in the quest for such knowledge has been the trailblazing work of Evelyn Hooker.

During World War II, when Hooker was a research psychologist at the University of Southern California in Los Angeles, she developed a close friendship with one of her brightest students. Over a period of time, he introduced Dr. Hooker and her husband to a number of his friends; and as a spirit of trust grew, the student revealed that he was living in a homosexual relationship, a disclosure that was quite risky in those times. Friends of his also told her about that part of their lives, and the student begged Hooker to study the homosexual people of whom they were representative: "homosexuals who function well and don't go to psychiatrists." Busy with her laboratory studies of neurotic rats, Hooker at first refused. Besides, she wondered, how could she study people who were her friends? But the student wouldn't give up. Finally, seeing the wisdom of undertaking such a study, Hooker applied for a grant from the National Institute of Mental Health. With a matched sample of thirty homosexual men and thirty heterosexual men, none of whom were in psychiatric treatment, she conducted a series of psychological tests and then turned the tests over to skilled clinicians for analysis. These psychiatrists and psychologists were unable to tell from the test results which men were homosexual and which were heterosexual. Furthermore, the study revealed no higher degree of pathology within the homosexual group than in the heterosexual group. And there were just as many homosexual men as heterosexual men who rated *superior* in the tests. The idea that homosexuality in and of itself is a mental illness simply didn't hold up under carefully monitored study.[31]

Hooker's mid-1950s study, along with the earlier Kinsey studies that had shown homosexual behavior to be more prevalent than had previously been thought, provided the opening wedge for a new look at the topic. Before this time, mental-health experts had considered it indisputable that homosexuality was an illness, although they differed significantly about whether it could be cured.

Through more thorough research, the way was being cleared for interdisciplinary efforts to find answers concerning whether it was an illness at all.

▼ REVISION BY PROFESSIONAL MENTAL-HEALTH ORGANIZATIONS

In 1967, Dr. Stanley Yolles, director of the National Institute of Mental Health, appointed a task force made up of behavioral, medical, and social scientists "to review carefully the current state of knowledge regarding homosexuality in its mental health aspects and to make recommendations for Institute programming in this area." Evelyn Hooker chaired the task force. Its attention to the topic engendered a large amount of research, which, in turn, began to have an effect on attitudes toward homosexuality. Gay and lesbian activists naturally seized upon the findings, and the word spread: homosexuality had been demonstrated to be not a destructive mental illness but simply a sexual variation. A number of state legislatures took a new look at laws prohibiting homosexual acts, and some states decriminalized sex acts between consenting adults in private. Various municipalities enacted anti-discrimination ordinances to protect the civil rights of homosexual people. The mass media began to treat the topic in a more sympathetic light.[32] And, in 1973, in a move that stunned many people and caused considerable controversy within its own membership, the American Psychiatric Association (APA) voted to remove homosexuality from its official list of mental disorders.

This was not a denial that disturbed homosexual people exist. They do exist, just as surely as do heterosexual people who are poorly integrated into society and have various mental, emotional, and social problems. What the APA was willing to acknowledge was that there are also many *healthy* homosexual people.[33]

The association's official news release declared that "homosexuality per se implies no impairment in judgment, stability, reliability, or general social or vocational capabilities" and should not be regarded as a psychiatric disorder, but simply as one form of sexual behavior. At the same time, the APA included under mental disorders a special category called "sexual orientation disturbance," a diagnostic classification for people whose "sexual interests are directed primarily toward people of the same sex and who are either disturbed by, in conflict with, or wish to change their sexual orientation."[34] In all other cases of homosexuality, it seemed to the APA unreasonable and unfair to diagnose people as psychologically maladjusted if (1) they were not bothering others and were staying out of trouble with the law, (2) they were capable of earning an independent living, and (3) they were capable of forming meaningful relationships with other people. Certainly such characteristics were to be considered signs of good mental health.[35]

In 1974, another professional organization, the Association for the Advancement of Behavior Therapy (AABT), also issued a formal statement, asserting that "homosexuality is in itself not a sign of behavioral pathology" and urging "all mental health professionals to take the lead in removing the stigma of mental illness that has long been attributed to these patterns of emotion and behavior."[36]

And in 1975, the American Psychological Association (which also uses the initials APA) likewise resolved to work for the removal of the stigma attached to the homosexual orientation and removed homosexuality from its list of mental disorders, just as the American Psychiatric Association had done.

In the decades since Hooker's pioneering study, numerous other studies of homosexual and heterosexual people have been conducted in which the two orientations have been carefully matched for adequate controls. Some have concentrated on gay men, others on lesbian women.[37] Again and again, these studies have indicated that, overall, homosexual people are as psychologically healthy and as well integrated into society as heterosexual people are.[38]

▼ DAMAGE CAUSED BY SOCIAL REJECTION

But isn't this picture a bit too rosy? After all, homosexual people are living in a hostile society and would have every reason to have psychological problems. Those homosexual men and women who seek out help toward a "cure" or a change of orientation often point out that they can no longer stand being stigmatized, discriminated against, joked and sneered about, and threatened with disclosure, blackmail, and even physical assault. They can no longer bear having to live two lives. The strain becomes too great, the self-hatred too strong, the anxieties too engulfing. But what about those homosexual people who *don't* seek out help? What is *their* level of anxiety?

Aware of such considerations, Martin Weinberg and Colin Williams conducted a large-scale cross-cultural study of nonpsychiatric homosexual men in the United States, Denmark, and the Netherlands. Like Evelyn Hooker, these sociologists had become interested in studying the topic after meeting a homosexual person whose very *being* served to explode the familiar stereotypes. After he had addressed the Social Problems class they were team teaching at a university in 1966, they wrote: "His very ordinariness reduced the aura of mystery surrounding the exotic label 'homosexual.'. . . His air of well-being led us to re-evaluate our thinking." Among other concerns, Weinberg and Williams wanted to find out if homosexual men differed from the general male population with respect to self-acceptance, psychosomatic symptoms, depression, and faith in others. The researchers found little difference between the two samples in two of the categories: self-acceptance and psychosomatic symptoms. They did find, however, that those in the homosexual samples in all three societies reported less happiness and less faith in others than did those in the samples of the general male population. Weinberg and Williams concluded that this finding was in line with the "societal rejection theory." According to that theory, homosexual people are forced to adjust to varying degrees of legal repression and social rejection that affect personal happiness and trust—even though at the same time they may be able to adapt in such a way as to maintain a positive self-image and avoid psychosomatic symptoms.[39]

The Weinberg-Williams study suggests that the "homosexual problem" is really a "heterosexual problem" in that the dominant society has refused to grant full human acceptance to homosexual people. The situation may be compared with what society has traditionally perceived as the "black problem," which is actually a problem of white racism. Because of this reality, black people cannot be expected to solve racial tensions and injustices on their own through some "pick-yourselves-up-by-your-own-bootstraps" approach. Similarly, gay men and lesbian women cannot by their own inner fortitude resolve the sadness, pain, and distrust they so often feel. Their anguish springs from the social pressures that make personal trust and happiness more difficult for them to achieve than for heterosexual people. In both cases, it is society— not the victims of discrimination—that must change.

▼ HEALTHY HOMOSEXUALS AND HEALTHY TRUTHFULNESS

One final study should be mentioned, since it provides some answers about different categories of homosexual people and shows why clinical studies have failed to provide the whole picture. Aware that many studies of homosexual men have been concerned either with psychiatric patients or with men who were referred for treatment after being in trouble with the law, British sociologist Michael Schofield decided to explore whether men in these categories differed from homosexual men who had never been in therapy and had never been convicted of homosexual offenses. He found that the men who had never been arrested and had never been in therapy were better integrated into the larger community in both work and leisure activities. They were more likely to be living in long-standing, stable relationships, and they were far less promiscuous than either the prison sample or the patient sample.[40] If the findings on only the patient and prison samples had been reported and then generalized, as though they applied to *all* homosexual men, the third group (the healthiest group) would have been completely misrepresented. Yet this has too often been the practice—especially in most of the older studies.

Developmental psychologist Elizabeth Gibbs makes a similar point about studies of homosexual women. She states that "research which uses nonclinic samples and appropriate comparison groups" shows lesbian and heterosexual women to be more alike than different. She goes on to emphasize that "studies have been unable to document the stereotypes of lesbian women as more mentally disturbed, lacking in self-esteem, or more prone to alcohol abuse or suicide."[41]

An awareness of behavioral-science research on homosexuality can help us to better understand and deal with questions surrounding the topic, and it is important that we avail ourselves of such knowledge as much as possible. Otherwise, it is all too easy to perpetuate old myths and stereotypes and thus to bear false witness against our neighbor.

▼▼▼▼▼▼▼▼▼▼

From Homophobia to Understanding

IF THE CHURCH takes seriously its responsibility to share Christ's love with all people, Christians must reach out to homosexual people as well as heterosexual people. That will mean not only giving serious attention to the findings of the social and behavioral sciences, but also facing up to a number of specific issues relating to the topic of homosexuality. First, we must deal with *homophobia*—the term coined by psychotherapist George Weinberg for the fear, anxiety, revulsion, and anger the subject tends to generate.[1] Second, we need to develop an understanding of gay people as a people or community. And third, we must ask ourselves if there needs to be a rethinking of homosexuality from a biblical and theological perspective.

▼ SOME FORMS OF HOMOPHOBIA

When a gay activist organization announced an "If You Are Gay, Wear Blue Jeans Today" campaign at the University of Illinois (Champaign), large numbers of students left their usual denim attire in the closet and wore dresses, skirts, slacks, and shorts. Some who inadvertently wore blue jeans went back to their rooms and changed clothes after other students made remarks or asked questions. The gay organization felt it had made its point: many people were actually afraid to wear jeans; they preferred to give up their customary attire rather than be suspected of homosexuality.[2]

Homophobia may take many forms: fear of being thought homosexual by others, fear of possible homosexual response in oneself, fear of "catching" homosexuality (as though it were a contagious disease), or fear that children will see homosexuality as a viable alternative to heterosexual marriage and will choose a homosexual life-style. A particularly virulent form of homophobia is to identify AIDS as God's judgment upon homosexuals. (One wonders: is, then, Legionnaires' disease to be interpreted as God's judgment on militarism? Is crib death God's judgment on babies? Is toxic-shock syndrome God's judgment on menstruating women?)

Among people who are aware of their own personal homosexual tendencies, homophobia often takes the form of self-loathing.[3] We have already encountered a clear example of this in Dr. Howard Brown's description of his feelings as an adolescent. Virginia Mollenkott remembers that when she was in high school and so dedicated to Christ that she resolutely avoided masturbation or any other sexual expression, the awareness of her lesbian impulses made her afraid to get into bed with her own body. She even attempted suicide because Christian leaders repeatedly told her that God had no use for homosexuals like her. And author Jeremy Seabrook recalls thinking in his youth that he was "the most monstrously perverted creature on earth." He points out that for people who first become aware of their orientation, the word *homosexual,* because it conjures up a certain stereotyped image, "has a repelling and contaminating power which makes people recoil and say, 'That can't be me.'"[4]

Some homosexual adolescents begin acting out sexually with members of the opposite sex in a desperate attempt to prove to themselves that they are not homosexual. Numerous pregnancies among lesbian teenagers are considered by some scholars to be "a way of either denying or testing their sexuality," reports Deborah Zera after reviewing the limited research studies on the topic. She also calls attention to the higher risk of suicide among homosexual adolescents than among heterosexual adolescents.[5] Eli Coleman, a medical-school professor who trains mental-health professionals in the area of human sexuality, has focused on the process homosexual people go through in admitting to themselves that they are homosexual. Having internalized society's negative attitudes, they often will "conceive of themselves in the same way society does—different, sick, confused, immoral, and depressed." They will probably deny, repudiate, or repress their feelings at first. Furthermore, writes Coleman, "individuals feel indirect rejection when they hear peers, religious leaders, or family make negative statements about homosexuals and homosexuality."[6]

▼ DISTORTIONS CAUSED BY HOMOPHOBIA

Many Christians think of homosexuality as topping the list in a hierarchy of sins. For that reason, homophobia may even result in a strange kind of "situation ethic," although that term would probably not be used. For example, one military chaplain with an evangelical affiliation reported to a civilian pastor friend that during overseas service he had encouraged the men in his charge to visit prostitutes in what was known as the local "meat market." When the pastor asked why he had given such advice, the chaplain replied simply, "To prevent perversion." Somehow it didn't occur to him that to use and exploit women in this way might in itself be a perversion of God's plan for sexuality. The chaplain's sole concern was to prevent homosexual acts; and to further this goal, even sex with a prostitute was considered acceptable since at least it was heterosexual. Such reasoning is all too common. For example, several years ago it was revealed that a state legislator had sired two children outside of marriage. Hearing the news, a conservative member of Congress from the legislator's state said he hoped this "does not depict someone that we want to represent us in politics or other serious endeavors—but at least it shows a preference by him for a heterosexual lifestyle."[7] And when the Justice Department investigated allegations that some members of Congress had lured teenage assistants into illicit sexual acts, one male constituent contacted his representative to say that he didn't mind what they were doing with his tax dollars "as long as they're doing it with little girls," but that "if they're doing it with little boys," it was an altogether different matter.[8]

Homophobia can also hinder or block even supposedly objective scientific research on homosexuality and obstruct the dissemination of accurate information. For instance, when the Kinsey

Institute made plans for its study of homosexuality in the 1970s, only the National Institute of Mental Health was willing to grant funds. Other sources of funding "lacked the courage to fund a large-scale objective study of homosexuality."[9] William Paul notes that various academic associations of social scientists, alerted to the problem, have found it necessary to pass resolutions urging more research on the topic and also calling for a halt to the discrimination experienced by many gay and lesbian scholars and clinicians. Researchers who are not gay or lesbian themselves have also run into similar prejudice if they have shown an interest in sexual-orientation research. According to Paul, scholars pursuing such studies have often had to face such career consequences as "stigmatization and job discrimination, not to mention avoidance by funding agencies."[10] Graduate students have sometimes been discouraged from projects examining various aspects of the topic.

Similarly, homophobia has long had a restraining effect on public dissemination of knowledge about homosexuality. Certain beliefs about gay and lesbian people have often been perpetuated even when this means deliberate denial of evidence to the contrary. Psychotherapist C. A. Tripp reports that a 1967 television documentary was purposely distorted when network officials felt that the program in its original, accurate version seemed "too supportive" of homosexual people and might antagonize an important segment of the viewing public. The interviews with "happy" homosexual people seemed so positive that they outweighed the "unhappy" examples. Careful editing and cutting of the sound track changed some of the content so drastically that one man threatened to sue the network and another entered a formal complaint of fraud and withdrew his release, thereby denying the network any future reruns.[11]

In a similar incident, after other serious factual distortions showed up in a 1980 television documentary called *Gay Power, Gay Politics,* a seven-month-long investigation resulted in the National News Council's censuring of CBS for deliberate misrepresentations of the gay community.[12]

Some school systems, after having reluctantly agreed to include family-life education in the curriculum, have directed instructors not to provide students with any information on homosexuality—

even if the students ask questions on the topic. William Paul tells of the Texas Department of Education's rejection of a sexual-hygiene text's brief mention of the fact that many psychiatrists no longer consider homosexuality a mental illness. "This is blatant restriction of free access to information," says Paul. "It is a form of thought control no different in principle from methods employed by totalitarian systems." And because of such censorship tactics, "Texas students have been prevented from discovering that there is a debatable issue when it comes to homosexuality and mental health."[13]

Homophobia also lies behind the long delay in providing the public with accurate information about AIDS. In 1981, when the first cases of AIDS showed up in the United States, the disease had attacked only a small number of men—all of them homosexual. The Public Health Service's name for the strange disease was GRID, an acronym for "gay-related immune deficiency." GRID became AIDS (acquired immune deficiency syndrome) not long afterward when some heterosexual people were also stricken. As long as it was considered a "gay disease" or the "gay plague" (a perception that still exists among many people), attempts to uncover its causes and find effective treatment received little attention and support from the public. Much of the blame rests with the government.

Dr. C. Everett Koop, the surgeon general during the decade when AIDS emerged, tells of his eagerness to give attention to what he saw early on as a serious societal health issue. But during the entirety of Ronald Reagan's first presidential term, Koop was forbidden to speak on the topic publicly! During that period, when he spoke on health issues at press conferences or speaking engagements or as a guest on television programs, he was instructed not to answer any questions on AIDS. Media interviewers were told by government public-affairs representatives not to *ask* Koop any questions on the topic. And although a government task force on AIDS had been formed, Koop was not invited to serve on it until 1985—the year that film star Rock Hudson (a personal friend of Ronald Reagan's) died of AIDS and public alarm over AIDS grew considerably.

In the meantime, Koop had been trying to learn everything he could about the topic. He recounts his careful efforts to keep current on biomedical research findings as they trickled in. He recalls that he had naively assumed at first that his exclusion from the AIDS discussion indicated nothing more than a division of labor. Soon he realized that he was facing a volatile political issue. In his memoirs, Koop writes:

> The Reagan revolution brought into positions of power and influence Americans whose politics and personal beliefs predisposed them to antipathy toward the homosexual community. This influenced the AIDS crisis in two ways. First, it slowed the understanding of AIDS. . . . Second, the conservative politics of the middle and late years of the Reagan administration attempted to thwart my attempts to educate the public about AIDS and tried to stir up hostility toward its victims. I tried to rise above the politics of AIDS, but it would cost me many friendships.[14]

In early 1993, the furor over newly elected president Bill Clinton's desire to overturn the ban against gay and lesbian people's serving in the U.S. armed forces was another manifestation of homophobia. People throughout the country—from the top military brass to members of Congress to ordinary citizens who spoke out on talk shows and lit up the switchboards of their representatives in Washington—joined in the debate. And while both compassion and reason were seen in some commentaries, much of the talk about the subject illustrated not only misinformation but the kind of deliberate distortion that has come to be known as *disinformation*. A 407-page report by the Rand Corporation, commissioned by Defense Secretary Les Aspin, was withheld from the public until August 27, 1993, over a month after President Clinton had acceded to the restrictive advice of his Joint Chiefs of Staff. The $1.3 million Rand report had concluded that there is no evidence that having acknowledged homosexuals in the military would hurt cohesion or performance,[15] but it was withheld by homophobic officials.

There is no one simple explanation for homophobia that applies to all people. Studies do show, however, that the people most likely to be characterized by high levels of homophobia are those who have never met a homosexual person (knowingly) and who hold excessively rigid beliefs about gender roles.[16]

Sometimes homophobic people are uneasy about their own sexual feelings. Tripp cites examples of high-ranking homosexual people (in fields such as politics and religion) who sometimes engineer moral crusades against homosexuality and seek the prosecution of known homosexual people. "The psychology of a high-ranking homosexual's antihomosexuality can be quite complex," explains Tripp. "Although he sometimes seems motivated by a simple desire to protect his own position, he more often exercises a complicated morality in which he justifies his own preferences by publicly attacking nearby variations as outrageous."[17] We are reminded of Christ's illustration of hypocrisy: seeking to remove a speck of sawdust from someone else's eye before removing the log from one's own. (See Matt. 7:3.) And we feel sure that the Christian community would be shocked indeed to learn that some of the most repeated attacks on homosexuality are coming from people who themselves engage secretly in homosexual practices. Of course, Tripp does not say, and we are not implying, that *all* moral crusades against homosexuality are conducted by people who are themselves homosexual. Yet, as Dr. Richard Green points out, in cases of very strong anti-homosexual feelings, one may suspect "conflict at some level."[18]

▼ Is Homosexuality on the Increase?

Other ways homophobia manifests itself are connected with the frequent assertions that homosexuality is on the increase and that if nothing is done to stop it, more and more people will choose to become homosexual. For one thing, these assertions betray a deep lack of faith in the attractions of heterosexuality. For another, there is no reliable evidence to support the assertion that sexual orientation is simply a matter of choice. If it were, why would there be so many gay and lesbian people in a society that rejects and punishes homosexuality?

Above all, there is no reliable evidence to support the declaration that homosexuality is on the increase. Rather, as Evelyn Hooker explains, the social *visibility* of openly declared homosexual people, the emergent homosexual organizations protesting public policy, and the widespread discussion of scientific research on the subject may make it *seem* that more homosexuality exists than ever before.[19] The evident increase, however, is in openness rather than in incidence. There is certainly no basis for the unexplained claim of one Christian author that "the incidence of male homosexuality has increased enormously—perhaps a hundred times—with the introduction of oral contraceptives"![20] Nor is there foundation for the claim of another Christian writer that "homosexuality is on the rise in today's society. And with the Women's Liberation Movement, more and more weak men are feeling threatened by women and choosing homosexual rather than heterosexual relationships."[21]

Such statements are indicative of the homophobic reactions of some Christians as attitudes toward gender roles have changed in recent decades. In 1975, national attention was drawn to the efforts of two independent Baptist ministers in New Milford, Connecticut, who threatened to go to court because sixth-grade children of both sexes were being required to take one half-year each of home economics and industrial arts. The ministers feared that the children—especially the boys—would become homosexuals if the schools didn't stick to traditional gender-based activities, the girls learning to cook and sew while the boys learned metalworking and carpentry.[22] In 1993, a woman told a television talk-show audience that she feared her little granddaughter would be influenced toward a life of lesbianism because a lesbian relative had given the toddler a plastic toy tool set for Christmas.

In a similar vein, a book on Christian child rearing contains a cautionary section titled "How to Develop Your Normal Child into a Homosexual." High on the list of warnings for parents of boys is this: "Teach him to sew and cook, and how to knit, too. After all, sexist attitudes about chores are out of date nowadays." Quoting 1 Cor. 6:9–10, the same author goes on to say, "Here God makes it quite plain that even being an effeminate boy is sin in His sight."[23] Think of the damage such statements can do to a boy or young man of a gentle, sensitive, artistic or poetic bent—or to a young man who, for hormonal reasons or because of certain chromosomal irregularities, is considered "effeminate" in physical appearance. Such a person is being told that his very *being* is sin!

The same book says that a mother can produce a lesbian by applying the list to her daughter in reverse; for example, "never make her wear a dress, and don't spend much time with her, since she prefers playing football with her father anyway."[24]

The important connection between negative attitudes toward homosexual people and an insistence on restrictive gender roles shows up in the very title of Suzanne Pharr's 1988 study, *Homophobia: A Weapon of Sexism*. This book contains an important analysis of the methods common to sexist, racist, economic, and homophobic forms of oppression.[25]

▼ THREE COMPONENTS OF SEXUAL IDENTITY

Part of the confusion and fear about homosexuality is related to a failure to distinguish among three components of sexual identity. As psychiatry professor Richard Green has noted, these components involve: (1) our basic conceptions of ourselves as being either male or female (our gender identities); (2) how we conform to expected gender behaviors as defined by our particular culture (our gender roles); and (3) whether, in terms of a sexual partner, we are attracted to someone of the same sex or the other sex (our sexual orientation).[26]

Gender roles (number two on the list) vary from culture to culture and are undergoing extensive rethinking and change in our own culture. Thus males may feel more free to be tender and to participate in activities traditionally thought "feminine," whereas females may feel more free to be assertive and to participate in activities traditionally considered "masculine." In such cases, people are following *individual* interests, abilities, and personality, instead of trying to fit into a mold determined solely by their having been born into a *category* of male or female.

A person may not conform to gender-role stereotypes and yet have a "gender identity" or self-concept (number one on the list) that matches his or her anatomy. Even though he may be knitting a sweater or changing a baby's diaper, the male thinks, "I am a boy" or "I am a man." Even though she may be repairing her bicycle or piloting a helicopter, the female thinks, "I am a girl" or "I am a woman." This is in contrast to the thinking of the *transsexual person,* who considers himself or herself to be a member of the opposite sex trapped in the "wrong body," and who may even seek hormonal treatment and sex reassignment through surgery.[27]

It should also be noted that a person who doesn't conform to gender-role stereotypes is not necessarily attracted to people of the same sex (number three on the list). Some homosexual people do not fulfill traditional gender-role expectations, but many do. In other words, many lesbian women look and act extremely "feminine" in the conventional sense of that word. And many gay men look and act extremely "masculine," as that term is traditionally understood. In the same way, heterosexual people may take on either traditional or nontraditional gender roles. Thus, taken by itself, number two on Green's list (gender roles) must not be confused with either number one (which may relate to transsexualism) or number three (which may relate to homosexuality). Confusing these three components of sexual identity can only serve to divide, distress, and misinform the Christian community.

▼ HOMOSEXUALITY—OR FRIENDSHIP?

Another area of homophobia that we Christians must face is our fear and suspicion about close same-sex friendships. Jesus said, "By this everyone will know that you are my disciples, if you have love for one another" (John 13:35). But how can we expect the world to *know* that—if we are afraid to love each other because somebody might think we're homosexual? People who are basically heterosexual need to realize that affectionate feelings toward friends of the same sex do not necessarily entail *genital-related* feelings. There is no reason to fear that, because of simply feeling affection, one is somehow "becoming" homosexual. It is certainly possible to feel and speak of love for someone else without the slightest desire to express that love through genital sexual relations. Shakespeare was affirming exactly that sort of close friendship when he wrote, "Let me not to the marriage of true *minds* / Admit impediments."[28] In his anthropological study *Friends and Lovers,* Robert Brain writes that "friendship need not derive from an unconscious sexual drive but a cultural imperative to exchange ideas, sentiments, and goods. . . . To me, it is the strangest thing that in Western Christian society, founded on the love of God and the fellowship of mankind, loneliness has become one of the hallmarks."[29]

In a world yearning for intimacy, we need to rid ourselves of the fears that keep us from knowing the depth of friendship displayed, for example, in Jesus' friendship with John, the beloved disciple, or in his friendship with Mary, Martha, and Lazarus. We are denying ourselves choice gifts of God if we let homophobia rob us of the joy of telling friends we love them and hearing them speak of their love for us, or of holding a friend who needs a shoulder to cry on, or of clasping a hand to show we care, or of hugging in a way that simply expresses a sense of affection and kinship. Similarly, we need to take care that we do not attribute homosexuality to others simply because we observe a deep and close relationship or see two persons of the same sex sharing a home. They may or may not be homosexual, but it is not our business to decide, and inferences are often unfounded. Needless gossip has caused a great deal of discomfort and pain to single persons who greatly need warm, intimate relationships and a sense of family. (In her Pulitzer Prize–winning play, *The Children's Hour,* Lillian Hellman forcefully illustrated the tragic outcomes that such situations can have.) In this regard, the Kinsey researchers showed great sensitivity by taking into consideration the human tendency toward suspicion and gossip. "It should be emphasized," they wrote, "that a high proportion of unmarried females who live together never have contacts which are in any sense sexual."[30]

▼ HOMOSEXUALS AND CHILDREN

One last way that homophobia manifests itself is through the belief that homosexuals are out to catch small children, either for purposes of recruitment into a "gay life-style" or for purposes of seduction or even rape.

The "recruitment" idea first received national publicity during the 1977 campaign that defeated the anti-discrimination ordinance in Dade County, Florida. People who oppose civil rights for gay and lesbian people have argued, without any basis in fact, that homosexuals want to increase their numbers and therefore recruit other people's children to make up for their inability to produce their own biological offspring. Such an assertion involves distortion on several fronts. For one thing, it shows a total lack of understanding of the multiple factors that contribute to a person's becoming homosexual. People cannot simply be "recruited" into homosexuality. As was pointed out in the preceding chapter, the propensity is already there at a very early age. And as we shall see later in this chapter, this propensity is apparently the result of a complex interaction of influences not yet fully understood, including both genetic/biological factors and social/psychological factors.[31] "Think of the efforts that have been made through the ages by heterosexuals to seduce homosexuals," argues Dr. Mary Calderone, one of the founders of the Sex Information and Education Council of the U.S. (SIECUS). "It doesn't work either way." She stresses a need to view sexual orientation, whether heterosexual or homosexual, not in terms of sexual acts but as a state of being. "Furthermore," she writes, "no one who was programmed by five years of age to be heterosexual can be seduced to become homosexual, any more than the reverse."[32]

The stereotype of the homosexual child seducer has arisen from sensationalized media reports of isolated instances in which a male schoolteacher, scout worker, camp counselor, minister, or priest is arrested for sexual activities with (perhaps even rape of) young boys. An extreme example is the case of the grisly sex-torture mass murders that took place around Houston, Texas, in the 1970s. Over a period of time, many teenage runaway boys were lured into a sadistic sexual situation and then killed. In Wisconsin and Ohio in 1992, the horrifying discovery of the remains of the seventeen sexually abused and dismembered young male victims of convicted serial-killer Jeffrey Dahmer shocked the nation. Such gruesome cases, however, are in a category by themselves. The fact that same-sex acts take place should not make us think of such disturbed men as representative of homosexuals in general, any more than we would want to think of rapists or molesters of little girls or serial murderers of women as representative of heterosexuals in general.

In fact, according to Kinsey Institute researcher Alan Bell, child seduction and child molestation are usually heterosexual phenomena. Many of us remain unaware of this because the word *hetero-*

sexual is never used in media reports about male attacks on girls or women, whereas news releases about male attacks on boys often use the word *homosexual*. Hence, the public has been lured into the false assumption that homosexual offenses occur more frequently than heterosexual ones. (This perception may be changing somewhat as television, radio, and print journalists in recent years have been informing the public of all that is entailed in child abuse and how widespread the problem is. More people are becoming aware that the tragedy of incest and other sexual abuses committed against both girls and boys is not primarily an issue of sexual orientation but a matter of exploitation and the flagrant misuse of adult power.) Bell reports that the Kinsey Institute's data show that almost never did homosexual males report being introduced to homosexuality during childhood through seduction by older males.[33] On a similar note, sociologists William Simon and John Gagnon have written that, contrary to popular stereotypes, seduction by an older woman does not appear to be a common "mode of entry into homosexuality" for most lesbian women.[34]

There is, of course, no denying that child seduction (both heterosexual and homosexual) does exist. Parents should certainly teach their children how to recognize and cope with sexual invitations and sexual overtures on the part of adults. *Pederasts* (men who are erotically attracted to young boys) are not necessarily exclusively or primarily homosexual; they may be married and sexually active with their wives and may even have children of their own. Sometimes they are just as erotically attracted to young girls and are more accurately classified as *pedophiliacs* or *pedophiles* (adults who desire sexual contact with children under the age of puberty).[35] In general, most homosexual people (like most heterosexual people) are sexually attracted to adults, not to children. No doubt it is wise to discourage pedophiles and pederasts from working closely with children.[36] But from the standpoint of the children's safety, there is no more reason for barring an ordinary homosexual person from teaching children than there is for barring an ordinary heterosexual person from the same job.

In fact, homosexual teachers may bring distinctive enrichment to many students' lives. University of Massachusetts researcher Pat Griffin found in her study of lesbian and gay educators that most of the participants felt that their homosexual orientation gave them a special perspective that "grew out of their experience as members of a stigmatized minority group." Some even spoke of "having a special mission" or "hidden agenda" beyond their academic responsibilities. "This agenda was not, as anti-gay groups claim, to recruit or molest children," writes Griffin. "Rather, participants believed that their personal sensitivity to prejudice and intolerance enabled them both to identify with students who were 'outcasts' in school and to help other students learn to accept difference rather than fear and ridicule it."[37] The sensitivity and social concern of these teachers encompassed not only gay and lesbian issues but all forms of discrimination—whether on the basis of race, physical or mental disability, or anything else. As one woman expressed it, having worked so hard at her own self-acceptance made her better equipped to help others. "I have more to offer than subject expertise," she told the researchers. "I can be there for special ed. kids, acting-out kids. I've got room in my heart and compassion because of my experience as a lesbian."[38]

▼ HOMOSEXUALS AS ROLE MODELS

Such positive findings notwithstanding, there is still considerable societal ambivalence about accepting homosexual people as role models—especially in the schools. Many people continue to perceive the problem as it was stated a number of years ago in a *Christian Century* guest editorial: "Children become adults and take their places in society by patterning their behavior after role models. . . . It is inescapable: sanctioning homosexual life-styles will affect the way the young perceive adult society, and it will have an effect on the kind of people they grow up to be."[39] According to this line of thought, for a school board to knowingly hire a homosexual person would constitute the social sanction of homosexuality. And the more effective and popular the homosexual teacher turned out to be in the classroom and larger school community, the more powerful (and, in this reasoning, dangerous) the teacher's influence would be. Such reasoning no doubt undergirded the outcome of a June 1992 Gallup Poll indicating that although 74 percent of Americans generally favor equal job opportunities for homosexual men and women, only 41 percent expressed a willingness for homosexual people to be hired as elementary school teachers and only 47 percent were favorable toward the hiring of gay and lesbian high school teachers.[40]

Fears about gay and lesbian people as role models, either inside or outside the schools, are based on the assumption that homosexuality is a matter of choice. But former Kinsey Institute director Paul Gebhard states that he has never known of anyone who is homosexual by choice. The only choice possible is whether or not to *accept* one's homosexual orientation. We have already seen that there are many contradictory theories about the origins of homosexuality. Dr. Gebhard stresses that the factors leading to homosexuality are extremely complex, while the orientation is not a matter of conscious choice.[41]

Dr. Anke Ehrhardt, a leading researcher in gender identity, sex differences, and sexual orientation, agrees. She comments that "homosexuality is still a phenomenon that we cannot really explain. Not only is the research inconclusive as far as hormones are concerned, but as far as environmental learning factors are concerned." She points out that in her research on lesbians, no one factor seems to predict the development of a homosexual orientation. There was nothing unusual about the parental background of the women in her sample, and in fact the sample showed an unusually low percentage of divorced homes.[42] Since parents form the first and frequently the most influential role models, it is important to remember that most homosexual people were brought up by heterosexual parents!

Children reared by gay and lesbian parents, on the other hand, are just as likely to turn out to be heterosexual as are children reared by heterosexual parents. An examination of the scientific literature on the topic led researcher Sharon L. Huggins to conclude that "parental homosexuality does not give rise to gender identity confusion, inappropriate gender role behavior, psychopathology, or homosexual orientation in children."[43] In Huggins's own study of thirty-six adolescent sons and daughters of both heterosexual mothers and lesbian mothers, only one adolescent was identified as a self-designated homosexual. Interestingly, that particular adolescent came from the *heterosexual* mothers' sample.

Developmental psychologist Elizabeth D. Gibbs writes that "the general consensus among researchers is that children raised by lesbian mothers develop an appropriate gender identity, follow typical patterns of acquiring sex-role concepts and sex-typed behaviors, and generally develop a heterosexual orientation."[44] (She hastens to say that, by pointing out this conventional pattern, she is not implying the undesirability of either androgynous gender behavior or the development of a homosexual orientation that may show up in individual cases.) She also calls attention to studies that indicate that children of lesbian mothers tend to show greater tolerance and openness than others to cultural diversity and individual differences.

Richard Green, in his studies of children being reared by either male-to-female or female-to-male transsexual parents and children reared by lesbian parents, likewise found that the children tended to develop as heterosexuals. The children were found in all respects to be typical children. This finding, along with data on other children who showed an inclination toward homosexuality or transsexualism even though their parents were heterosexual and tested in no way unusual on clinical tests and attitude scales, led Dr. Green to conclude that "maybe parents don't have a lot to do with the sex typing of children."[45] His findings provide a whole new dimension for reasoning about role models: parents are the first and most intimate role models a child knows, and "typical" children are being brought up by "atypical" parents, while "atypical" children are being brought up by "typical" parents! One conclusion seems clear: close proximity to adults of either homosexual or heterosexual persuasion does not in itself cause children to become either homosexual or heterosexual.

A number of researchers are convinced that there is an interaction between neuroendocrine factors and social learning, not yet fully understood, that may predispose people toward homosexuality or transsexualism.[46] Psychology professor Heino Meyer-Bahlburg has pointed out that we have "very little knowledge of sexual orientation in general," including heterosexual orientation. "What we need are prognostic longitudinal developmental studies that will have to take into account sex-dimorphic behavior in general, peer-group socialization and pubertal maturation. When we are able to identify the factors that contribute to the development of heterosexual orientation, then we will probably be able to delineate those which lead to homosexual development." Meyer-Bahlburg goes on to speculate that perhaps in human beings "endocrine factors contribute to the development of sexual orientation by way of facilitation of specific sexual learning."[47]

Alertness to the great complexity of factors involved in the development of homosexuality prompted Kinsey Institute researcher Alan Bell and his colleagues to undertake one of the largest studies of homosexual men and women ever attempted.[48] Some of their findings were already discussed in chapter 6. But it is also worth noting that, on the basis of their own study and an examination of other relevant scientific literature, they concluded that "a large body of convincing research appears to suggest a biological foundation for homosexuality, at least among some people"—a point that other scientists have been making as well.[49] From all available evidence, the message is clear: adult role models—whether heterosexual or homosexual—do not influence a child's sexual orientation.

There is no question that teachers influence their students for better or worse in those areas where students are able to exercise choice. Since basic sexual orientation is not one of those areas, the hiring of gay and lesbian people in the schools is best approached as the kind of issue it really is: an issue of civil rights. Here the fairest and most responsible approach would seem to be a *single standard* for both heterosexual and homosexual people. In other words, as far as jobs are concerned—including teaching jobs—the sexual orientation and behavior of any individual should be irrelevant as long as it is reasonably private, and unless actual performance on the job can be shown to be negatively affected.[50]

Russell Baker reminisces in the *New York Times Magazine* that at least two of his high school teachers were homosexual in orientation. One of them, he remembers, had encouraged a classmate to become proficient in an art for which he is now world renowned, and did so without affecting the classmate's heterosexual orientation. The other taught Baker himself that life can be witty—and wit is the hallmark of Baker's success—without affecting Baker's enthusiastic heterosexuality. Beneath his grin, Baker supplies an important corrective to the fear that a teacher's way of life, whatever that may be, will be copied by students: "If the teacher was a 'role model,' parents were obviously unaware of it, for most of them surely did not want their children to grow up to be spinsters. Yet, despite almost constant tutelage by spinsters, I never felt the slightest temptation to indulge in spinsterism."[51]

First-rate teachers, whether heterosexual or homosexual, can provide valuable role models in effective use of language, in attitudes of compassion and social concern, in disciplined work habits, in graceful behavior under stress, in love of life and learning, and the like.[52] (In fact, good homosexual teachers have been doing exactly those things for many years. Their homosexuality is unknown for two reasons: because of society's desire not to know, and because of their personal belief that their sexual orientation is nobody's business but their own. True, it can be argued that changes in societal attitudes cannot occur until more homosexual teachers go public; but only those who have the required economic independence and spiritual stamina should take the plunge.)

While few elementary school students are aware of the sexual orientation of their teachers, middle school, junior high, and high school students are given to such speculation, often very acute and accurate. For a student who knows that he or she is developing in a homosexual direction—frequently a terrifying and guilt-ridden secret—becoming aware that a certain admired teacher is homosexual could have extremely positive results. The young person would see in that teacher the possibility of a self-accepting rather than a self-hating attitude, and might realize that it is possible for homosexual people to contribute something valuable to the world and to relate constructively to other people. Such a young person might thus be spared a painful and destructive involvement in the promiscuity of the cruising scene, or spared from entering into heterosexual marriage in the mistaken hope that the marriage will "cure" his or her predisposition toward homosexuality.

Psychoanalyst Theodore Isaac Rubin has argued that "any relationship, professional or otherwise, that ultimately reduces self-hate and enhances compassion contributes to a long term and possibly permanent therapeutic effect. This process in turn makes self-growth, creativity and constructive relating possible. We invariably relate better to other people when we relate better to ourselves."[53] Surely we would not want to deny the opportunity for self-acceptance and creative living to our neighbor the homosexual!

▼ WHAT DOES GAY MEAN?

As we pointed out in chapter 4, one of the biggest reasons for widespread homophobia is the wide gap, the social distance, heterosexual people maintain between themselves and the homosexual world. Not knowing homosexual women and men as people, many heterosexual Christians can think only in terms of an abstract category to be feared and held in disdain. Naturally, effective ministry is blocked by such an attitude. And one term especially repulsive to many heterosexual Christians is the word *gay* as it is applied by homosexual people to themselves.

There are a number of different theories about the origin of the specialized use of the word *gay* as an adjective or noun meaning "homosexual." But there is agreement that it served originally as a code word for secret communication among homosexual people who felt the necessity of keeping their identity hidden from a hostile society. The primary meaning of the word *gay* is "happy," and with the growth of the homosexual liberation movement and the movement toward gay pride, many homosexual people prefer to use that term almost exclusively. The term *gay* deliberately provides a counterimage to prevailing stereotypes of the neurotic, maladjusted, unhappy homosexual person. It is intended to convey a sense of self-acceptance and of high self-esteem.[54] "I'm gay and I'm proud" and "Gay is good" have become familiar slogans in the homosexual subculture.

Christians who are accustomed to thinking only in terms of "Gay is sin" are likely to reject out of hand—or even fail to hear—what the gay community is trying to say. "Gay is proud" seems to go against all we've ever been taught about homosexuality; it seems a deliberate flaunting of disobedience to God. Consequently, we may close our minds, our ears, our hearts. But for members of the gay community, "Gay is proud" is an effort to say, "I am a person, a human being, just as you are. Recognize me. Accept me. Respect me. I bring to the world my share of talents. I have contributions to offer the society that is rejecting me. I am learning what it means to be accepted by others who are like me and understand me and who have helped me to see that I am not alone. I am learning to accept myself. But can you—will you—accept me?"

▼ WHAT IS THE GAY COMMUNITY?

The gay community is not a particular geographical location, but rather an aggregate of people, places, and activities. Members of the gay community share a sense of social and psychological unity and common interests stemming from their sexual orientation and the societal reaction to that orientation. Through getting together and through information networks and publications, gay people find collective support and acceptance.[55] Actually, it is misleading to speak of the gay community as though it were some sort of monolithic institution composed of a homogeneous population. Perhaps it would be better to speak in the plural: gay communities or homosexual subcultures. What these communities have in common is their members' sense of being an oppressed minority. They seek a social life together and support from one another to help them cope in a society that stigmatizes them. But beyond that, there are enormous variations in the "gay worlds" within the larger gay world.

Perhaps the biggest distinction that needs to be made is between the public (and often more sensational) gay world and the quiet, invisible world of homosexual friendships and networks. The more public gay world includes people who are open about their homosexuality and active in the gay-rights movement, working for changes in laws, public attitudes, and so on. But there is another dimension of the public gay world as well. That dimension consists of settings conducive not only to social activities but also to initiating sexual contacts.

From the standpoint of Christian ethics, the depersonalized sexual encounters of "cruising" (looking for partners solely for casual sexual contact) have elicited some of the strongest arguments for condemning what is erroneously labeled *the* "gay life-style." It

must be kept in mind, however, that such behavior is not even remotely connected to the way many homosexual people conduct
their lives, and thus it is wrong to consider "homosexual life-
style" and "cruising" to be synonymous terms—just as it would
be wrong to equate "heterosexual life-style" with "canvasing singles bars for pickups." Furthermore, it is only fair to point out
that 54 percent of the males who frequent public men's rooms for
sex would not label themselves gay and in fact are married and
otherwise "respectable," often church and community leaders.
They are seeking impersonal sex because that least jeopardizes
their family and job connections and their standing in the community.[56] Obviously, however, these 54 percent constitute terrific
threats to the health of their wives and future children, their own
health, and that of their casual partners. Nevertheless, having said
all this, we are well aware that "cruising" in gay bars and seeking
out anonymous sexual encounters in gay baths and sex clubs have
been acknowledged practices within the gay male subculture and
have been major factors in the spread of the human immunodeficiency virus (HIV) among gay men. However, the gay community
is to be commended for its vigorous educational efforts in response to the threat of AIDS, efforts that resulted in a reevaluation
of risky sexual behavior and a drastic reduction in depersonalized
"cruising." As a result, the annual rate of new HIV-positive cases
among homosexual males has been dropping.

Perhaps the heterosexual world should ponder its own share of
responsibility for the cruising scene. In one university town, after
same-sex dancing was prohibited at a favorite student gathering
place, one young man expressed his disappointment in a letter to
the local newspaper. "Why does society persist in forcing gays into
strictly sexual situations?" he asked. "By not allowing gay people
to participate in healthy social activities, society is forcing us into
the bedroom, or the bar room, and even into the restroom, while
everyone else is allowed to socialize freely and display affection in
countless ways that would indeed be considered sexual were it
performed by a same-sex couple."[57] What many Christians fail to
realize is that many people who are cruising are searching for
something much more meaningful than casual sex. Many yearn
for a life partner, even though they may be too confused and

frightened to know how to sustain a long-term relationship and thus drift in and out of casual sexual encounters. "Where else can I go?" some ask. Whereas a heterosexual Christian can find a life partner at church or college socials, homosexual people (including some homosexual Christians) often feel forced to slip off to the big city to seek out homosexual bars and clubs, even if they are extremely uncomfortable in those settings.

Even those who are already settled in permanent committed homosexual relationships may occasionally visit the gay bars, but not for reasons related to cruising. Rather, they long for a sense of social acceptance as a couple, something denied them in society at large. "It is impossible to know to what extent love is strengthened by being public," writes Dennis Altman, "yet romantic ideals of secret love notwithstanding, I suspect that after a time lovers have a real psychological need for the support that comes from being recognized as such. . . . The very concealment of love tends in time to produce strains a more open relationship could better handle."[58] Could those churches that refuse to provide social acceptance to homosexual people be forcing them to rely on the very resources of the gay communities that the churches are so quick to condemn?

When cruising for casual sex has occurred, it has been primarily a male phenomenon. Kinsey Institute researchers Alan Bell and Martin Weinberg found in their extensive 1970 study of diverse homosexual life-styles that only 17 percent of lesbian women reported purposely searching for a casual sex partner, as compared with 85 percent of gay men.[59] As Bell points out, "the highly charged sexual atmosphere of the gay world" has not only failed to support sexual monogamy but conspired against it.[60] The cruising scene characteristic of a certain segment of the gay community, especially in the pre-AIDS era, has been described by Evelyn Hooker: "A standardized and essential feature of interaction in bars, baths, streets, and parks is the expectation that sex can be had without obligation or commitment. Sexuality is separated from affectional and social life and is characterized by promiscuity, instrumentality, and anonymity."[61] In the early 1990s, health officials were beginning to express concern that "a relapse" to such "pre-AIDS recklessness" was occurring among many gay men in their teens and early twenties, resulting in an increase in diagnosed cases of AIDS among this age group at a time when such cases had decreased among homosexual men overall.[62]

▼ PROMISCUITY AND THE "EX-GAY" MINISTRIES

Dr. Ralph Blair, a psychotherapist who directs New York's Homosexual Community Counseling Center, explains that cruising and promiscuity are not so much expressions of the sex drive as they are the futile attempts of people with low self-esteem to find ego stroking and self-acceptance. As a counselor and an evangelical Christian, Dr. Blair is cognizant of the various "ex-gay" ministries that claim that Christ can and does "cure" the homosexuality of those who seek healing. He has talked with some leaders of such organizations who have admitted in private (but rarely in public) that their own desires are as homosexual as they ever were. In some cases, certain leaders of such ministries have admitted to engaging in homosexual practices even though purportedly striving to free others from homosexuality. One leader privately admitted that he was misleading people who, expecting his ministry to change them into heterosexuals, found only that the "liberation" or "deliverance" promised them was simply a desperate day-to-day struggle against sexual expression.[63]

Undoubtedly, however, there are some sincere Christians who believe that they have been "cured" of homosexuality. We do not wish in any way to question the sincerity of these people. Some of them may have been true bisexuals, able to respond romantically and erotically to people of either sex (number three on the Kinsey continuum described in chapter 6). Others may have been predominantly heterosexual and were engaging in homosexual practices as a matter of choice (ones and twos on the continuum). In either case, it is understandable that through faith in Christ these people have returned to a sexual expression that satisfies social norms without violating their own true nature. But what about people who are predominantly or exclusively homosexual (fours through sixes on the continuum) and who claim a change in orientation? Dr. Blair, who through counseling has helped hundreds of homosexual people overcome their need for promiscuity, explained to us by letter what may be occurring in the lives of these Christians:

As people begin to see that they can associate with others on a basis that is not just genital, either with others who are "getting their heads together" through therapy or with other believers in Christian fellowship, they are opened up to much more meaningful interaction than they have known before. It is easy to misunderstand these newer experiences as evidence of a diminishing homosexuality. Actually it is a diminishing of the use of sex for non-sexual [self-esteem] purposes. Sooner or later, the person realizes that the authentic homosexual orientation remains intact. Sex can now be something to use . . . as an expression of affection and no longer as an inadequate means for self-acceptance.

As founder of Evangelicals Concerned, a national task force of homosexual Christians and their friends, Dr. Blair has heard from many people who once sincerely thought they had undergone a change of orientation and who later discovered that such a change had not in fact occurred. His hope is that Evangelicals Concerned will provide such people a place to find Christ's acceptance and meet other gay and lesbian Christians who are seeking to work out and live out a responsible ethic for homosexual Christians.[64]

▼ THE PRIVATE, ORDINARY HOMOSEXUAL COMMUNITY

In addition to the public manifestation of "gay life" that is often featured in media reports, there is another "gay world" that heterosexual Christians need to know about: the private homosexual world made up of people who go about their daily lives, jobs, and religious and social activities just as heterosexual people do. Sex is only one small aspect of their lives and is likely to be confined to the partnership in a context not unlike heterosexual marriage. Thus, Hooker is careful to draw attention to those sectors of the homosexual community where "sexuality is integrated in the affectional, personal, and social patterns of individuals who establish relatively stable and longlasting relationships." In this invisible gay world, contrasting dramatically with the cruising of the "baths and bar scene," social occasions are apt to consist of a gathering of friends (often homosexual couples in one another's homes) for dinners, picnics, birthday celebrations, holidays, anniversaries, and so on.[65]

Perhaps it is lack of awareness of the very *ordinariness* of everyday life in the vast hidden homosexual world that accounts for the insensitivity shown by some well-meaning Christians in their zealous opposition to gay civil rights or in their efforts to break up social relationships. After the dean of a Christian college had expelled a young gay student and advised him to break off all contact with the gay community, the young man exclaimed, "But these people are my *friends!* They are very nice people! Why must I cut myself off from them when I really like them?" To a counselor he later said, "Where else can I go? Those are the people who understand me and accept me. They're interesting people who have taught me all sorts of things about art and music. So *much* of what we do has nothing at all to do with sex."[66]

Yet many Christians fail to be sensitive on this point in their warnings to "avoid contact with all former homosexual friends" and to "avoid places where such people gather."[67] Sometimes this insensitivity extends even to the terminology they use, as in this statement by a prominent theologian: "The church of Christ must never forget that the homosexual has little disposition to seek help while he associates only with his 'queer' cohorts."[68] We need to move out of such homophobia and into an understanding of why gay communities exist and what they're really like.

The Debate in American Christendom

HOWARD BROWN writes of a Baptist minister's son in a small midwestern town. Upon finding out that his son was homosexual, the minister told him daily that he would go to hell for committing an abomination. During the boy's senior year in high school, his father ordered him to eat his meals in his room, away from the rest of the family. Although he was an outstanding musician and had won state and national music contests, he was told he could not play the church piano and, indeed, was not to attend the church at all. On graduation day, the father sent the boy's brothers and sisters out of the house and handed the young man his "gift." It was an envelope containing a small amount of spending money and a one-way train ticket to New York. His mother was sad, but could only say that she thought it was "best for the family."[1] In another case described by Dr. Brown, a mother put her arm around her son's shoulders after learning that he was homosexual—which he took to be a sign that she was going to accept him. Then she spoke, saying she had made only one mistake in her life. "What do you mean?" he asked, whereupon his mother told him that she should have had an abortion twenty-two years earlier. Since that conversation she has been telling everyone that her son is dead.[2]

In other cases known to the authors, young women and men have committed suicide because they were unable to endure the severe castigation they experienced from Christian parents and other church members. One deeply devoted lesbian Christian, educated for a career in Christian service, put a gun to her head in desperation after hearing one more time that she was condemned by God and the church. In another case, a young gay man was highly regarded in his community for his artistic talents. A gentle, loving man, he was committed to Christ and to his life partner, a university professor. But his Christian mother constantly bombarded him with letters and long-distance phone calls, telling him he was going to hell because of his homosexuality. Lovingly, he tried to reason with her. He sent her books (including the first edition of this book). He introduced her to materials telling of other parents who had homosexual sons or daughters. He visited her whenever he could. But all to no avail. She kept escalating her pressure on him to repent and change, until he felt he could stand it no longer. One day, after receiving one of her condemning letters, he attached a hose to the exhaust pipe of his car and ended his pain by ending his life.

Rick Huskey, a former Methodist deacon who had planned to become a minister, fared better in his dealings with his Christian parents. Upon the revelation of his homosexuality, his church had withdrawn plans to make him an elder and later removed him from deacon's orders. His parents had been stunned to learn of his homosexuality, but they lovingly accepted him and stood by him. Willing to share their story with the readers of a Christian family magazine, the Huskeys told it to a free-lance writer, who reported that "fear of rejection kept them from asking for help from the church." They felt that on the topic of homosexuality the church was playing the role of follower rather than leader, "following popular opinion instead of leading toward compassion and acceptance."[3]

▼ DOES RETHINKING MEAN WORLDLY COMPROMISE OR CHRIST-LIKE LEADERSHIP?

Some Christians would argue that any trend toward acceptance of homosexuality *is* following popular opinion, rather than standing fast on Christian principles and calling homosexuality sinful.

As we have seen, the Bible clearly condemns certain kinds of homosexual practices (in the context of gang rape, idolatry, and lustful promiscuity), just as it condemns certain kinds of heterosexual practices. However, it appears to be silent on certain other aspects of homosexuality—namely, the matter of a homosexual orientation as described by modern behavioral sciences and also the matter of a committed love relationship analogous to heterosexual monogamy. Because of these silences and gaps in biblical teaching, many Christians are reconsidering the subject. This rethinking has been given added impetus by the growing awareness of personal incidents such as those described in the opening section of this chapter and by debates on the ordination of openly lesbian and gay people, debates about the religious celebration of same-sex unions, concerns about gay civil-rights ordinances, and the like.

In the *Christian Medical Society Journal,* Lewis Penhall Bird commented on the decision of the American Psychiatric Association to declassify homosexuality as a psychiatric disorder: "As with other controversial subjects, the issues used to be firmly settled. Now 'everything that was nailed down is comin' loose.'" Bird went on to point out that Christians—including those in the conservative evangelical camp—have revised their views on at least three other sexual practices: sexual intercourse during menstruation, masturbation, and oral-genital sex. Although he did not attempt to resolve the problems surrounding the homosexuality issue, Bird did raise a number of questions to help Christian counselors think through this and other matters relating to human sexuality.[4]

To Bird's three sex-related issues on which Christians have been changing their minds over a comparatively recent period, we could add a fourth—contraception. Although the official Roman Catholic position allows for no "artificial" form of birth control (as opposed to "natural" methods that require carefully timed periodic abstinence), the majority of Catholic couples in the United States and Canada use some form of contraception, including the so-called nonnatural methods and sterilization.[5] And so do most Protestant couples. Protestant denominations today generally emphasize that wise family planning is part of responsible Christian marriage and family living. Yet in the first several decades of the twentieth century, official Protestant pronouncements on contraception were as disapproving of the practice as any Roman Catholic statement ever was. Statements were issued by various denominations—Episcopalians, Lutherans, Methodists, Presbyterians, Baptists, and others. These official statements were peppered with claims that the practice of contraception "violated nature" and was "both anti-social and anti-Christian," a "menace to the family," "demoralizing to character," "hostile to the national welfare," an indication of "grave immorality," and a succumbing to "that pagan atmosphere of life which the early church endeavored to cleanse." There were warnings that if churches moved away from their traditional teachings on birth control, the "whole Christian ethic" would be destroyed and along with it "the whole social order." Debates over the issue heated up conferences, committees were formed to study the issue, and statements were drafted and redrafted in efforts to provide guidance for the people in the pews. Meanwhile, the people in the pews were reaching their own conclusions. The social climate was changing; and while the churches debated whether or not contraception was moral, families were having fewer and fewer children. In the early 1930s, the Committee on Marriage and the Home under the old Federal Council of Churches saw the need for serious rethinking of the topic and issued a report endorsing contraception for all the reasons the majority of people accept the practice today. But various denominations within that body voiced strong opposition, with some threatening to withdraw from the council rather than have any part in an association that approved of birth control. The adoption of the report was blocked, and the topic was referred back to the executive committee for more study.[6]

It isn't difficult to see the parallels between these debates over contraception and the debates over the church's position on homosexuality today. It is also clear that issues surrounding sexuality probably are more volatile and produce more fear and anger among Christians than the issues in any other area of human concern.

In Lewis Bird's listing of masturbation, oral-genital sex, and coitus during menstruation as issues that have prompted rethinking by many Christians, he noted that at one time such practices were considered *deviant* (in the sense of being labeled unnatural, unhealthy, abnormal, and as such, sinful). Now many Christian writers and counselors have reclassified them as *variant* sexual practices (sexual conduct considered to fall within normal limits, simply a variation).

The Bible is silent on the topics of masturbation and oral-genital sex, although the church has by no means been silent over the ages and has condemned both as sins in God's sight. It might be wise for us to focus on the third of the topics on which thinking has recently been revised—namely, sexual intercourse during menstruation—because it is more parallel to the case of rethinking homosexuality. Both intercourse during menstruation and abusive homosexual practices are condemned in Scripture.

▼ An Illuminating Parallel

Bird's only comment on this topic is that "few modern evangelicals would advocate excommunication (Leviticus 18:19–30) for couples who engage in intercourse during menstruation." However, not only have there been few negative attacks; some Christian writers and counselors positively *encourage* the practice, and some do not so much as *hint* that any prohibition of the practice is found in the Bible.

Medical doctor Ed Wheat, for example, has provided this advice: "A wife's sex drive ordinarily does not diminish during the menstrual period; so if both partners desire intercourse at this time, it's perfectly all right. If the wife has a diaphragm for birth control, she may insert it during the time of light bleeding and even have intercourse without any blood coming into the lower vagina."[7] Another counselor, Herbert Miles, uses a variant on the natural-law argument, claiming that if the Creator made woman in such a way that her peak sexual desire is right before, during, and after her menstrual period, God "must have meant for her need to be satisfied under the right circumstances."[8] However, if a gay or lesbian person were to claim that God intended his or her sexual needs "to be satisfied under the right circumstances," that person would likely be accused of twisting Scripture. This observation is mentioned only to show that even in the most conservative Christian circles, a consistent system of interpreting Scripture is seldom applied. In spite of declarations of firm adherence to principle, there is far more accommodation to human experience in interpreting and applying Scripture than many Christians would care to admit.

In their book on sex in Christian marriage, Tim and Beverly La-Haye recognize the problem and address themselves to the biblical prohibition. Pointing out that intercourse during menstruation is not viewed as harmful by most medical authorities, they suggest that it should not be viewed as sinful because, according to Christian theology, the death of Christ did away with all the ceremonial laws and rituals. Furthermore, they explain, "those laws were given thirty-five hundred years ago, before showers and baths were so convenient, before tampons, disinfectants, and other improved means of sanitation had been invented."[9] The authors refer only to the instructions about menstruation in Leviticus 15, and do not quote from Leviticus 20. Verse 18 of chapter 20 says that "if a man lies with a woman during her monthly period and brings shame upon her, he has exposed her discharge and she has uncovered the source of her discharge; they shall both be cut off from their people"(NEB). Although the LaHayes neglect chapter 20 of Leviticus while discussing coitus during menstruation, they latch on to that chapter in their discussion of homosexuality. As we saw earlier, they put great stress on verse 13: "If a man lies with a male as with a woman, both of them have committed an abomination; they shall be put to death; their blood is upon them."

One could, of course, attempt to resolve the inconsistency in treatment by arguing, as the LaHayes do, that in the one case the command relates to ceremonial law, while in the other it is part of moral law. But such a distinction simply will not hold up in the light of the twenty-second chapter of Ezekiel. In that chapter, sins are listed that call forth God's judgment, including violations of sexual prohibitions that are also found in Leviticus 20, and which seem to imply a moral violation rather than merely a breaking of ceremonial taboos. Singled out in the Ezekiel passage are incest, adultery, and intercourse during menstruation. Homosexual acts, on the other hand, are not mentioned at all! Furthermore, a number of commentators think that all the transgressions on the list are equally serious to Ezekiel. Referring specifically to the statement about intercourse during menstruation, Bible scholar H. L. Ellison writes: "What needs to be stressed is that Ezekiel sees in offenses against the natural modesties of sex (verse 10b) and in adultery (verse 11a) evils as great and as deadly as incest and promiscuity of the worst sort."[10] Rabbi Maurice Lamm points out that, among observant Jewish couples today who abide by the concept of family purity (*taharat ha-mishpachah*), abstinence during the wife's menstrual period continues to be required.[11]

In making these points, we do not wish to argue that intercourse during menstruation should be considered sinful for Christians. We could direct attention, for example, to Paul's instructions that married couples not abstain from sexual relations except for specific periods set aside for prayer by mutual consent (1 Cor. 7:5), or to Jesus' breaking of the taboos against touch with regard to the woman "who had been suffering from hemorrhages for twelve years" (Mark 5:25–34). We could also point to passages that present Christian teachings on changes in the ceremonial law, although no passage is *specifically* addressed to the regulations concerning menstruation. What is important to notice is simply that in view of medical opinion and personal experience, Christians have been willing to ignore commands about coitus during menstruation. Therefore, couldn't it be looked upon as a parallel case that some Christians are also rethinking the matter of homosexuality? As in the case of coitus during menstruation, the rethinking is partially due to medical opinion and other research, and partially due to the personal experience and needs of individuals. The parallel is worth pondering.

▼ CANDIDATES FOR HELL, OR FOR GOD'S GRACE

In the thinking, writing, and speaking of many Christians, probably no other group has been singled out as "candidates for hell" as consistently as homosexual people. Usually such condemnations are backed up with 1 Cor. 6:9–10, because the list of those who will not "inherit the kingdom of God" includes the two distinct Greek words that have been been joined together in some translations and assumed to apply to all homosexual people. In our chapter 5, we discussed in detail the misunderstandings that have arisen because of how this passage has been interpreted and translated. We also pointed out that other categories in that passage are often overlooked, such as that of the covetous or greedy, who are never singled out by Christians for the kind of judgment categorically passed on homosexual people. This select use of Scripture becomes even more clear when we turn to Gal. 5:19–21, which again describes those who "will not inherit the kingdom of God." Nothing about homosexuality is mentioned, but "enmities, strife, jealousy, anger, quarrels, dissensions, factions" *are* mentioned—and all of them are sins that seem to be very much at home in the average church! People who engage in them are seldom the subject of sermon topics setting forth God's judgment; it is much easier to make scapegoats of homosexual people. But Jesus warned us that judgment is a boomerang (Matt. 7:1); and the cumulative effect of scapegoating has been a legalistic and fearful withdrawal from the unlimited and unconditional love of God, and from the glorious liberty of the children of God.

For the sake of honesty in our interpretation and application of Scripture, as well as for the sake of justice and compassion, the time now seems ripe to take an altogether new approach to homosexuality. Some Christians are beginning to do this. Both independently and in mainline denominations, groups of homosexual Christians and their supportive heterosexual friends have been formed in recent years. A representative sampling of such groups includes Dignity (Roman Catholic), Integrity (Episcopal), Lutherans Concerned, Affirmation (United Methodist), American Baptists Concerned, Brethren/Mennonite Council for Lesbian and Gay Concerns, Friends for Lesbian and Gay Concerns (Quaker), Presbyterians for Lesbian and Gay Concerns, New Ways Ministry (Roman Catholic), Affirm (Gays and Lesbians of the United Church of Canada), National Gay Pentecostal Alliance, United Church Coalition for Lesbian and Gay Concerns, and the Universal Fellowship of Metropolitan Community Churches.[12] In various denominations, study groups and task forces have brought together homosexual and heterosexual Christians for dialogue, understanding, and policy decisions. Such dialogue played an important role in a change of attitudes toward gay and lesbian people in the Netherlands. As we mentioned earlier, in the United

States, a national task force called Evangelicals Concerned was founded by psychotherapist Ralph Blair. The heterosexual and homosexual evangelicals who make up the group are "concerned about the lack of preparation for dealing realistically with homosexuality in the evangelical community and about the implications of the Gospel in the lives of gay men and women."[13]

There is also an interdenominational movement of local churches that have publicly declared themselves to be open to the full participation of lesbian and gay people in all aspects of church life. Among United Methodists, such churches are part of the Reconciling Congregation Program. American Baptist supportive churches are known as Welcoming and Affirming, while Mennonites simply use the term Supportive Congregations. Among Presbyterians, such congregations go by the name More Light Churches. The counterpart among Lutherans is the Reconciled in Christ Program. United Church of Christ congregations and Disciples of Christ congregations that extend a special welcome to gay men and lesbian women are called Open and Affirming churches. And Unitarian Universalist groups that specifically seek gay and lesbian participation call themselves Welcoming Congregations.

▼ THE CURRENT CHRISTIAN SPECTRUM, PART ONE: HOMOSEXUALITY AS SIN

Even apart from such specialized groups, there has been a great deal of discussion on the topic of homosexuality in virtually every denomination. A continuum or spectrum of views on homosexuality has been developing among Christians of various persuasions. On one end are those who take the absolute position that homosexuality is sin. "The New Testament blasts homosexual activity as the lowest, most degraded kind of immorality," claims one person of this persuasion.[14] On the other end of the spectrum are those who would agree with Ralph Blair that it is time for Christians "to abandon un-Biblical crusades against homosexuality and to help those who have quite naturally developed along homosexual lines to accept themselves as Jesus Christ has accepted them—just as they are—and to live lives which include responsible homosexual behavior."[15] A similar view is held by Troy Perry and the Universal Fellowship of Metropolitan Community Churches.[16] Between these two ends of the spectrum are a variety of views, some of which include a great deal of compassionate and concerned questioning.[17]

Even those who stand firmly on the "sin perspective" end of the continuum are increasingly careful to draw a distinction between homosexual *orientation* and homosexual *activities*. According to this perspective, *being* a homosexual isn't sinful, but *practicing* homosexuality is. In 1975, when over two thousand evangelicals gathered in St. Louis for a national conference called the Continental Congress on the Family, an official statement was issued that opposed the "unjust and unkind treatment given to homosexuals by individuals, society, and the Church" and called for ministry "to those who are homosexually oriented in order to help them to change their life-style in a manner which brings glory to God." While expressing the belief that "the Bible teaches homosexuality to be sinful," the congress stated "that a homosexual orientation can be the result of having been sinned against." Thus, the call was for understanding, forgiveness, and spiritual support on the part of Christians who care about helping homosexual people.[18]

▼ THE CURRENT CHRISTIAN SPECTRUM, PART TWO: CONCERN FOR PEOPLE AND RELATIONSHIPS

Already in the 1970s, there were signs that some Christians were taking a new look at the homosexual person as an individual human being, rather than thinking about homosexuality only in the abstract. An example was this candid confession of evangelical author Joseph Bayly: "For years I have been troubled by a strict application of the Bible's strong condemnation of homosexuality, and total judgment of the homosexual person. . . . I accept the Bible's authority; at the same time I have wondered—as with suicide—about a precise identification of every person of this type with the biblical model."[19]

Other Christians, besides moving beyond the matter of homosexual acts to consider the homosexual person, have been taking a fresh look at homosexual *relationships*. "Perhaps we have been asking the wrong questions about such relationships," suggests

Margaret Evening. "The emphasis seems to have been merely on whether or not homosexual acts are morally permissible . . . when the primary consideration should be: 'Is this friendship going to radiate love *out* to others and draw them *in* to its circle . . . ?'" Her belief is that "every loving relationship should be a center of healing and comfort, open and available to all amid the wounds and sores of society."[20]

Many religious groups—Roman Catholic, Protestant, and Jewish—have come to realize that their faith in a God of love and justice requires them, *at the very least,* to stand up for the civil rights of gay and lesbian people. For example, the Union of American Hebrew Congregations in 1977 called for equal protection under the law for homosexual people and an end to discrimination in housing and employment. The 1990 National Conference of Catholic Bishops likewise argued for the honoring of the basic human rights of homosexual people, reaffirming earlier statements that had been issued in the 1970s and 1980s. The bishops pronounced as "deplorable" the verbal and physical violence that has been directed toward gay men and lesbian women. Representative of Protestant statements is a Lutheran appeal for Christians to "be more understanding and sensitive to life as experienced by those who are homosexual" and to "take leadership roles in changing public opinion, civil laws, and prevailing practices that deny justice and opportunity to any persons, homosexual or heterosexual."[21]

A number of religious leaders wrote to representatives in Congress who were considering a lesbian/gay civil-rights bill in 1985. "Our religious traditions teach us the importance of providing equal justice to all persons and respect for the dignity of each person," they wrote. "We believe that the basic rights of employment, housing, and access to public services should not be denied anyone merely by reason of their sexual orientation." They felt a sense of responsibility to "provide moral leadership in improving public understanding of this issue and the persons it affects." Among those signing were representatives of the Church of the Brethren, the Christian Church, the Union of American Hebrew Congregations, the Presbyterian Church (USA), the Lutheran Council in the USA, the Episcopal Church, the United Methodist

Church, the United Church of Christ, the American Ethical Union, and the Unitarian Universalist Association.[22]

As James Nelson, a professor of Christian ethics, has written, "The church's unequivocal support of civil rights for gay people ought not depend upon Christian agreement about the theological and moral appropriateness of homosexuality. The matter of civil rights is a matter of basic Christian commitment to social justice for all persons."[23]

▼ THE CURRENT CHRISTIAN SPECTRUM, PART THREE: ACCEPTANCE OF HOMOSEXUAL UNION

A growing minority of Christians are suggesting that a compassionate and creative solution to the question of homosexuality lies in the acceptance of committed, permanent homosexual relationships between two people who love each other and want to spend their lives together. "I have posed the thesis that there is the possibility of morally good homosexual relationships," wrote John McNeill in *The Church and the Homosexual,* suggesting that "the love that unites the partners in such a relationship, rather than alienating them from God, can be judged as uniting them more closely with God and as mediating God's presence in our world."[24]

Louie Crew, the essayist and poet who founded Integrity to bring together gay Episcopalians in a national organization, has pointed out the hypocrisy of many Christians who disparage homosexual relationships. "On the one hand, the church condemns us for allegedly not forming stable relationships," he writes. "On the other, the church strictly forbids us to form such relationships."[25]

A number of years ago, an associate professor of theology at Drew University, Darrell J. Doughty, presented a paper to a local meeting of United Presbyterians that was then made available to the denomination at large. Drawing an analogy between the homosexual issue and the first-century issue concerning whether all non-Jewish converts to Christianity should have to be circumcised, an issue that "stirred up passions of ferocious intensity," Professor Doughty pointed out that the first-century problem was solved by a triumph of grace over law. Similarly, although the

rabbis taught that "a man without a woman is not a man," neither Jesus nor Paul was married; and when Paul discussed marriage in 1 Corinthians 7, he made no appeal to nature or to
creation or to the necessity of procreation, but only to the relationship between the people directly involved. Defining sin as "the
manipulation and exploitation of other persons in the attempt to
establish and elevate ourselves," Doughty argued that "if we condemn homosexuality as contrary to the Will of God, and refuse
ordination and perhaps even church membership to homosexual
persons, then the burden is on us to show that homosexual relationships cannot be relationships of love . . . and that our decision
is not simply an attempt to justify ourselves."[26]

At the 1975 annual meeting of the Christian Association for
Psychological Studies, a symposium on homosexuality brought together a panel of Christians in the mental-health professions. They
explained that behavioral-science research and the realities of their
clinical practice had forced them to take a new look at the traditional biblical interpretations that consider all homosexual behavior to be sinful. They suggested an alternative view—namely, that
promiscuity, fornication, and adultery should be regarded as sinful
for both homosexual and heterosexual people, but that a loving,
committed, permanent relationship between two people of the
same sex was in an entirely different category and was not condemned in Scripture. According to a *Christianity Today* news report, the majority view expressed by members of the panel was
that "God's 'perfect' will is for the monogamous heterosexual
family. However . . . Christians burdened with an involuntary homosexual orientation could choose a committed homosexual relationship as within God's 'permissive' will rather than an unwanted
celibacy."[27] Many gay and lesbian people might not appreciate the
implication of second-class Christianity in that statement. But
since the acceptance of committed same-sex unions would solve a
great many problems and provide helpful guidelines for both ethical living and ordination decisions, this alternative to traditional
attitudes is worth exploring in greater depth.

▽ ▽ ▽ ▽ ▽ ▽ ▽ ▼ ▽

Proposing a Homosexual Christian Ethic

FOR MANY CHRISTIANS, to accept same-sex covenantal partnerships would require a major shift in thinking—a shift from one "model" of viewing a theologically based ideal for human sexual expression to another model in which there is no less a desire to know what is pleasing to God and to live accordingly. On the next page we describe the two models in graphic form.

For most Christians, such a shift in thinking will not come easily. It is, after all, a different way of looking at the topic, and it goes against teachings that are familiar to most people. Some Christian leaders, sensitive to the problems on both sides of the issue, seem to reach the alternative view rather grudgingly or adopt some position in between the two views. Lewis Smedes, an evangelical theologian and ethics professor, provides one example of what we might call "cautious accommodation."

▽ CAUTIOUS ACCOMMODATION

In his book *Sex for Christians,* Smedes has suggested that a homosexual Christian should seek a change in sexual orientation if at all possible. But if change is impossible and "constitutional homosexuality" is real, says Smedes, then two other options exist: celibacy, and "optimum homosexual morality." According to Smedes, celibacy is to be preferred—even though he admits that such a course is likely to be difficult. The emphasis is not on converting to heterosexuality but on abstaining from homosexual practices. Admitting that "ordinarily no one has the right to prescribe celibacy for another person," Smedes nevertheless urges homosexual Christians to give serious consideration to such a course on the basis of his belief "that homosexual life is ethically unwarranted and personally unsatisfying."

SEXUAL ETHICS: TWO MODELS

Model 1 THE TRADITIONAL VIEW	Model 2 THE ALTERNATIVE VIEW
God's Ideal for the Sexual Expression of Love	*God's Ideal for the Sexual Expression of Love*
Heterosexual, monogamous marriage (A relationship between a man and a woman; it is accepted as a given that all people are heterosexually oriented)	A covenantal relationship (For heterosexual people, the uniting of a man and a woman in what is known as marriage; for homosexual people, a committed relationship between two men or two women who are united in a loving covenantal union)
Abuses of the Ideal	
Fornication (sexual intercourse without the commitment of marriage)	*Abuses of the Ideal*
	Sex with people with whom there is no committed, covenantal relationship
Adultery (sexual intercourse with someone other than one's spouse)	Unfaithfulness to the covenantal partner, or behavior causing another person to be unfaithful to the one to whom she or he is pledged
Promiscuity (sexual intercourse with many different people, casual sex based on lust, exploitation of others, etc.)	
Homosexuality (sexual acts between people of the same gender)	Promiscuity (sex with many different people, casual sex based on lust, exploitation of others, etc.)

Being a realist, however, Smedes points out that neither change nor celibacy may work out for some homosexual people. What then? He suggests that one should develop the "best ethical conditions" for living out one's sexual life. Specifically, that would mean "no exploitation, no seduction, and no enticement of youth into the homosexual sphere." It would also mean intense development of the nonsexual aspects of life, and efforts toward building stable relationships, "associations in which respect and regard for the other as a person dominates their sexual relationship." But Smedes emphasizes strongly that, in his view, "to develop a morality for the homosexual life is *not* to accept homosexual practices as morally commendable. It is, however, to recognize that the optimum moral life within a deplorable situation is preferable to a life of sexual chaos."[1]

In a somewhat similar vein, Roman Catholic moral theologian Charles E. Curran has suggested the application of what he terms a "theory or theology of compromise." This is a principle that allows for accommodations to be made that would not be necessary if sin had not entered the world. He illustrates by pointing out that some Roman Catholic moral theologians have argued that, although ideally all property should be shared by all people in loving community, private ownership may be justified in the less-than-ideal real world in which we live—the original world order having been changed because of sin's presence. Just as private property is permissible, though less than the ideal, so too may homosexual expression be permissible in certain cases. Curran emphasizes that by speaking of the "sin of the world" he is referring to "the sinful structures and realities present in our world and in no way to personal guilt, blame, or responsibility." He states that "the phrase 'sin of the world' is used to emphasize that heterosexuality is the ideal" and thus he is talking about "a true lack—something which falls short of the human ideal."[2] However, he acknowledges that this ideal may not be possible for the homosexual person, nor may such people in all cases find celibacy and sublimation to be a reasonable way of dealing with their sexuality. Curran has recognized the existence of "many somewhat stable homosexual unions which afford their partners some human fulfillment and contentment" and has pointed out that "obviously such unions are better than homosexual promiscuity" and may be "the only way in which some people can find a satisfying degree of humanity in their lives."[3] In some of his writings, he goes so far as to affirm that "for an irreversible, constitutional, or genuine homosexual, homosexual acts in the context of a loving relationship striving for permanency are objectively morally good." But at the same time, he stresses that heterosexual relationships remain the ideal and urges striving toward that way of relating if at all possible.[4]

Counselors who think of homosexuality in more positive terms are also sometimes careful to suggest that the person who feels he or she is developing in a homosexual direction should be absolutely *sure* of a homosexual orientation before embarking on a course based on such an assumption. Societal attitudes can make the lot of the homosexual person a difficult one. It is especially hard to sustain a long-term, faithful sexual union when social pressures are all in the direction of divisiveness. Whereas pressures on heterosexual married couples offer great incentives and rewards for staying together, homosexual unions are beset with pressures to split them apart. Because of these and similar practical handicaps, it is a kindness to advise people whose drive could be channeled in a heterosexual direction to go in that direction if at all possible. (On the other hand, it is *not* a kindness to push young people into heterosexual marriage if they still have some doubts about their orientation.) The Anglican theologian Norman Pittenger, one of the few writers who dared to pioneer the development of "an ethic for homosexuals," has a brief but pertinent discussion of such considerations in his book *Time for Consent: A Christian's Approach to Homosexuality.*[5]

On the other hand, John McNeill, who made similar points in the first edition of his own book *The Church and the Homosexual,* reported in a later edition that he had changed his mind on the topic and "would no longer place the same emphasis on 'exploring every avenue toward the achievement of normal heterosexual capacities and relationships'" because he is convinced that most homosexual people are aware of their sexual orientation at an early age. Yet in spite of this awareness, large numbers have tried "to deny or repress their homosexuality and live out a heterosexual life." From his work as a therapist, McNeill believes such denial and repression are a more serious psychological problem for such individuals than is the far less frequent problem of someone's mistakenly worrying about being homosexual and then finding out he or she is actually heterosexual.[6]

▼ THIELICKE'S ETHIC FOR HOMOSEXUAL PEOPLE

Helmut Thielicke, the renowned German Protestant theologian, provides a thought-provoking and well-informed discussion of homosexuality in his book *The Ethics of Sex*.[7] Having studied the relevant medical and psychological research that had become available by the 1960s, when he was writing, Thielicke expresses dismay over the inaccurate and uninformed statements about homosexuality in the literature of Protestant theology. He recognizes that "constitutional homosexuality . . . is largely unsusceptible to medical or psychotherapeutic treatment, at least so far as achieving the desired goal of a fundamental conversion to normality is concerned." He argues that when an "ailment" is "recognized as incurable," our attitude toward it must change; we must "accept" it. He defines acceptance rather courageously: "to accept the burden of the predisposition to homosexuality only as a divine dispensation and see it as a task to be wrestled with, indeed—paradoxical as it may sound—to think of it as a talent to be invested (Luke 19:13ff.)."

Thielicke establishes that constitutional homosexuality is an ethical issue and definitely not a matter for criminal prosecution, except when it involves acts with minors, indecent public display, or prostitution. In other words, the standard is no different from that applied to heterosexual people. And, according to Thielicke, homosexual people must realize their "optimal ethical potentialities *on the basis* of [their] irreversible situation." It is in the reality of their actual situation that they must seek to "achieve the optimal ethical potential of sexual self-realization."

Thielicke rejects the widespread solution of requiring celibacy of all homosexual men and women who want to live Christianly, pointing out that "celibacy is based upon a special calling and, moreover, is an act of free will." He does not want to require of homosexual people "a degree of harshness and rigor" not demanded of heterosexual people. In light of the various special problems faced by the homosexual person who wants to live biblically, Thielicke recommends that other Christians exhibit a great deal of pastoral care that does *not* expose the homosexual person to "defamation" of that which is natural to him or her.

While recognizing the possibility of the homosexual person's living in an "acceptable partnership" and even citing evidence of stable, monogamous homosexual relationships, Thielicke nonetheless believes that, in general, Christian pastoral care will have to focus on helping homosexual people *sublimate* their urges. He believes that the enormous pressures brought to bear upon homosexual men and women make the achievement of monogamous relationships truly exceptional.

Foremost among the pressures endured by homosexual Christians, according to Thielicke, is the fact that "the homosexual does not have the benefit of living within a supportive order that is informed by a traditional ethos such as that of the institution of marriage." Such a person does not have at his or her disposal "a set of prefabricated decisions" provided by tradition that would make it easier to find one's way. Rather, according to Thielicke, the homosexual person is left to work out his or her own path of ethically responsible behavior "to an unimaginably greater degree" than other people.

▼ ETHICAL STANCES IN THE NETHERLANDS

J. Rinzema, pastor of a Reformed church in the Netherlands, is another pioneering author in the call for "a viable homosexual ethic." He has urged Christian moralists to "develop a morality for homosexuality in consultation with homosexual people." Such a morality would encourage permanent relationships for constitutional (unchangeable) homosexual people and would include the provision of guidelines for such matters as courtship and decisions to form a permanent union, and then for living within that union. "As there are rules for the relationships between married people," writes Rinzema, "we believe that society must both create room for and find rules by which homosexual people can live together in permanent relationships."[8]

Rinzema knows what he's talking about in suggesting that heterosexual Christian leaders get together with homosexual people for discussion, because that is exactly what has been done in the Netherlands. Holland is one of the few places in the world where there is relatively little discrimination against homosexual people. Educational efforts, changes in laws, scientific research, and changing attitudes within the churches have all had an impact on public awareness of lesbian and gay people as human beings of dignity and worth who have much to contribute to society. In the early 1960s, a working group of Roman Catholics and Protestants was formed for discussion of the issue. Through this organization (Pastoral Help for Homophiles), heterosexual and homosexual Christians could share their perspectives in an effort to develop a sensitivity to and an understanding of one another.

Similarly, the churches of the Netherlands made an effort to rethink Scripture and theology with regard to homosexuality, and some efforts were made toward the formation of ethical principles as well. For example, a Roman Catholic priest issued a set of guidelines that, among other suggestions, encouraged ministers to help gay and lesbian people build stable relationships. The ministers were advised to recognize that sexual abstinence "is not to be seen as a natural thing for the homosexual and is in fact exceptional." Pastors were instructed to help homosexual people see the importance of faithfulness within a relationship. Near the top of the list were two especially crucial guidelines: (1) "A stable relationship must never be broken," and (2) heterosexual marriage must be rejected as a solution for homosexuality.[9]

These two guidelines need to be heard by those Christians who have caused excruciating mental and emotional torture by trying to break up a relationship between two persons who deeply love each other. Any counselor who gets involved with the real hurts of human beings is likely to have run into some cases of this sort. Likewise, the problems of homosexual people who have entered heterosexual marriages in the hope that this will bring about a "cure" or change of orientation are also familiar to counselors.

The tragedy here is not only the homosexual person's pain, but also the anguish suffered by the spouse—which is intensified all the more if children have been born of the union. Unfaithfulness and eventual marital breakup are not at all uncommon in such situations. Better these unions had never been entered into in the first place.

Some Christians in the Netherlands, like some Christians the world over, remain unconvinced that homosexual acts can *ever* be right—even in a stable, committed relationship. Certain Dutch Christians have argued that "if some women who cannot find husbands can abstain from sexual contact, so can the homosexual."[10] A similar position is taken in an InterVarsity publication, *The Returns of Love,* which candidly describes the struggles of a young Christian fighting to resist his homosexual impulses and live a celibate life.[11]

▼ CELIBACY: A SPECIAL GIFT, OR A CONDITION FOR SALVATION?

But if these Christians find it impossible to reconcile the idea of homosexual expression with Christian theology, others find it difficult to reconcile required homosexual celibacy with Christian theology. We have already mentioned the view of Helmut Thielicke that celibacy is a "special calling" and "an act of free will." Similarly, theology professor Daniel C. Maguire takes issue with the Vatican's 1976 "Declaration on Certain Questions Concerning Sexual Ethics." Maguire argues that, in Catholic theology, celibacy is seen as "a precious gift" given by God only to certain persons. "Yet when we move with the Declaration to homosexual persons," says Maguire, "the precious gift is normative and a necessary condition for salvation. . . . For the heterosexual person the Declaration recalls St. Paul's practical advice that it is better to marry than to burn." Yet for homosexual people as a group, "there is no alternative to burning . . . unless, of course, they are all charismatically gifted" with the "precious gift" of celibacy.[12] Thus, Maguire points out that the Vatican is more strict concerning homosexuals than heterosexuals. The Vatican's stance is especially ironic in the light of John Boswell's discovery that the oldest Greek liturgical document in the Vatican library contains a ceremony celebrating the union of two clerics (both of them male).[13] Thus the contemporary church is denying to its members and clergy that which was fully acceptable in the fourth century.

▼ THE CREATION ACCOUNTS: HETEROSEXUALITY OR COHUMANITY?

As we discussed in our chapter on the Bible, the biggest barrier to accepting the possibility of homosexual unions is, for some Christians, their understanding of the creation accounts in the first two chapters of Genesis and in Jesus' commentary on them in Matthew 19. David Fraser, for example, relates the creation account to the Song of Solomon and argues thus: "That God's image is both male and female, not simply being-in-community, has ramifications beyond Genesis one. The Song presumes erotic love to be heterosexual and the rest of revelation reinforces that conviction."[14] To John Stott, another proponent of this view, the second chapter of Genesis "affirms the *complementarity* of the sexes, which constitutes the basis for heterosexual marriage." He states further that "the complementarity of the male and female sexual organs is only a physical symbol of a much deeper spiritual complementarity."[15]

Theologian Theodore Jennings, however, takes a different perspective, suggesting that our being created male and female in the image of God is a way of understanding that "the crucial determinant of our humanity" is *cohumanity.* "That our humanity is cohumanity cannot be interpreted only in a sexual or genital way," says Jennings. "If this is done, nothing remains of the symbolic and thus ethical significance of cohumanity. We have then literalized the metaphor so as to deprive it of its general ethical significance."[16]

Rosemary Radford Ruether, a professor of historical theology, applies the concept of cohumanity specifically to homosexual unions:

> Once sex is no longer confined to procreative genital acts and masculinity and femininity are exposed as social ideologies, then it is no longer possible to argue that sex/love between two persons of the same sex cannot be a valid

embrace of bodily selves expressing love. If sex/love is centered primarily on communion between two persons rather
than on biological concepts of procreative complementarity,
then the love of two persons of the same sex need be no less
than that of two persons of the opposite sex. Nor need their
experience of ecstatic bodily communion be less valuable.[17]

It seems to us that the Genesis creation accounts imply that
male and female are meant to relate to one another *as* male and female, both of them made in the image of God and both of them
responsible for the stewardship of the created world. But if we
take the creation accounts to mean that relating as male and female can mean only genital relating in heterosexual marriage, we
have excluded all people who are single (for whatever reason—illness, disabilities, preference, orientation, lack of opportunity, and
so forth) from any place in the cooperative union of cohumanity.

It should be obvious that male-female relating in society goes
far beyond genital relating. (It may be less obvious, in view of prevailing stereotypes and misinformation, that homosexual men continue to think of themselves as male and homosexual women
continue to think of themselves as female, with members of each
gender continuing to enjoy nongenital friendships with the other
gender—whether homosexual or heterosexual.) The points that
need to be emphasized are these: heterosexual men and women
can relate authentically as male and female in a social group without having genital relations with everybody of the other sex. And
single heterosexual people can participate in social activities with
the other sex, affirming cohumanity, without having genital relations with any representative of the other sex. Similarly, homosexual Christians who enter a same-sex union can do so without
breaking the cohumanity of creation, because they can continue to
relate to the other sex as male and female in nongenital ways.
Clearly, the point of the creation accounts is not the establishment
of normative heterosexuality or even the *complementarity* of the
sexes (as though each gender is incomplete and requires a union
with the other in order to be whole). Rather, we are simply told
that "when God created humankind, [God] made them in the like-
ness of God. Male and female [God] created them, and [God]

blessed them and named them 'Humankind' when they were created" (Gen. 5:1–2). It is a statement of cohumanity—nothing
more, nothing less.

▼ ARE WE PERPETUATING THE "FALLEN ORDER"?

Another issue brought up by certain Christians is this: if heterosexual monogamy is the *ideal* according to God's design for
human sexuality—even if the establishment of stable homosexual
relationships might lie within the "permissive" will of God for
people incapable of heterosexual relationships—aren't we failing
homosexual people if we don't help them strive for the "ideal"? If
homosexuality entered the world some time after the fall described
in the third chapter of Genesis (since only two heterosexual people
were in the world before that), these Christians ask, then aren't we
perpetuating the "fallen order" by not steering homosexual people
toward a change of orientation and heterosexual marriage? And if
we say that such change is impossible, aren't we denying the re-
demptive power of Jesus Christ to "save to the uttermost" and
make all things new?

For those who link homosexuality to the fallen order, the issue
is a complex one. Some would reply to the questions in the previous paragraph by stating that it is necessary to proceed from an
understanding of psychological research, including an awareness
of how deep-rooted sexual self-identity is, and then go on to speak
of God's meeting individuals *where they are* and bringing good
out of what appears to be "less than the ideal." Others would say
that if certain persons are equally heterosexual and homosexual,
or if their homosexual urge is weaker than the heterosexual one,
they should certainly be encouraged to structure their lives in ac-
cordance with social norms and "God's ideal." (Of course this
view does nothing for those who are predominantly or exclusively
homosexual.) Still other Christians would take issue with the notion that heterosexuality is God's ideal in the first place—at least if
the idea carries with it the implication that homosexual Christians
are somehow "second-best" or "second-class." Thus John Mc-
Neill asks, "How can Christian homosexuals accept themselves
and their homosexuality with any sense of their own dignity and

value as long as they must see themselves and their actions as organically expressing the effects of sin in the world . . . ?" In McNeill's view, "the homosexual is here according to God's will," and "God had a divine purpose in so creating human nature that a certain percentage of human beings are homosexual."[18]

James Nelson, professor of Christian ethics at United Theological Seminary of the Twin Cities, would agree. He argues that "same-sex relationships are fully capable of expressing God's humanizing intentions," and views the "homosexual problem" as "more truly a heterosexual problem" (that is, a problem of homophobia and heterosexism), just as the gender-discrimination issue that is often called the "woman problem" is in reality a problem of "male sexism." He commends the 1973 statement of the Executive Council of the United Church of Christ concerning the full acceptance of homosexual people symbolized by ordination: "In the instance of considering a stated homosexual's candidacy for ordination the issue should not be his/her homosexuality as such, but rather the candidate's total view of human sexuality and his/her understanding of the morality of its use."[19]

▼ THE HIGH PRICE OF CARING

At this point, it should be clear that the questions surrounding homosexuality in Christian perspective are far from settled. There is no uniform opinion among Christians; in fact, there is a great deal of disagreement. But as more and more people become less afraid of the topic and more sensitive to the issues involved, a solid groundwork is being laid for creative rethinking on the theological/biblical/ethical level and for compassionate counsel on the practical/personal level.

Those who dare to pioneer and persevere in such rethinking must be prepared to pay a price. Deeply ingrained attitudes toward taboo subjects do not disappear overnight. Even to suggest a reexamination of the subject can call forth charges that a person is guilty of heresy, of leaving Christian teachings and going against the will of God. For instance, when the ecumenical radio minister for the Netherlands prayed for homosexual people during one of his broadcasts in 1959, he received an avalanche of mail, not only from grateful homosexual people and "confused homosexuals who could not believe that he as a minister could do such a thing," but also from confused and angry colleagues and people who accused him of blasphemy and ignorance of the Bible. Yet his courage in bringing the topic out in the open helped pave the way for the change of attitude that took place in his country.[20]

In spite of known discrimination against homosexual people, "it has not yet become fashionable to champion the cause of this minority group," wrote law professor Walter Barnett in 1973. Today, although there have been some encouraging signs of changing attitudes here and there, his observation continues to hold true. Barnett pointed out that a civil-rights enthusiast could stand up for the cause of a racial minority without worrying that others might raise questions about his or her own skin color (not that it should matter!). Skin color won't rub off on someone else, but "the aura of 'immorality' can."[21] The implications of this for concerned, compassionate Christians come through in a statement from Erving Goffman's classic work on stigma: "In general, the tendency for a stigma to spread from the stigmatized to his [or her] close connections provides a reason why such relations tend either to be avoided or to be terminated where existing."[22]

John McNeill, alert to the same problem, writes that an effective counseling ministry to homosexual people can ruin a minister's career and destroy his or her reputation. He quotes a report of the National Federation of Priests' Councils that notes, "Individual priests and ministers, working with homosexuals, usually encounter a social and psychological stigma as a result of their work, and this stigma is the single most effective obstacle to ministers who want to work with homosexuals."[23]

▼ THE BIG QUESTION FOR US ALL

The big question is this: are we willing to face the cost in order to share the love of Jesus Christ? In chapter 2 we noted how, in Mark Twain's novel *The Adventures of Huckleberry Finn,* Huck wrestles through a moral dilemma about demonstrating true friendship to a stigmatized person of his day—a man who bore the dual stigma of blackness in a racist society and slavery in an exploitative one. To help his friend Jim escape meant violating not only human law but also divine law as it had been interpreted in that society, because to help a slave escape meant stealing property from his or her owner. Not only did Huck worry about God and about going to hell for obeying the impulse of his heart, but he also worried about what people would think of him. "It would get all around that Huck Finn helped a nigger to get his freedom; and if I was ever to see anybody from that town again I'd be ready to get down and lick his boots for shame."[24] But such worries did not prevent him from doing what he felt to be right.

Jesus knew all about stigma. He never hesitated to move among the oppressed people of his day, including the most despised social outcasts. He went about his ministry without worrying about the aspersions cast upon his character, his motives, his righteousness. "If this man were a prophet," said some, "he would have known who and what kind of woman this is who is touching him—that she is a sinner" (Luke 7:39). He ignored the insinuations and seemed unconcerned about reputation. "Look," said those who criticized Jesus and passed judgment on him, "a glutton and a drunkard, a friend of tax collectors and sinners!" (Luke 7:34).

Jesus was not afraid of being called names, nor was he afraid to be identified with the most hated, discredited people in the society in which he lived. He cared about them. He felt their pain, knew their hunger and thirst, recognized their humanity, saw the image of God in them. In short, he loved them. And he longed to minister to them—even if others misunderstood and vilified him. Name-calling was as common then as it is now, and to label someone with a scornful term identified with a stigmatized group has always been considered an extreme insult. Today, terms of insult are frequently associated with homosexuality—"queer," "dyke," "flit," "butch," "faggot" or "fag."

During the time that Jesus walked the earth, the stigmatized people were the Samaritans, and the term of insult was "You Samaritan!" When some who opposed Jesus yelled, "Are we not right in saying that you are a Samaritan and have a demon?" he replied that he did not have a demon—that he honored God (John 8:48–49). But he made no effort to deny their charge that he was a

Samaritan. Why? Because he refused to dissociate himself from this disdained group.

We are reminded of an incident in Laura Z. Hobson's novel *Gentleman's Agreement*, in which she writes about a Gentile journalist in the late 1940s who pretended to be Jewish for a number of months in order to expose and combat anti-Semitism through publishing a revealing personal account of discriminatory practices. "Perceived as a Jew, he is treated like a Jew and begins to recognize the pain of his Jewish friends and both the prejudice and the patronization of the Gentiles around him," wrote Jacqueline Wexler of the National Conference of Christians and Jews in an introduction to a 1983 paperback edition of the novel. Distinguishing between *sympathy* and *empathy*, Wexler wrote that "we sympathize from a privileged position, recognizing the ill fortune of another," but "we empathize with one another when we share directly or analogously common wounds and comparable pain."[25]

In one scene in *Gentleman's Agreement*, the journalist's young son runs into the house and tells of the ugly anti-Semitic names he has been called by other children, who told him no "dirty little Jew" could ever get in their games. His father asked, "You didn't want to tell them you weren't really Jewish?" The boy looked startled that his father would even ask the question. "Good boy. I like that," his father said proudly. He told his son, "Lots of kids just like you are Jewish," and explained that, had the boy chosen to deny and dissociate from them, "it'd be sort of admitting there *was* something bad in being Jewish and something swell in not."[26]

In just this way, Jesus did not dissociate himself from the Samaritans, the group "respectable" people had no dealings with. Rather, as we discussed in chapter 3, he chose the example of a Samaritan to illustrate the principle of neighbor love. Are we willing to follow his example? Even when our fulfilling the second great commandment may seem to go against tradition and public opinion?

The Reverend Paul Oestreicher, an Anglican priest active in Amnesty International, remarked on a British Broadcasting Corporation program that "the hero of . . . [Jesus'] best-known parable was a Samaritan, the Jew's most hated enemy. 'Go and be like him,' said Jesus . . . like that atheist, that communist, that fascist, that homosexual . . . like whomever we most love to hate."[27]

"Love your neighbor as yourself" we are told (Matt. 22:39). "Greater love has no one than this, that one lay down one's life for a friend" (John 15:13, from the *Inclusive Language Lectionary*[28]).

Who *is* my neighbor? Who *is* my friend?

Could it be the Samaritan?

Could it be the homosexual?

▽ ▽ ▽ ▽ ▽ ▽ ▽ ▽ ▽ ▼

The Continuing Challenge

THOMAS MERTON, the Trappist monk whose untimely death in 1968 did not end his capacity to enrich the world through his spiritual writings, once composed an essay on the Good Samaritan. He pointed out that the lawyer who asked Jesus, "Who is my neighbor?" was perplexed by the second great commandment. The first commandment, enjoining us to love God with our entire being, posed no problem for this expert in religious law. After all, God is good and deserving of our love. But to love one's neighbor as oneself? Wasn't that asking more than seemed reasonable? Thus, says Merton, what Jesus' questioner really wanted to know was "where to draw the line. Who is the neighbor to be loved, who is the alien not to be loved?" The lawyer was trying "to protect himself against loving an unworthy object and thus wasting his love." He wanted to know how to "classify people, and judge them accurately as worthy of love, or of hatred, or of indifference." But by refusing to provide any such guidelines for separating human beings from one another, Jesus was teaching him "that classifications are without significance in this matter of love."[1] The story Jesus told made that point clear.

▽ PREJUDICE AND MISCONCEPTIONS

In his classic work, *The Nature of Prejudice*, psychologist Gordon W. Allport points out that we human beings tend to use

categorization to simplify our lives. Our previously held generalizations—no matter how faulty—make it easy for us to prejudge a
new person or situation without having to think about it. Erroneous prejudgment, of course, lies at the heart of prejudice. However, not all overgeneralizations necessarily indicate an underlying
prejudice. Allport argues that *some* "overblown generalizations"
are nothing more than *misconceptions* based on how we have
mentally organized wrong information. What distinguishes prejudice from a simple misconception is *emotional resistance to new
evidence*. "We tend to grow emotional when a prejudice is threatened with contradiction," Allport explains. "Thus the difference
between ordinary prejudgment and prejudice is that one can discuss and rectify a prejudgment without emotional resistance."[2]

Our hope in writing this book is that many of our readers will
be willing to examine the evidence and correct any misconceptions
they may have held about gay, lesbian, and bisexual people, learning to love *all* their neighbors as themselves. At the same time, we
know that some readers may be emotionally resistant to new evidence and new ways of looking at their homosexual neighbor. In
so doing, they illustrate Allport's definition of prejudice as "an
avertive or hostile attitude toward a person who belongs to a
group, simply because he [or she] belongs to that group, and is
therefore presumed to have the objectionable qualities ascribed to
the group."[3] It makes no difference to the biased person if little or
no factual basis exists for the blanket assignment of such negative
characteristics to the detested group.

One woman wrote to us several years after publication of the
first edition of *Is the Homosexual My Neighbor?*, telling us she
had picked up the book "with fear and trepidation." She explained that she was afraid she would find that we had answered
the title's question in the affirmative and feared the implications if
that turned out to be the case! When she found that we did indeed
apply Christian neighbor love to the homosexual person, she said,
she became so angry that she was unable to write to us for two
years after reading the book. And she was still angry then!

When confronted with new information that contradicts faulty
generalizations, prejudiced people often use what Allport calls a
"re-fencing device" to keep their prior views intact. For example,

upon learning about the homosexual orientation of some acquaintance or public figure, they might admit that she or he really is a nice and honorable person. They can't deny that this particular *individual* contradicts their stereotyped image of the group they hold in disdain. But at the same time they hastily pull up the drawbridge to distance themselves from the group as a whole (claiming, in this illustration, that the particular person being discussed is different from homosexuals-as-a-group, who "everybody knows" are promiscuous, anti-God, and out to destroy the family).

"When a fact cannot fit into a mental field, the exception is acknowledged, but the field is hastily fenced in again and not allowed to remain dangerously open," writes Allport.[4] He uses the example of the racist's question—But would you want your daughter or sister to marry one?—which often elicits just the negative response or hesitancy the racist hopes for in order to obliterate the other person's positive statements about members of a particular ethnic group. Thus, the group remains "fenced off" as being inferior, its members undesirable. In the early 1990s, such re-fencing occurred often during the debates over whether gay and lesbian people should be permitted to serve in the military. Many military and government personnel acknowledged the fine job performance of numerous homosexual people, but their positive comments were often quickly followed with the question, But would you want to live in close quarters with homosexuals and have to sleep and shower near them?

Allport asserts that "there are two conditions under which a person will not strive to re-fence his [or her] mental field in such a way as to maintain the generalization." One is the condition of "habitual open-mindedness," in which there is a constant willingness to examine and reexamine evidence, while making every effort to avoid boxing people into rigid categories. Such open-mindedness is, according to Allport, rare (although it is certainly in keeping with what Jesus was teaching about neighbor love and should not be rare among those who profess to follow him). The other condition for modifying previously held concepts is "plain self-interest." Allport uses the example of a man who is prejudiced against people of Italian descent until he falls in love with a wonderful Italian woman and comes to appreciate her and her family.

"Then he finds it greatly to his self-interest to modify his previous generalization and act thereafter on the more correct assumption that there are many, many kinds of Italians."[5]

There are also many, many kinds of gay and lesbian people, just as there are many, many kinds of heterosexual people.[6] Yet it is not uncommon to hear Christians speak derisively of "the gay life-style"—a term they consider synonymous with debauchery. "If you've ever seen yourself in a fun-house mirror, you may under-stand what I and millions of other gay and lesbian Americans are going through," wrote Tracy Thorne, at the time a lieutenant in the United States Navy, during the 1993 national debate over lifting the Pentagon's ban on homosexual people in military service. Thorne, whose public admission of his homosexual orientation brought about his dismissal from the navy in spite of his exemplary record as a jet pilot, bombardier, and tactician, told of being deeply troubled over the way gay and lesbian people were being carica-tured. He found especially disturbing the efforts of the religious right to "distort the debate by linking homosexuality with every-thing from pedophilia to a maniacal lack of sexual self-control." Decrying the portrayal of gay and lesbian people as "sexual preda-tors" whose primary aim is to lure their heterosexual colleagues into sexual liaisons, he argued that the notion "that homosexuals lack self-control is a myth based in fear and ignorance."[7]

▼ THE DEBATE OVER THE MILITARY'S "GAY BAN"

Thorne decided to speak publicly about his homosexual orienta-tion because of his increasing distress over the incongruity between the military's discriminatory policy and the principles it professed to uphold. He explained his feelings to the Senate Armed Services Committee a year after he had made his decision to come out of the closet. "When I took the oath of a naval officer," he said, "I swore to defend my country against all enemies, foreign and domestic. I believe—as I hope that you do—that discrimination is a domestic enemy." He went on to tell of having sworn to defend fundamental values of America. Yet the military's policy against gay men and lesbian women ignored those values. He became convinced that someone had to stand up and say, "No more."

Thorne was willing to be that someone. "I knew it was going to upset some people," he told the committee and an audience of over one thousand people, mostly military personnel, attending the special hearings at the Norfolk Naval Base in May 1993. "And I knew I was going to challenge the status quo. But I couldn't allow this domestic enemy of discrimination to continue unchallenged." His words rang out forcefully, with deep conviction and sincerity:

> I challenge discrimination with *truth*, the most powerful
> weapon I have. Personally, I couldn't reconcile being a part
> of a military that was supposed to defend liberty and justice
> for all when "all" didn't include *me*.

He went on to tell of paying dearly for telling the truth: he was immediately removed from the cockpit, grounded, and eventually given a job running a photocopier in the navy safety office until his discharge was finalized. His name on the jet he had flown so proudly was painted over. And the $2 million that he estimated the navy had invested in his "Top Gun" flier training was essentially thrown away.[8]

Thorne is only one of several outstanding military personnel whose chosen careers have been abruptly ended because they have bravely disclosed their homosexuality. Many, in the early 1990s, had hoped that the revelation of their sexual orientation would counter the prevailing negative stereotypes of homosexual men and women and hasten a change in the Pentagon's policy. The hostile climate toward gay men and lesbian women had appeared to be showing some signs of change—particularly in view of the campaign promises of the newly elected U.S. president, Bill Clinton. Clinton was determined to lift the ban that since the early 1940s had officially barred gay and lesbian people from military service. Pointing out that, in the decade of the 1980s alone, it had cost taxpayers over $500 million to discharge nearly seventeen thousand homosexual people from various branches of the military, the president spoke of the difficulty he often encountered in attempting to help people see that "we don't have a person to waste."[9]

During the controversy, the General Accounting Office issued a report saying that the Pentagon spent over $28,000 to recruit and train replacements for each enlisted person it dismissed from the service, and nearly $121,000 for each officer kicked out. It was estimated that, solely in economic terms, it had cost taxpayers $27 million for the one thousand gay and lesbian military personnel discharged in 1990 alone.[10]

But of course the costs cannot be measured solely in economic terms or even in terms of wasted talent. The personal and social costs are immeasurable. The pain, shattered dreams, and humiliation suffered by thousands of loyal, highly skilled American servicemen and servicewomen would be difficult to describe.

At the time we were writing the first edition of this book, Leonard Matlovich, a sergeant in the U.S. Air Force with an impeccable service record that included three tours of duty in Vietnam, was making history by challenging the rule that disallowed his continuing in military service after he had acknowledged his homosexual orientation. Matlovich had been awarded the Bronze Star for heroism and a Purple Heart after stepping on a Vietcong land mine. Knowing that his homosexual orientation would not interfere with his duties, he had decided to be open with his commanding officer. He told the African-American officer that his decision to challenge military policy on gays could be compared with the civil-rights challenges that led to the Supreme Court's landmark 1954 decision on desegregation of the schools. Given a general discharge from the service, Matlovich began a lengthy legal battle to become reinstated. He was aware that air-force regulations allowed the retention of homosexual people in the military under "most unusual circumstances." But what were these circumstances? Matlovich and his lawyers went to court to require the air force to spell out the conditions under which homosexual people would or would not be allowed to continue in military service. After five years in which the air force issued various contradictory statements, a U.S. district court ordered the air force to readmit Matlovich because of its "perverse behavior" in failing to define its standards. However, by that time the political climate and likely makeup of the Supreme Court resulted in Matlovich's decision to drop his crusade for reinstatement and to accept instead an out-of-court settlement. In 1980, the air force paid him $160,000 to cover back pay and fringe benefits as well as other compensation. He was also given an honorable discharge. After his death from AIDS in 1988, Matlovich was buried with full military honors in the Congressional Cemetery in Washington, D.C., where his tombstone announced: "A Gay Vietnam Veteran." It was inscribed with his statement: "When I was in the military they gave me a medal for killing two men and a discharge for loving one."[11]

At the time that Matlovich was waging his battle for reinstatement, another, lesser-known gay man was challenging the military's practice of giving homosexual people an other-than-honorable discharge. Vernon E. Berg III, the son of a navy chaplain, was a 1974 graduate of the U.S. Naval Academy at Annapolis and had trained as a missile officer. Removed from the navy after the disclosure of his homosexuality in 1975, he objected to the "other than honorable" discharge he was given, and he sued. The court's decision on his behalf established a precedent for permitting the granting of honorable discharges (along with the veteran's benefits such discharges provide) to persons whose military service was terminated because of their homosexuality.[12]

Up until 1975, code numbers printed on discharge papers, even for honorable discharges, recorded the *reason* for such dismissals, the end result for gay and lesbian people being what one writer has called "a forced outing" that would follow the individual from one job to another.[13]

Formal guidelines issued by the Defense Department in 1981 directed that homosexual military personnel not guilty of any misconduct *should* be granted honorable discharges. However, author Randy Shilts reports that, as a punitive measure against homosexual service members, some commanders continued to issue less-than-honorable discharges even after the issuing of that directive.[14]

Since the 1975 legal challenges of Matlovich and Berg, countless other gay men and lesbian women have also filed lawsuits or in other ways taken a public stand against the military's discriminatory policies.[15] Among them are the Reverend Dusty Pruitt, a Metropolitan Community Church pastor and a captain in the army reserves who was in line for promotion to major when her identity as a lesbian caused her to be forced out of the military;

Joseph Steffan, near the top of his class at the U.S. Naval Academy at Annapolis but denied graduation privileges because he revealed his homosexual orientation during the last semester of his senior year; Keith Meinhold, a twelve-year navy veteran who had been considered one of the navy's most outstanding airborne sonar analysts and instructors and who had made no secret of his homosexual orientation among his colleagues and superiors but was booted out of the military after announcing his homosexual orientation on national television; Margarethe Cammermeyer, a colonel with a doctorate in nursing and twenty-six years of military service, who, at the time of her dismissal at age fifty for having revealed her lesbian orientation during a security-clearance interview, was the chief nurse of the Washington National Guard; and Gulf War veteran Jose Zuniga, a highly decorated junior noncommissioned officer and military journalist whose heroism as a combat medic and recognition as the U.S. Sixth Army's 1992 Soldier of the Year did not alter the army's decision to discharge him after he announced his homosexuality during the April 1993 March on Washington for Gay and Lesbian Rights.[16]

Legal challenges have continued in spite of the U.S. Supreme Court's refusal in 1990 to hear appeals in the two cases that reached the highest court. One of these was the case of an army-reserve drill sergeant, Miriam Ben-Shalom, who had been waging court battles for sixteen years at the cost of her life savings and her home. She argued that the army had violated her constitutional rights of free speech and equal protection by not permitting her to reenlist after she announced her lesbian orientation. The other case was that of James Woodward, a naval flight officer who admitted his homosexual orientation at the time he enlisted in 1972 but said he had never engaged in sex with a person of the same gender. Two years later, when seen sitting in an officer's club with a man who was being discharged because of homosexuality, Woodward was again confronted about his homosexual tendencies and shortly thereafter released from active duty. He had sued for reinstatement but was denied.[17] And nothing changed even when his case reached the Supreme Court, which left standing the rulings of the lower courts.

▼ WHY THE BAN?

Arguing that the military's ban on homosexual people has had nothing to do with morale and national security but rather has signified "baseless prejudice founded on fears and ignorance" and "the same mind-set that resulted in the exclusion of millions of black Americans and millions of women and other minorities," Senator Howard Metzenbaum of Ohio in July 1992 proposed legislation to end the ban. Representative Patricia Schroeder of Colorado had already introduced such a bill in the House of Representatives.[18] These were only two of an increasing number of efforts to change the military's policy. Suddenly it seemed that members of Congress, the media, the presidential candidates, and citizens throughout the nation were engaged in a conversation about homosexuality—a topic that not too long ago was seldom mentioned in public discourse. During the heated controversy over gay and lesbian civil rights in general, many questions were raised. One centered around the rationale for the Pentagon's undisguised and rigorously defended discrimination. What was the basis for the ban?

Author Randy Shilts, who spent five years researching the military's treatment of gay and lesbian people in the armed services, reports that the codification of punishment for homosexual soldiers first appeared in military law during World War I. "Assault with the intent to commit sodomy" was listed as a felony. "This law, the first revision of the Articles of War in more than a century," writes Shilts, "did not name sodomy itself as a crime." But a few years later, a new revision of the Articles of War did, with the crime now designated as "the sexual act itself, whether it involved assault or was consensual." For the next two decades, "homosexuality was dealt with as a criminal act, a move that saw huge numbers of gay sailors and soldiers imprisoned."[19]

Shilts reports that the new science of psychiatry also was at this time laying the groundwork for excluding people from the armed services solely on the basis of *being* homosexual. During the mobilization of troops to fight in World War II, military officials sought the help of psychiatrists to weed out persons deemed unfit for service. Since most psychiatrists at that time considered homosexuality a mental illness, regulations were issued in 1942 stating that persons who engaged in homosexual practices, whether "habitually or occasionally," should not be considered for military service. In 1943, the final version of the exclusionary policy was instituted.[20]

Nearly four decades later, in light of the Matlovich and Berg court challenges, the Department of Defense realized the policy needed to be refined and clarified, and a restated policy was issued in 1981. One change was the elimination of any exceptions to the ban so that others could not seek reinstatement on the grounds Matlovich had used in arguing his case. "Homosexuality is incompatible with military service," the policy now declared simply and unequivocally. It specified those who would be considered homosexual and the reason for their rejection: "The presence in the military environment of persons who engage in homosexual conduct or who, by their statements, demonstrate a propensity to engage in homosexual conduct, seriously impairs the accomplishment of the military mission." Shilts points out that the mere *desire* to engage in a same-sex sexual act at some future time, even if never acted upon, was now considered sufficient reason for discharge. "The military had, in effect, banned homosexual thoughts," he wrote—something that no other modern nation has done except Nazi Germany.[21]

Shilts provides evidence that the rationale behind the ban varies with the societal winds. During the McCarthy era, national security was the designated reason for the ban, the belief being (without any shred of proof) that homosexual people posed greater security risks than heterosexuals because they might betray their country if threatened with exposure of their sexual orientation, or they might be lured into compromising sexual situations by espionage agents and leak confidential information. More recently, the argument has turned in another direction: the presence of homosexual people in the military is said to jeopardize "discipline, good order, and morale."[22]

At the same time, during times of war, the military relaxes its policy. (Even such a temporary loosening of the ban, of course, demolishes arguments about the supposed "unfitness" of gay and lesbian people for military service.) Not long after the ban was initiated during World War II, when the army found that more military personnel were needed, new orders were quickly issued for retaining "reclaimable" homosexuals after a time of hospitalization.[23] In more recent years, many gay and lesbian reservists were called to serve in the war in the Persian Gulf. However, many were told they would be removed from the reserves as soon as the war ended.[24] "They were just going to use me, throwing their standards aside in light of Desert Shield–Desert Storm, then kick me out if I returned," said one lesbian reservist, adding that she was "upset, in tears, outraged." After going to the media with her story, she was given an honorable discharge.[25]

The Defense Department's own studies over the years have contradicted the rationale behind its ban on homosexual men and women. In 1957, a board appointed by the Secretary of the Navy published over six hundred pages of documentation that provided no evidence whatsoever that gay and lesbian people were unfit for military service, or that they posed a security risk. It acknowledged many instances of persons who had served "honorably and well, despite being exclusively homosexual." "In fact," said the report, "there is some evidence that homosexuals are quite good security risks." However, the report was kept secret for nearly twenty years, its existence denied by the Defense Department until it was uncovered by Vernon Berg's lawyers in 1976 under the Freedom of Information Act.[26]

Another study, which the Pentagon commissioned and financed in the late 1980s and then rejected because of disagreement with the findings, concluded that a person's sexual orientation was totally irrelevant and was "unrelated to job performance in the same way as is being left or right-handed."[27] The results of this study by researchers Theodore Sarbin and Kenneth Karols were suppressed by the Department of Defense and brought to light only after months of untiring effort by U.S. representatives Gerry Studds of Massachusetts and Patricia Schroeder of Colorado (who was serving as chair of the House Armed Services Subcommittee).[28] Studds and Schroeder also were made aware of a second analysis prepared by Michael McDaniel for the Defense Personnel Security Research and Education Center that, because of the furor over the first report, was never submitted to the Department of Defense officials who had commissioned it. That report had concluded that the suitability for military service demonstrated by gay and lesbian people was "as good or better than the average heterosexual."[29] The secretary of defense at the time, Richard Cheney, even admitted that the belief that homosexual people pose a security risk is "a bit of an old chestnut."[30]

Defense Department officials were not pleased with the results of the study by Sarbin and Karols, because the findings were at odds with the established policy of banning gay and lesbian people and showed the reasoning behind the ban to be both seriously flawed and unsupported by factual data. Officials also refused to consider the practical suggestions of these two highly credentialed researchers. These scholars suggested that the military regard homosexual people as a *minority group* and work with social-science specialists in developing programs to combat discrimination against them. Pointing out that such a strategy had already been used in combating racial discrimination, they emphasized that "the social construction of homosexuals as minority group members is more in tune with current behavioral science theory than the earlier constructions: sin, crime, and sickness."[31] Once again, as it had done with the 1957 study, the Defense Department rejected the conclusions of its own policy review. As we mentioned in chapter 7, this history repeated itself in 1993 when the defense secretary rejected the results of the Rand Corporation study that he himself had commissioned.

▼ PREJUDICE BY ANY OTHER NAME . . .

Many observers have compared the military's ban on gay and lesbian people with the arguments once used to segregate black troops from white troops. For example, a navy memorandum issued in December 1941 contained this justification for discrimination against black sailors:

> The close and intimate conditions of life aboard ship, the necessity for the highest possible degree of unity and esprit-de-corps; the requirement of morale—all these demand that nothing be done which may adversely affect the situation.

Past experience has shown irrefutably that the enlistment of Negroes (other than for mess attendants) leads to disruptive and undermining conditions.

The memo went on to warn that incorporating minorities into defense efforts was a major objective of "subversive agents" intent on breaking down efficient organization.[32]

But the nation was at war, and the armed forces had to accommodate the thousands of black soldiers and sailors who wore their country's uniform. At first, black people were relegated to traditional service roles much like those they were assigned in civilian society, where racism had long kept them "in their place." Black sailors, for example, were usually assigned to the Steward's Branch, their duties being to "prepare meals, clean rooms, and press uniforms for the ship's officers," writes Phyllis Jordon. Even when one ship was eventually assigned an all-black crew, every one of its officers was white. "The Army created entire divisions of black soldiers and squadrons of black pilots," and "segregation was the order of the day."[33]

When, in 1948, President Harry Truman ordered the integration of the armed forces, the heated debates within Congress and the military and among the citizenry foreshadowed the debates over gay and lesbian service members in the 1990s. "Politicians catering to Negro votes will abolish segregation and force the white boys from every section of the country to be obliged to associate and eat and sleep with Negroes," lamented one southern senator.[34] In addition to the argument that privacy would be invaded, it was said that black people would spread diseases, that morale would break down because members of the armed services would be forced to work alongside people they disliked, that white service members would refuse to take orders from black officers, and that the mingling of the races at dances and other social events would offend some people. The parallels between past justifications for racial discrimination in the armed forces and recent rationalizations for anti-homosexual bias are truly astounding.

Some African-Americans dislike this analogy, however, saying that homosexuality is different—that it's a matter of behavior rather than an innate characteristic such as race. Or that gay and lesbian people are trying to ride the coattails of an established civil-rights movement without having experienced the unique struggles of a group still suffering from the legacy of slavery and the ongoing indignities encountered because of skin color—something that cannot be hidden, as sexual orientation can.[35] This type of reasoning has been criticized by Barbara Smith, a black lesbian feminist author who argues that *all systems of oppression are intertwined* and that becoming aware of one kind of oppression can help us understand another oppression. "I have found in teaching and in speaking to a wide variety of audiences," she writes, "that making connections between oppressions is an excellent way to introduce the subjects of lesbian and gay male identity and homophobia, because it offers people a frame of reference to build upon." She also reminds her readers of the factual inaccuracy and strategic error of treating the topic of homosexuality "as if all gay people [are] white and male."[36] On a similar note, the late poet Audre Lorde said that her personal experience as a member of three categories—"lesbian," "black," and "feminist"—along with other categories that are considered unacceptable in some circles, taught her that "there can be no hierarchies of oppression."[37]

▼ MARCHING AS TO WAR

When the Senate Armed Services Committee took its hearings on the military's "gay ban" to the Norfolk Naval Base in May 1993, national media attention was drawn to the only two persons to testify publicly that they opposed the ban. Tracy Thorne, whose story we told earlier, was one. The other was Lieutenant Richard ("Dirk") Selland, who had received glowing evaluations for his work until he acknowledged his homosexuality. He was then dismissed from the nuclear submarine where he had served as supply officer and was told that discharge proceedings would begin immediately.

A devoted Christian, Selland had grown up in the Lutheran Church (Missouri Synod). Only a few months before his appearance before the Armed Services Committee, he had come to feel God's loving acceptance of him as a homosexual person. Now, facing dismissal from the navy, he longed for the support of a

Christian community. He and his partner each quietly took the necessary steps to join a local Evangelical Lutheran Church of America congregation. But after the church council voted to accept them into membership, the president of the congregation resigned, a petition to call a congregational meeting to overturn the council's decision was circulated, and a number of church members threatened to walk out if the couple was accepted.[38]

This anecdote pointedly illustrates sociologist James Davison Hunter's observation that, "as the strongest institutional bulwarks of traditionalist ideals of gender roles and sexuality, the military establishment and the churches are barometers of how the conflict over homosexuality fares in the larger social order."[39]

In American tradition, both the military establishment and religious institutions have symbolized order, authority, and convention. They have provided many people with an anchor, offering the security of clearly defined standards and rules and the knowledge that violators can expect to be punished. Both institutions use the language of war—the one fighting actual battles while the other stands ready to "sound the battle cry" over symbolic battles.

▼ HOMOPHOBIA AND GENDER ROLES

Both the armed forces and the churches have also traditionally symbolized societal ideals for male and female behavior. And by delineating the "proper role" in which each gender has been expected to serve God and country, both institutions have played a significant part in reinforcing stereotypical definitions of masculinity and femininity.[40]

During World War I, for example, one soldier summarized a prevailing sentiment when he wrote that although the death of a son in battle would be a "bitter blow, . . . what more could a real mother ask than to be the mother of a real man?"[41] Toughness, aggressiveness, bravery, boldness, the will to power, and other qualities associated with militarism were thought to define manliness. Womanliness was defined in terms of weakness, gentleness, and dependency on men for guidance and protection.

The battlefield was said to be the place that separated the men from the boys. The military culture was designed to take a boy and "make a man out of him." In recent decades, however, especially since the controversy over the war in Vietnam, such notions have been increasingly questioned and challenged by both women and men. And as society has been changing through efforts to promote gender equality, the armed forces and the churches have been forced to make changes as well—but only after a great deal of resentment and resistance. This legacy of resentment and resistance has much to do with the uneasiness reflected in current discussions about homosexuality, which is a phenomenon that many people don't understand but vaguely associate with the blurring of gender distinctiveness.

In the debates about permitting women to serve in combat, writes Randy Shilts, "the discussion among the nation's top military men revolved less around questions of military effectiveness than around a defense of manhood."[42] Similar thinking has also played a significant part in the relentless efforts to weed out homosexual service personnel of either gender. This concern over traditionally ascribed gender roles also helps explain Pentagon statistics showing that women have been dismissed from the military on charges of homosexuality at a rate three times that of men.[43] Shilts says that "the hunt for lesbians in the U.S. military in the 1980s was not merely a preoccupation, it was an obsession."[44] He asserts that, since many men have opposed the entrance of women into the armed services, military policies banning homosexuality have provided a way to get rid of unwanted women—especially those who succeed at jobs traditionally held by men. "Until proven otherwise, women in the military are often suspect of being lesbian," explains Shilts. "Why else, the logic goes, would they want to join a man's world?"[45] Many women have complained of being harassed and expected to yield to sexual advances or else be subject to discharge through accusations of lesbianism—regardless of their actual sexual orientation.

In 1990, a special memo was issued to officers in charge of the nearly two hundred ships and forty shore installations that make up the navy's surface Atlantic fleet. The document expressed concern over a seemingly lax implementation of the policy on homosexuality when applied to women and called for stricter enforcement, claiming that lesbian women tended to be aggressive, intimidating, and prone to use "subtle coercion" or make outright sexual advances, thereby setting up a "predator-type environment" from which vulnerable young female sailors needed to be protected. The vice admiral who sent out the message pointed out that because "the stereotypical female homosexual in the Navy is hardworking, career-oriented, willing to put in long hours on the job and among the command's top professionals," charges against such a person were all too often not being taken seriously or were "pursued half-heartedly." Upon reading the memo, U.S. Representative Gerry Studds said that by producing such a document "the Navy almost caricatures itself." He wondered what in the world was going on "if it is the Navy's policy to root out top performers."[46]

What is going on, according to one navy lieutenant who resigned her commission after eight years of service, is that "for Navy women, superior achievement is the litmus test for lesbianism, and threatening to label a woman 'lesbian' is an effective social and professional control to ensure she complies with sexual advances, or at least fails to outperform her male counterparts." She reports that during her years of service she was "subjected to blatant and damaging sexual harassment from senior Navy men, and improper sexual advances and subtle disrespect from junior Navy men" but had never experienced, nor could she remotely imagine, the predator-type behavior of *women toward women* that the memo warned about. She views the memo as supporting an open sanction of "homophobia as a motivation to harass and discharge women."[47]

Of course, enlisting homophobia to limit women's aspirations and activities is not confined to the military. It is rampant in civilian life as well. As Suzanne Pharr has written, "If lesbians are established as threats to the status quo, as outcasts who must be punished, homophobia can wield its power over all women through lesbian baiting." She explains:

> Lesbian baiting is an attempt to control women by labeling us as lesbians because our behavior is not acceptable, that is, when we are being independent, going our own way, living whole lives, fighting for our rights, demanding equal pay, saying no to violence, being self-assertive, bonding with

and loving the company of women, assuming the right to our bodies, insisting upon our own authority, making changes that include us in society's decision-making; lesbian baiting occurs when women are called lesbians because we resist male dominance and control. And it has little or nothing to do with one's sexual identity.[48]

Pharr also calls attention to the threat *gay men* pose for those heterosexual men who define their manhood in terms of exercising control over women. "Visible gay men are the objects of extreme hatred and fear by heterosexual men because their breaking ranks with male heterosexual solidarity is seen as a damaging rent in the very fabric of sexism," she writes. "They are seen as betrayers, as traitors who must be punished and eliminated."[49] Men whose affection is directed toward other men "are perceived as not being 'real men,' that is, as being identified with women, the weaker sex that must be dominated and that over the centuries has been the object of male hatred and abuse," writes Pharr. "Misogyny gets transferred to gay men with a vengeance and is increased by the fear that their sexual identity and behavior will bring down the entire system of male dominance and compulsory heterosexuality."[50]

Her analysis sheds some light on certain anxieties expressed by many men who have opposed lifting the military's "gay ban." They fear that homosexual advances will be made toward heterosexual men in showers and in the close sleeping quarters common to many military situations and that straight men will find themselves ogled as sex objects in the way that they have evaluated women's bodies. Much of this anxiety springs from the sex-as-conquest attitude that has pervaded heterosexual military culture the world over throughout history—as witness the horror stories of girls and women of all ages being raped during wartime, or the widespread exploitation of poor women who work as prostitutes near military installations in third-world countries, or the pregnant women and fatherless children left behind when troops leave an area, or the "boys-will-be-boys" partying such as the navy's infamous Tailhook Convention scandal in which over one hundred officers were implicated in either sexual offenses or the ensuing cover-up of the events. All of this springs from what one commen-

tator has called "a cocky sense of entitlement to women's bodies."[51] The predatory atmosphere that many heterosexual men
fear will occur if homosexual men are permitted to serve in the
military may well be a projection of their own attitudes toward
sexuality.[52]

▼ STATUS POLITICS AND CULTURE WARS

There is something else going on, too, in the anxieties many
people express about homosexuality. Homosexuality is a phenomenon outside most people's frame of reference, and many are not
ready to make room for it in their way of viewing the world. It is
not something they understand, and what people don't understand they often fear. Many people find it unsettling to question
beliefs they have long taken for granted. They cling desperately to
familiar ways of thinking. And they want to make sure their children grow up seeing the world as they do.

Sociologists have long studied the conflicts between competing
groups in society, each promoting their particular way as the ideal.
Social theorists use the term "status groups" for groups defined by
their members' devotion to a common life-style and belief system.
As groups struggle to defend, maintain, and promote their particular worldview, they engage in "status politics." Social scientists
Ann Page and Donald Clelland suggest that a better term might be
"the politics of life style concern." When societal changes are perceived as a threat to a particular status group, members of that
group resist and mobilize for battle. "Protestors are expressing a
direct concern about the erosion of their control over their way of
life," write Page and Clelland.[53] Such people would like to make
sure their viewpoint is given official status, protected, and promul-
gated through those institutions that socialize and influence the individuals that make up a society—the public schools, religious
organizations, statutory law, the media, the arts, and so on.

Thus, when they see various groups struggling against discrimination and oppression and working for just and equitable treatment, they often feel threatened. Heavily invested in the status quo,
they fear their own rights will be encroached upon if civil rights are
extended to these other categories of people. Nowhere has this

argument been voiced more strongly than among those who oppose civil rights for gay and lesbian people. The argument goes that if gay, lesbian, and bisexual people are granted protection from discrimination as a basic civil right, they are being granted "special rights." And furthermore, the argument continues, they will be advancing their "hidden agenda" of "mainstreaming a deviant lifestyle," "legitimating immorality," and "overturning family values."

"Gays are at the cutting edge of the cultural war," argue opponents of the lesbian and gay rights movement, warning that this movement will prove to be the "first step in the criminalization of Christianity" because Christians in the United States will no longer have a right to their beliefs about homosexuality.[54] Such fears are, of course, ill founded, but they illustrate what has been called not only a culture war, but a religious war.[55]

In the 1970s, as we were writing the first edition of this book, there were well-organized efforts (usually spearheaded by fundamentalist Christians) to overturn local ordinances protecting homosexual people from discrimination in jobs, housing, and public accommodations. But by the 1990s, anti-gay forces no longer considered opposing and overturning such ordinances to be strong enough measures in their battle against gay and lesbian civil rights. Instead, money and energy were poured into efforts to make it illegal to pass such anti-discrimination ordinances in the first place.

In November 1992, voters passed an amendment to the Colorado state constitution denying local governments the right to prohibit discrimination on the basis of sexual orientation and rescinding the gay-rights laws of Denver, Aspen, and Boulder.[56] Empowered by the successful anti-gay-rights campaign in Colorado, right-wing religious coalitions immediately began targeting other states to work for legal changes that would deny the extension of anti-discrimination ordinances to homosexual people.

In Oregon, however, a proposed anti-homosexuality amendment to the state constitution was defeated by voters in the same general election in which the Colorado measure was passed. The proposed Oregon amendment would have gone even further than Colorado's by requiring the government to take a moral stand, condemning homosexuality as "abnormal, wrong, unnatural and perverse," and lumping it together with pedophilia and sado-masochism as something that must be actively discouraged. At all levels of state authority, no tax money was to be spent in any way that would condone or promote homosexuality. The vagueness of the wording caused concern among legal scholars, as well as librarians, public officials, public school teachers, university professors, and others who received public funding. For example, would it affect what books were permitted on library shelves, what ideas were permitted to be discussed in classrooms, what jobs could be held by gay and lesbian people? No one was sure—although supporters of the anti-gay measure admitted that part of its intent was to keep homosexual people out of any public position that would involve contact with Oregon's children.[57]

The fear and hatred stirred up by the campaign were enormous. One target of a smear campaign was Portland's chief of police, Tom Potter. Accused of setting a "bad example," he received nasty phone calls, hate mail, and weekly death threats because of his personal stand on gay and lesbian rights and his loving support for his lesbian daughter, also a police officer. At the same time, he received encouragement from other parents of gay and lesbian children and from homosexual young people. But he also learned of parents whose condemnation of homosexuality was so extreme that they wished their homosexual child would die of AIDS![58] Potter told a newspaper journalist that he had grown up in an evangelical home where he had formed "all these perceptions of gay people as child molesters and unnatural" but changed his mind through the disclosure of the homosexual orientation of one of his best friends. And then there was his daughter. "I believe my daughter was born that way. In the same way I was born left-handed," he said. Yet, he said, his parents had tried to change him into a right-handed person. "As a result, I developed a stutter whenever I tried to write with my wrong hand."[59]

▼ WHY SHOULD DIFFERENCE MAKE ANY DIFFERENCE?

"Recent discoveries about handedness, inconclusive as they may be, argue—if argument is necessary—for an ever-deepening appreciation of human diversity," writes Jack Fincher in his book

Lefties.[60] Fincher himself endured the humiliating experience of being slapped by a first-grade teacher for trying to write with his left hand. "Just why left-handedness should be academically forbidden was neither evident nor ever explained. Something, we were given vaguely to understand, was wrong with it, *psychologically.*"[61] Never mind the great contributions made by people like Leonardo da Vinci and Benjamin Franklin, and countless other left-handed people throughout history. Or the fact that many left-handed people today are exercising leadership in every field. (One of the lesser-known distinguishing marks of the 1992 presidential race was the left-handedness of all three major candidates.) In 1915, only 3 percent of Americans admitted they were left-handed. In today's more accepting climate, one out of ten acknowledges being left-handed.[62]

An intolerance of difference lies behind the outmoded thinking that relegated left-handed people to second-class treatment, paid no heed to the distinctiveness of the "different wiring" of their brains, and tried to force them to conform to the majority pattern of right-handedness. Elements of such thinking have not entirely disappeared, as in such examples as these: a Postal Service employee who, after thirteen years of sorting mail with his left hand, was told he must follow the manual instructions and use his right hand or lose his job; a left-handed police officer who was fired for wearing his holster on his left hip because he was afraid he would shoot himself in the foot if he tried to grab his gun with his right hand; and a grocery-store cashier who lost her job for using her left hand to ring up sales.[63]

It isn't hard to see a parallel between the situation of the left-handed person and that of the homosexual person, as we mentioned in chapter 6. In both cases, people are discriminated against for something that is part of their very nature but that differs from the majority. Both are expected to fit into a world that is organized without their needs in mind, catering instead to the comfort and convenience of the majority.

A spokesperson for Lefthanders International reports that, as an equal-opportunity employer, the organization employs both left-handers and right-handers but that all the office equipment and desk items are built for left-handers—which provides right-handers with a comparable experience of the difficulties left-handers go through in everyday life as they use various tools, musical instruments, scissors, pencil sharpeners, and so on, that have been designed for the right-handed majority.[64]

No doubt many gay and lesbian people wish there were a similar way to help heterosexual people experience some of the difficulties homosexual people go through in everyday life. For example, heterosexual people might imagine a world in which husbands and wives would not be permitted to show any affection in public and must pretend their relationship is simply platonic or else risk losing their jobs. A world in which advertisements would never feature pictures of a man and woman together. A world where newspapers would refuse to print wedding announcements except for same-sex couples and would not include the person's life partner in an obituary list of survivors because society didn't consider such a person "family" and disliked seeing someone's heterosexuality "flaunted." A world in which heterosexual people could not tell work colleagues about their weekends unless they changed pronouns and pretended to have been with someone of the same gender. A world in which the partner in only homosexual relationships could be included in a person's health-insurance coverage. Gay and lesbian people say such an imaginary topsy-turvy world is very much like the real world in which they live daily. It is a reality that is foreign to most people.

▼ CONSTRUCTING REALITY

Social scientists tell us that the reality by which we order our lives is "socially constructed." In other words, through our interaction with other human beings and our participation in the society in which we live, we form our perception of the world. This shared perception of "the way things are and should be" provides a sense of order that members of a particular society don't like to have disrupted. That their society's way of seeing and doing things is the right or only way may be so taken for granted that they find it hard to comprehend the different perspective of another culture. "The appearance of an alternative symbolic universe poses a threat because its very existence demonstrates empirically that one's own universe is less than inevitable," explain sociologists Peter Berger and Thomas Luckmann.[65]

People who like to think that everything is settled once and for all are terrified at the thought of viewing social phenomena in new and different ways. That's why some individuals and groups have been reacting with such fierce abhorrence to gay and lesbian civil-rights efforts. Since their own world is a heterocentric one, they have already made up their minds from a heterosexually based vantage point and are positive they know God's mind as well (often viewing the two minds as one and the same).[66] Thus they refuse even to consider another perspective—one that takes into account homosexual people as equally worthy human beings. And the idea of homosexual Christians strikes them as heresy. "It's as absurd as saying 'adulterers for Christ,'" one woman told us.

Sociologist Kai Erikson has shown that such certitude character-ized the Puritans of the Massachusetts Bay Colony, a society in which "the very idea of intelligent controversy seemed absurd: after all, the truth was as plain as the print on everyone's Bible." If there were any souls "capable of entertaining doubt after this truth had been interpreted for [them] by the godly clergy," Erikson ex-plains, they were considered to "either suffer from a crippling de-fect or be caught in the snares of Satan." There was always the suspicion that "some devilish mischief was afoot" if a Puritan's cer-tainty was ever jarred by a "persuasive argument" or "clever line of reasoning." However, there was a problem in that human expe-rience could not be fitted so neatly into the system the Puritans were trying to devise. "For all its commanding tone, the Bible had few passages that could be read as statutes," writes Erikson. "Every day the courts seemed to discover some frightful new sin for which there was no precedent in Biblical history."[67] In time, the members of the elite group designated to interpret and apply the Bible in such ambiguous cases came to be resented for their tremen-dous power over people's everyday lives.

This problem is still with us. Michael Guinan, a Franciscan priest and professor of Old Testament studies and Semitic lan-guages, calls attention to some of the inhumane ways the Bible has been used throughout history—the justification of South Africa's apartheid policy being one example. "We should not be surprised then to find the Bible being quoted in the current debate over the rights and dignity of persons who are homosexual," he writes, suggesting that among those who so misuse the Bible perhaps "the basic underlying problem has to do with faith." He explains:

> For all their "religious" talk, such self-righteous people really do not have faith in God as much as faith in their own faith. The God of the Bible is a God of surprises, a God who calls us forward to new depths and new understanding.

He suggests that a "healthy sense of doubt" in our own faith should be "an integral part of our faith."[68]

Some Christians cannot feel comfortable with such questioning and openness to new understandings—particularly on such a hot topic as homosexuality. They share the conviction of the Massachusetts Bay Puritans that "truth [has] been forever discovered in its entirety."[69] When challenged to take a new look at this or any other controversial social issue (for example, gender roles or reproductive rights), such people are quick to echo the words of an angry parent who opposed the use of certain textbooks in the schools: "It's an insidious attempt to replace our periods with their question marks."[70] They want to feel that everything is settled.

Homosexuality is particularly difficult for such people because it doesn't fit into their perception of the world. It violates their sense of an orderly system that decrees the loving union of a man and woman and the children that issue from that union. They speak of revulsion—of actually being sickened—at the thought of a loving union of two men or two women. The nausea they express is real—a kind of psychological vertigo as the ordered system of the universe they understood so clearly seems to spin around out of control. Order appears to have given way to chaos.

Cultural anthropologist Mary Douglas has studied the ways human beings handle anomalies—those things that don't fit into the usual scheme of things but are exceptions to the rule.[71] In a heterocentric society in which heterosexuality is viewed as the norm, homosexual people are in a sense anomalies. Douglas points out that one way societies deal with anomalies is to ignore them by simply not perceiving them. The "don't ask, don't tell, don't pursue" policy concerning gay and lesbian people in the military takes such an approach.[72]

A second way societies deal with anomalies is to condemn them and get rid of them. Douglas uses the example of certain West African tribes that killed twins at birth to eliminate a phenomenon that contradicted their belief that two human births could not issue from a single womb at the same time. They thus constructed their own reality—a reality in which *of course* double births did not exist. After all, there weren't any around, were there?

It isn't hard to see how this second way of dealing with anomalies applies to the harsh treatment of homosexual people over history. Persons of homosexual orientation have been put to death, imprisoned, committed to mental hospitals against their will, or forced to undergo bizarre treatments (such as aversion therapy) to "cure" them. They are punished simply for existing. They must either be put away, separated from those who consider themselves the standard of normality, or they must change. When Christians talk this way, they often do so under the guise of love and compassion, saying that they do not hate homosexuals but love them and thus want to free them from homosexuality.

An analogous situation comes to mind. In the eighteenth century, Dr. Benjamin Rush, a political leader, author, physician, and friend of John Adams and Thomas Jefferson, put forth a theory that the skin color of black people resulted from a congenital disease, that they were not happy with their skin color, and that efforts should be made to "cure" the disease and turn them white, as nature intended the human race to be!

Rush had learned about a slave who had begun developing white blotches in his skin, gradually becoming white all over his body. The slave was eventually able to purchase his freedom from the fees collected for his appearance in public exhibitions. We now know that he had vitiligo, a disease in which the skin gradually loses its pigmentation. (New attention was drawn to this disease in 1993 when singer Michael Jackson revealed in a television interview with Oprah Winfrey that he was afflicted with a skin condition that is thought to be vitiligo.)

Benjamin Rush, however, believed the former slave's change of color indicated nature's healing. Psychiatrist Thomas Szasz comments that nothing about the case is more striking than that Rush considered a black person's biologically natural color to be a disease and viewed the man's disease as a "spontaneous cure."[73] At a 1797 meeting of the American Philosophical Society, Rush presented his theory about a hereditary mild form of leprosy that had no other symptoms than black skin. Historian Winthrop Jordan points out several effects Rush suggested his theory might have.[74] (It's a simple step to see in Rush's faulty and condescending reasoning some analogous attitudes displayed by many Christians toward homosexual people today.)

Rush felt, first of all, that his theory would permit people to be compassionate toward black people (they were allegedly victims of an illness, after all), while at the same time whiteness was being emphasized as the norm. A second supposed benefit of his theory was the rationale it provided for maintaining social distance even though black people should be accepted as fellow human beings. In other words, interracial dating and marriage were to be avoided. Care must be taken not "to infect posterity with any portion of their disorder." True, the mild form of leprosy they were said to be afflicted with was not generally regarded as infectious. But Rush argued that there might be some slight risk in that he knew of two white women who were said to have turned darker after marrying black men. However, Rush believed that the less intimate contact involved in the employment of black people as domestic servants did not pose a threat.

A third significant effect his theory could have, Rush emphasized, was the verification of Scripture. It would be a way of reconciling the Bible with what people saw with their own eyes. The assumption being that Adam and Eve were white, it could be reasoned that all the descendants of the original pair logically should have been white, too. And yet some were not. Rush's disease theory could explain the discrepancy and vindicate the truth of the creation account.

Fourth, Rush saw his theory as providing an incentive for science to find a "cure" for black skin and thereby end the justifications that had been used to enslave a race of people (namely, that dark skin was a divine curse or that it meant that certain peoples were designed for labor in the hot sun).

A final outcome Rush saw for his theory was the happiness it would supposedly bring to black people, "for however well they appear to be satisfied with their color, there are many proofs of their preferring that of white people."

Jordan sums up Rush's overall reasoning in these words: "If only blackness were leprosy, slavery and intermixture stood condemned and Scripture and humanitarian benevolence confirmed."[75] The theory, so scientifically false, never gained acceptance; but it serves as an excellent illustration of the ethnocentric reasoning that can take place as members of a dominant group try to deal with that which differs from themselves.

▼ FROM DEVIANCE TO DIVERSITY

Having examined two of the ways Mary Douglas describes in which individuals and societies deal with anomalies (ignore/deny and condemn/eliminate), let's look at the third way she gives. "Positively," she writes, "we can deliberately confront the anomaly and try to create a new pattern of reality in which it has a place."[76] It is this approach that many people of faith are taking as they seek out ways to show biblical love to their lesbian, gay, and bisexual neighbors. Human variation is accepted as part of God's good creation.

Douglas's third way also fits with trends in social-science studies of homosexual people as a social group. Under the older conceptual framework for conducting such research, homosexual people were usually studied as "deviants." Today, the research is more likely to be organized around such concepts as "social reaction,"[77] minority status,[78] and "oppression theory."[79]

The sociological concept of deviance simply refers to behavior that deviates in some way from the behavior a given society requires of its members. It's important to keep in mind that value judgments were never intended by the social scientists who studied deviance in this sense; they were not saying that certain behaviors were inherently "deviant," nor were they using the term (as most people do) to mean immoral, degenerate, or sinful. They were simply pointing out that certain individuals or groups may deviate from the standards a particular society holds up as normal and proper. For example, it is certainly not an act of deviance, in the popular sense of that word, for a black woman to refuse to give her seat to a white person. But such an act *was* considered deviant under the Jim Crow segregation rules of the South at the time Rosa Parks kept her seat and thereby inaugurated the civil-rights movement. Her act violated the acceptable standards for behavior at that time and in that place. Deviance of this sort, emphasizes sociologist Joseph Julian, can "warn society that certain rules are not just or reasonable" and "can be one of the factors that effect needed changes in the organization of society."[80]

Rather than focus upon the personal behavior of persons who have been labeled deviant or search for causes of their deviance, most specialists in deviance-as-a-sociological-phenomenon are now concentrating on why certain behaviors are labeled deviant in a particular society, how such labeling comes about, and especially the effects of societal attitudes and reactions on those who have been labeled deviant. "For example, what makes homosexuality 'deviant,' according to social reaction theory," write Weinberg and Williams, "is not anything about the behavior per se but rather the fact that people differentiate, stigmatize, and penalize alleged homosexuals."[81]

A different way of looking at homosexuality sociologically is simply to conceptualize gay and lesbian people collectively as a *social group with minority status*, much like an ethnic group, rather than as a group that has broken societal rules. Many social scientists now take this approach. What determines the designation *minority group* is a group's relative lack of power, privilege, and prestige and not necessarily its having fewer numbers than a majority group. As sociologist Louis Wirth points out, we may think of a minority as a group of people whose physical or cultural characteristics result in their being treated differently than others in their society "and who therefore regard themselves as objects of collective discrimination."[82]

▼ THE CLASH OF TWO PERSPECTIVES

What we are seeing today in the heated debates over homosexuality that are taking place in religious groups, political factions, the military, and in society in general is a clash of two distinct perspectives. On the one side are those who embrace a *deviance* perspective, viewing homosexual people as breakers of society's rules and thus "abnormal perverts." On the other side are those who take a *diversity* position, in which gay and lesbian people are seen as constituting a minority group like other minority groups in today's pluralistic society. These two societal models parallel the two ethical approaches we presented in our chart in chapter 9. The deviance and diversity perspectives are at odds with one another, and communication between the two sides is difficult to establish.

Instead of seeking to understand gay men and lesbian women as *persons* who live and work and love much like anyone else, those who stress the deviance perspective tend to be most concerned with sexual expression. They would agree with the newspaper letter writer who said, "When you believe that some forms of sexual activity are deviant, you respond negatively to people who practice them and, on top of that, are proud and vocal about it."[83]

As sociologist Edwin Schur explains, statements such as this illustrate "a process of social typing through which people who, for whatever reason, feel threatened seek to avoid the persons and negate the conditions they find objectionable." He points out that "this process depersonalizes the offending individuals—who are treated as mere instances of a discreditable category, rather than as full human beings—thus imposing personal stigma and providing a basis for collective discrimination against them."[84]

The deviancy perspective provides a way for groups and organizations to maintain and strengthen boundaries. In his study of Puritans who deviated from that society's standards for acceptable behavior, Erikson noted how the punishments meted out to them functioned to teach the community where the lines were drawn. Such dealing with offenders also enhanced the Puritan community's group cohesiveness and its members' sense of righteousness and uniqueness. "Deviant forms of behavior, by marking the outer edges of group life, give the inner structure its special character and thus supply the framework within which the people of the group develop an orderly sense of their own cultural identity."[85]

The person that a group classifies as "a deviant," then, becomes a depersonalized entity that the group uses to make a statement to the world: *See this person! This is behavior we will not tolerate. This is the kind of person we righteous people refuse to be like—or to associate with. By our attitude toward him or her, we are reinforcing our standards, strengthening our moral position, reaffirming our distinctiveness. We will not compromise.* The group may offer acceptance if the person defined as deviant will only repent. Explaining the Puritans' insistence on repentance, even while the accused deviant was being led to the gallows (when restoration to the community was out of the question), Erikson writes that "a public ceremony of admission" was what they desired. "To repent is to agree that the moral standards of the community are right and that the sentence of the court is just."[86]

In our own day, a lesbian minister whose denomination denied her the right to accept a local church's call had such an understanding of repentance in mind when she said, "This decision says either lie or repent. I will not lie and I will never repent." She explained why. "We are talking about who it is that God made me."[87] The eight-hundred-member Downtown United Presbyterian Church of Rochester, New York, hired the Reverend Jane Adams Spahr to be one of their co-pastors because she was far and away the best, most qualified candidate they had interviewed; and their decision was upheld by the Presbytery of the Genessee Valley and by the Synod of the Northeast. But it was overturned at the national level when the denomination's highest judicial body ruled she could not be a pastor because of her committed long-term lesbian relationship with the Reverend Connie Staff of the Universal Fellowship of Metropolitan Community Churches.

What was unique about this situation was that Spahr was already an ordained Presbyterian minister, having been ordained before the Presbyterian Church U.S.A. had issued its 1978 declaration that "unrepentant homosexual activity does not accord with the requirements set forth in the Book of Order," thus forbidding ordination to any lesbian or gay person who was not living a celibate life. Since a "grandparenting" provision exempted the application of the ruling to persons who had been ordained prior to

1978, Janie Spahr and her supporters believed that the 1978 ruling would not affect her calling to the Rochester church. Denominational officials, however, argued that "the exemption for those ordained before 1978 was designed to prevent investigations into the activities of ministers prior to the church's first definitive ruling on the matter—not as a license for practicing gays and lesbians to continue as ministers."

At the same time, the widow of the man who had been the denomination's moderator during the formulation of the 1978 ruling said her husband had introduced the exemption to prevent the efforts by some to withdraw the ordination rights of previously ordained gay and lesbian people. Kathryn Connor said that her husband, John T. Connor, had intended the exemption to apply throughout such ministers' lives. "John knew those already ordained had been called by God, had satisfied the trials for ordination, had served the body of Christ for many years . . . and as a matter of justice as well as love should continue their ministries throughout their lives regardless of their sexual orientation and practice."[88] Nevertheless, the church's general assembly voted in June 1993 to uphold the denomination's disallowance of "self-affirming, practicing homosexual" clergy.[89]

This is but one of many examples of the struggles over the question of homosexuality that continue in various religious bodies. After taking eleven years to decide, the National Council of Churches in November 1992 refused to grant not just membership but even observer status to the Universal Fellowship of Metropolitan Community Churches (whose congregations are predominantly gay and lesbian). This rejection prompted the UFMCC's ecumenical officer, Nancy Wilson, to exclaim that "it's easier to get into heaven than into the N.C.C."[90] That same month, the American Baptist Churches' general board adopted the posture of many other denominations and declared homosexual practice to be incompatible with Christian teaching.[91]

Earlier in 1992, many people were shocked by a statement sent to all U.S. Catholic bishops in which the Vatican called homosexuality "an objective disorder" and endorsed discrimination against gay and lesbian people in such areas as teaching and coaching, foster-child care, adoption, housing, health benefits, and the military, asserting that homosexual behavior debases traditional family life.[92] And in a move called "unprecedented" in the nearly one and a half centuries of Southern Baptist history, a constitutional amendment was passed in June 1993 granting the nation's largest denomination power to expel from membership any congregations "which act to affirm, approve, or endorse homosexual behavior."[93] Such a move goes against such Baptist traditions as respecting the autonomy of the local church, allowing room for differences of opinion, and emphasizing the exercise of one's own conscience before God. No wonder the *Christian Century* declared that "discussion of homosexuality has reached the boiling point" in most church bodies![94]

On the other hand, those Christians who follow a diversity model rather than a deviance model would agree with San Francisco's oldest Southern Baptist congregation. Dolores Street Baptist Church emphasizes that "every member of the body of Christ is called to minister and exercise her or his gifts." This church made a formal congregational decision to "remain open and loving to all persons and to encourage them to minister." When the congregation learned of the Southern Baptist Convention's planned amendment to oust churches that were supportive of homosexual people, it voted to withdraw from the denomination, even before the measure passed. The Dolores Street congregation issued a statement in 1993 saying, "We cannot support and stand with a denomination that as a matter of policy condemns and excludes a part of our family: lesbian, gay, and bisexual women and men."[95]

The diversity perspective provides insights into the gay, lesbian, and bisexual experience that are totally missed in a deviance approach. With this awareness in mind, researchers Sherry Woods and Karen Harbeck speak of three advantages of applying the "oppression theory" conceptual framework to studies of minority groups. First, in this perspective, minority-group members portray their *own* life experience "rather than merely juxtapose their behavior against the majority's definition of what is normal. Second, the focus of the problem and potential solutions shifts from the minority population onto the majority's abuse of power." And third, say these authors, "each minority group's experience can be more precisely analyzed within its own context rather than further stigmatized by the majority's distortions."[96]

Earlier in this book, we spoke of the importance of listening to the voices of gay and lesbian people as they share their own stories, whether in person or through helpful books and other means. And we urged followers of Christ not to bear false witness against their neighbor the homosexual. Sadly, however, many heterosexual Christians are so intent on promoting the deviance approach that they distort the facts and mislead people, stirring up fear and hatred. For example, no sooner had New Jersey become the fifth state in the nation to pass a law against discrimination that included sexual orientation as a protected category (January 1992) than the small but vociferous Orthodox Presbyterian Church filed a federal suit against the state. The group erroneously claimed that the law would jeopardize their own freedom to preach and practice their beliefs.

Others have sought to discount the status of homosexual people as a discriminated-against group by saying their numbers are too small to be taken seriously as a bona fide minority deserving special protection under the law. When a new national study was released in 1993 showing that only 2.3 percent of the representative sample of men aged twenty to thirty-nine years had experienced same-gender sexual activity over a ten-year period and only 1 percent had been exclusively homosexual,[97] many opponents of gay rights "were giddy" over the possibility that the lower estimate of numbers might undermine gay power and slow down the momentum of the gay civil-rights movement.[98]

Other arguments intended to undermine the diversity approach center around claims that gay and lesbian people aren't really discriminated against and that gay and lesbian people want "special rights" beyond what ordinary citizens have. People who use "They aren't really discriminated against" arguments sometimes cite demographic material showing that, as a social group, gay people tend to have higher education and income than the national average.[99] Opponents of gay rights then say, "Where is the discrimination?" They say they don't hate homosexual people and they don't want them to lose rights but simply that they shouldn't have more rights than anyone else. "Everyone should have the same rights." But in the next breath they speak of their real fear that a national anti-discrimination bill will be passed. And they especially fear that new definitions of the family will become accepted and that homosexual marriage and adoption of children will be permitted.[100]

Those on the diversity side parry those arguments by pointing to the real discrimination that takes place daily in the lives of lesbian and gay people. When opponents of gay rights claim they want homosexual people to have the same rights as everyone else, but no "special" rights, they are guilty of either hypocrisy or a lack of logic or both—because they don't want gay couples to have the right to marry; to have spousal rights in health insurance, estate settlements, and tax laws; and to enjoy other privileges extended to married people. They oppose domestic-partnership policies. They don't approve of homosexual people being granted custody of their own children from prior marriages or having children through artificial insemination or adoption. They don't want homosexual people to serve in the military, or have ministries in churches, or be protected from discrimination in the workplace. How can these ordinary rights of everyday life be considered "special rights"?

When, in 1979, Senator Paul Tsongas proposed the first national legislation to prohibit employment discrimination on the basis of sexual orientation, he said he saw this as "a matter of equal rights and privacy." He pointed out that "most employees don't let their sexual orientation interfere with their work." His bill was not calling for affirmative-action programs, he stated, but simply provided "a legal recourse for persons fired or denied jobs because of this aspect of their private lives." He went on:

> Employment discrimination against homosexual persons generally occurs after the individual has been hired. Typically, the supervisor discovers that an individual is gay, and has the employee dismissed on that ground alone. In the absence of legal protection, the accused person's livelihood is

jeopardized for a lifetime, causing undue mental anxiety, and robbing the community of that individual's talents and productivity. This is wasteful and unjust.[101]

Many highly successful gay and lesbian people would like to see such national legislation pass, but in the meantime they are forming networks in the workplace in order to bring about environments free of harassment and the threat of discriminatory job loss. Many companies are becoming more sensitive to the needs of their gay and lesbian workers as such employees increasingly want to be open without feeling they are committing career suicide. "As in the military, managers confused the *invisibility* of their gay and lesbian employees with *rarity*," write Jay Lucas and Mark Kaplan, "and the willingness of gays to stay in the closet kept corporations from acting on these issues."[102]

And then there is gay bashing. Gay and lesbian people are frequent victims of hate crimes, many of which go unreported. A 1991 study of five major metropolitan areas in the United States revealed that over eighteen hundred anti-gay and anti-lesbian crimes had taken place, nearly a third more than in the previous year.[103] The anti-gay backlash creates an atmosphere of fear and hatred that is conducive to violence against homosexual people. Can there be any honest doubt that gay and lesbian people are discriminated against?

Those taking a deviance perspective insist on defining gay and lesbian people, even attempting to invalidate personal experience. Columnist Pat Buchanan once wrote that gay pride celebrations were not actually celebrations but rather were "masquerades where men and women 'put on a happy face' to cover up doubts, insecurities, or a sadness inside."[104] Like Benjamin Rush in his assertion that black people could not possibly be happy unless they were white (while not acknowledging that any unhappiness he observed might very well have originated in unjust treatment by the dominant white population), those who reject the diversity model in favor of a deviance one do not want to believe that gay and lesbian people can experience joy and contentment and lead fulfilled, productive lives. They don't want to hear that gay and lesbian people can be happy; and when they do hear it, they call it "pseudo-happiness" that conceals loneliness and maladjustment.

▼ DIVERSITY WITHIN DIVERSITY

Again, we stress the importance of letting gay and lesbian people define their own lives rather than superimposing on them what many people would like to believe in order to support the deviance model. This desire to learn what homosexual people themselves say about their lives was a driving force behind a massive study sociologists Alan Bell and Martin Weinberg conducted. "A primary focus of this investigation is upon diversity—the ways in which homosexual persons differ from one another," they wrote.[105] One finding that emerged was a typology of five major groups of homosexual people. Some were in "close-coupled" relationships analogous to marriage,[106] others were in "open-coupled" relationships in which strict monogamy was not preserved between the partners, and still others lived as "singles" (either, in the researchers' terms, "functionally" or "dysfunctionally") or were primarily asexual.

Diversity in life-styles is but one of the realizations we come to as we endeavor to learn more about our neighbors, the people who are homosexual.[107] As we listen to their stories and learn about their lives, we also become aware of the many issues that are being discussed within the gay and lesbian subculture today.

There are, for example, such issues as privacy, identity management, and the phenomenon called "outing" (forcing gay and lesbian people out of the closet by revealing their identity publicly even though they wish or wished to keep their homosexuality secret). Sometimes outing is done to unmask someone who is attacking gay and lesbian people or working against their best interests in order to provide a smokescreen for his or her own homosexual activities. There is little disagreement among homosexual people and supportive heterosexual people that exposure of a person's hypocrisy in such cases is deserved.[108] But opinions differ over the wisdom of forcing other gay and lesbian people out of the closet simply for political clout. Those who have not walked in their shoes do not know what such exposure might cost them, and it is sheer arrogance to suppose that someone else knows what is best for them without knowing their circumstances. Privacy does not necessarily mean dishonesty in every case; it may mean that some people want to retain the right to reveal only as much of themselves as they wish to reveal at a given time and place. On the other hand, many gay and lesbian people speak of the empowerment and freedom they have gained from a *voluntary* revelation of their homosexuality at a time that seems right to them.[109]

Another issue illustrative of the diversity among homosexual people today centers around choice. As the staff of the Sex Information and Education Council of the United States (SIECUS) has pointed out, the term "sexual preference" is now outdated "because sexual orientation is no longer commonly considered to be one's conscious individual preference or choice" but is thought to be rooted in a "complicated network" of biological and social factors.[110]

However, among some lesbian women, there has been a debate over the determinism they feel is implied in such research findings. In an article in *Ms.* magazine, Lindsay Van Gelder writes, "Virtually every self-identified gay man I've ever met has been convinced that his sexuality is a biological given, but lesbians are a mixed bag."[111] She and others point to the "complexities of the lesbian world" and the varied experiences of many women who, like her, have had satisfactory relationships with men before making a conscious decision to enter a relationship with a woman and "come out" as a lesbian. She objects to being regarded as "sexually handicapped" due to some "genetic flaw" that has caused her to be the way she is. She objects to the notion that she is considered a victim of something beyond her control, something she can't help but *would* if she could. The implication she sees behind such views is that being gay or lesbian is a bad thing and that such a person is to be pitied.

But, of course, such an implication is not the intent of those of us who emphasize diversity and believe in the human variation that has arisen out of God's wisdom and manifests itself in many distinct ways, including differences in sexual orientation. Being "different from" does not imply "better than" or "inferior to" one another.

However, since we do not want to discount anyone's experience, we acknowledge the emphasis upon choice that is so important to some women in the current debate. Women have for all too long felt that others determined their destiny and are now awaking to their own power to make their own decisions. Becoming aware of and choosing to act upon their lesbian feelings at a later point in life *is* the experience of some women. The reverse sometimes happens, too. As we pointed out in our discussion of the Kinsey continuum in chapter 6 and in the description of the research on bisexuality cited in note 3 of that chapter, people are located at various points between an exclusively heterosexual and an exclusively homosexual identity.

One researcher, Beverly Burch, has suggested a continuum within lesbianism itself, with "primary lesbians" on one side and "bisexual lesbians" on the other. Primary lesbians are aware of their homosexual orientation from an early age, whereas bisexual lesbians move toward woman-to-woman relationships after having had serious heterosexual relationships.[112]

Earlier, in a similar way of thinking, sociologist Barbara Ponse had proposed the terms "primary lesbians" and "elective lesbians," emphasizing that those in her research sample whom she categorized as elective lesbians spoke of a "late realization of their true lesbian nature." They reported that this awareness did not occur until their twenties, thirties, forties, or even later. "The primary lesbian is disposed to describe lesbianism as an orientation or condition that informs the whole character of her self," writes Ponse. Such a woman says of her lesbian identity, "I was always that way." In contrast, the elective lesbian "interprets discontinuous life experiences so that they demonstrate a true, underlying lesbian identity." In other words, according to Ponse, "elective lesbians are likely to invoke the notion of the essentiality of their lesbianism (as do the primary)" and may also view lesbianism as an orientation or condition, but they differ from primary lesbians in emphasizing that their sexual-emotional *behavior* is a voluntary choice.[113]

Such a way of conceptualizing the life experiences of lesbian women does not contradict the scientific research cited in chapter 6 and may be a way of bringing together the arguments of the *essentialists* (who argue that their lesbian identity has been essential to their concept of self from their earliest memories and who know from their innermost feelings and experience that a homosexual person is something one *is* and not something one *becomes*) and, on the other side, the *constructionists* (who gradually form their sense of lesbian identity as they interpret their feelings and life events over a long period).

▼ THE AIDS CRISIS: CALL TO ACTION AND COMPASSION

Doubtless no other issue has had the impact on homosexual people as a social group that the disease AIDS has had. It has helped bridge the gap between gay men and lesbian women and has galvanized the overall homosexual community into political activism as nothing else has done.[114] And because the first cases of the disease that came to light in the United States occurred among gay men and its spread was most pronounced among that group, it has made the larger society much more aware of homosexual people. (Responses to that awareness have been a mixture of hate and fear on the one hand and compassion and admiration on the other, as society has watched—often in awe—the loving concern, care, and support homosexual people have given each other and the strength and wisdom that the community has demonstrated in dealing with death in such large numbers and at such young ages.)

It is wrong to call AIDS a "gay disease" or "gay plague." What was a strange, unnamed disorder when it was first noted in the United States among a few gay men in 1980 and 1981[115] also came to light in Africa in the early 1980s, where it spread mainly among heterosexuals, virtually decimating numerous city populations. Of the 12 to 14 million people worldwide who have been infected with the human immunodeficiency virus (HIV), the virus that causes AIDS, between 7 and 8 million live in the sub-Saharan region of Africa.[116] The World Health Organization reported at the 1993 International Conference on AIDS that there were known to be 2 million cases of full-blown AIDS worldwide and estimated a tripling of both HIV infections and the cases of AIDS by the end of the 1990s.

In the United States, gay men make up 62 percent of AIDS cases, although they account for only 39 percent of new HIV infections, indicating that preventive measures have resulted in a decline in the virus's spread within that population, as we noted earlier. Infections are now spreading most rapidly among African-American people, women, the urban poor, drug users and their partners, and children.[117] Such infections have increased among heterosexual people.

Research continues into a virus that keeps changing, and continuing efforts are being made to develop an effective vaccine. Scientists now point to research that suggests that "HIV is not a new virus but an old one that grew deadly."[118] At the same time, long-term survivors have provided hope by dispelling the fatalistic view that AIDS always and inevitably spells death.[119]

The concept of Christian neighbor love allows no room for the irresponsible and ignorant claims of those who portray AIDS as having been sent by a vengeful and cruel God to show God's displeasure with homosexuality. As former surgeon general C. Everett Koop admonished in the report on AIDS he drafted while in office, we must remember that "we are fighting a disease, not people."[120]

Dr. David Schiedermayer, a Christian physician who has worked with many AIDS patients, has expressed concern about the lack of compassion in certain Christians who, in the midst of the AIDS epidemic, look for scapegoats to blame and persecute. He compares such attitudes with attitudes displayed during other periods of history, notably the time of the Black Death in fourteenth-century Europe, when Jews were the group singled out as scapegoats. They were severely persecuted because of irrational fears that they were poisoning wells, infecting the air, and spreading the deadly plague. Schiedermayer lists three choices that people have when faced with the spread of diseases that kill large numbers of people—whether in the case of bubonic plague during the Middle Ages or in the case of AIDS today. "When finally confronted by plague," he writes, "we can each choose to desert, to persecute, or to care."[121]

The Benedictine Brothers of Vermont's Weston Priory, whose recorded music has enriched many of our lives, remind us that "a person's own well-being is tied up with that of those he or she loves." They refer to the philosopher Robert Nozick's observation in *The Examined Life* that "love can place you at risk," because bad things that happen to people we love also happen to us—as do good things. The monks urge us to see that "the AIDS pandemic raises the question of love in a painfully urgent and concrete manner." They continue:

> Who are the ones with whom our own well-being is tied up? If we *are* the Body of Christ, and if some part of that Body is infected with the HIV virus, are we not *all* affected? Is not our own well-being tied up in the lives of men, women, and children living with AIDS? Do we believe that we have something to give, and much to receive, by reaching out lovingly to persons-with-AIDS? To help bear them up in their suffering, and to be gifted by their courage? To comfort those who mourn the deaths of their loved ones? We are all affected.[122]

Again, the Word comes to us: *You shall love your neighbor as yourself. Your own well-being is tied up in giving and receiving such love.* We agree with Thomas Merton's sentiments given at the beginning of this chapter: there can be no boundaries, no separation-by-classification, in this matter of love.

"Those who say, 'I love God,' and hate their brothers and sisters, are liars; for those who do not love a brother or sister whom they have seen, cannot love God whom they have not seen. The commandment we have from [God] is this: those who love God must love their brothers and sisters also" (1 John 4:20–21).

"God is love, and those who abide in love abide in God, and God abides in them" (1 John 4:16).

Notes

CHAPTER 1 ▼ WHO IS MY NEIGHBOR?

1. As quoted in John Lauritsen, *Religious Roots of the Taboo on Homosexuality* (New York: privately printed, 1974), 23–24.
2. Jerry Falwell, in an undated Moral Majority fund-raising letter sent out during the 1980s.
3. Such statements were made by Anita Bryant during her successful campaign to overturn a Dade County, Florida, ordinance that banned discrimination against homosexuals. See "Battle over Gay Rights," *Newsweek,* 6 June 1977, 20.
4. See "Vatican Declares Support for Discrimination Against Gays," *Virginian-Pilot and the Ledger-Star,* 18 July 1992; and Robert A. Bernstein, "Gays and the Vatican: A Religious Call to Hate," *San Francisco Examiner,* 24 July 1992.
5. This summary is based on several newspaper reports appearing in the *Virginian-Pilot* 27 Jan. 1992 and 5 Feb. 1992. Also see Felice Yeskel, "The Price of Progress," *Women's Review of Books,* February 1992, 21.
6. "Gays Under Fire" (cover story), *Newsweek,* 14 Sept. 1992, 35–41.
7. Donna Minkowitz, "It's Still Open Season on Gays," *Nation,* 23 Mar. 1992, 368–69.
8. "Gays Under Fire."
9. "Gays Under Fire."
10. Quoted in "Platform," *National Courier* 2 (15 Apr. 1977): 21.
11. Sigmund Freud, "The Psychogenesis of a Case of Homosexuality in a Woman," in *Collected Papers* (New York: Basic Books, 1959), 2:206–7.
12. "Torture, Homosexuality, and the Cry for Hope," *Other Side* 13 (April 1977): 6.
13. Interview with Paul Cameron on the nationwide syndicated call-in talk show *Point of View,* produced by International Christian Media, Dallas, Texas (Marlin Maddoux, president). The undated cassette tape of this broadcast, distributed by International Christian Media, is entitled "Paul Cameron: Homosexuality and AIDS." See also the discussion in Sara Diamond, *Spiritual*

Warfare: The Politics of the Christian Right (Boston: South End Press, 1989). Diamond calls Cameron "the most rabid of the anti-gay propagandists" (p. 101).

14. Eric Marcus, "They're Not Telling the Truth," *Newsweek,* 14 Sept. 1992, 41.

CHAPTER 2 ▼ THE RISKS AND CHALLENGES OF MORAL GROWTH

1. Richard Lettis et al., eds., *Huck Finn and His Critics* (New York: Macmillan, 1962), 187.

2. Lettis, *Huck Finn,* 188–89.

3. "The task of the southern apologists for slavery was to convince their opponents that if they argued that slavery was contrary to biblical teaching they could properly be classed as 'infidels,'" writes Robert Ferm, pointing out that "a 'biblical' defense of slavery was the key to much of their argument." See Robert Ferm, "Slavery: Introduction," in Robert Ferm, ed., *Issues in American Protestantism* (Garden City, NY: Doubleday Anchor Books, 1969), 181. For a detailed discussion of the religious arguments for slavery that were prevalent at the time that *Huckleberry Finn* was written, see Willard M. Swartley, *Slavery, Sabbath, War, and Women* (Scottdale, PA: Herald Press, 1983), chap. 1.

4. See Letha Dawson Scanzoni and Nancy A. Hardesty, *All We're Meant to Be: Biblical Feminism for Today,* 3d ed. (Grand Rapids, MI: Eerdmans, 1992); Paul K. Jewett, *Man as Male and Female* (Grand Rapids, MI: Eerdmans, 1975); and Virginia R. Mollenkott, *Women, Men, and the Bible,* rev. ed. (New York: Crossroad, 1988).

5. G. C. Berkouwer, *Holy Scripture* (Grand Rapids, MI: Eerdmans, 1975), 137.

6. Berkouwer, *Holy Scripture,* 137.

7. As cited in Berkouwer, *Holy Scripture,* 138.

8. John Milton, *Samson Agonistes,* line 41. For a discussion of Milton's brilliant dramatization of Samson's final hours, see Virginia R. Mollenkott, "Relativism in *Samson Agonistes,*" *Studies in Philology* 67 (January 1970): 89–102.

9. John Calvin, *Institutes of the Christian Religion,* trans. Henry Beveridge (Grand Rapids, MI: Eerdmans, 1975), 2:137.

CHAPTER 3 ▼ THE HOMOSEXUAL AS SAMARITAN

1. "Can the Risk Be Cut?" *Newsweek,* 6 Oct. 1975, 20; "'Gays' and the Press," *Newsweek,* 20 Oct. 1975, 93–94; Fred W. Friendly, "Gays, the News Media and All Americans' Right to Privacy," *Virginian-Pilot and the Ledger-Star,* 14 Apr. 1990, A-8.

2. Pierre Berton, *The Comfortable Pew,* U.S. ed. (Philadelphia: Lippincott, 1965), 78.

3. Personal interview, February 1976. For a full report, see Letha Scanzoni, "Conservative Christians and Gay Civil Rights," *Christian Century* 93 (13 Oct. 1976): 857–62, and "Gay Confrontation," *Christianity Today* 20 (12 Mar. 1976): 633–35.

4. "God Is Just a Prayer Away," a radio broadcast originating in Lynchburg, Ohio. The sermon described was presented on the 31 October 1976 program.

5. Tim LaHaye and Beverly LaHaye, *The Act of Marriage* (Grand Rapids, MI: Zondervan, 1976), 261.

6. See John Lauritsen and David Thorstad, *The Early Homosexual Rights Movement (1864–1935)* (New York: Times Change Press, 1974), 74; and Edwin J. Haeberle, "Swastika, Pink Triangle, and Yellow Star: The Destruction of Sexology and the Persecution of Homosexuals in Nazi Germany," in *Hidden from History: Reclaiming the Gay and Lesbian Past,* ed. Martin Bauml Duberman, Martha Vicinus, and George Chauncey, Jr. (New York: New American Library, 1989), 365–79.

7. All of these people are described in A. L. Rowse, *Homosexuals in History* (New York: Macmillan, 1977).

8. Except for Mary Woolley, all of these people are described in Barbara Grier and Coletta Reid, *Lesbian Lives* (Baltimore: Diana Press, 1976). On Willa Cather, see Sharon O'Brien, "'The Thing Not Named': Willa Cather as a Lesbian Writer," *Signs: Journal of Women in Culture and Society* 9 (Summer 1984): 576–99. On Virginia Woolf and Vita Sackville-West, see Louise DeSalvo, "Lighting the Cave: The Relationship Between Vita Sackville-West and Virginia Woolf," *Signs* 8 (Winter 1982): 195–214. See also Jane Rule, *Lesbian Images* (New York: Pocket Books, 1976); and Lillian Faderman, *Surpassing the Love of Men: Romantic Friendship and Love Between Women from the Renaissance to the Present* (New York: William Morrow, 1981). Faderman's book includes a discussion of Mary Woolley and Jeannette Marks, whose loving companionship spanned over half a century and ended only when they were parted by Woolley's death. The story of their life together is told in Anna Mary Wells, *Miss Marks and Miss Woolley* (Boston: Houghton Mifflin, 1978). A controversy arose shortly before the publication of Wells's book when word leaked out that, in the course of her research, the biographer had found letters indicating the lesbian nature of the relationship between Woolley and Marks. A number of shocked Mount Holyoke alumnae protested the book's publication. See Molly Ivins, "Book Calling Ex-Holyoke Head a Lesbian Is Assailed," *New York Times,* 21 Aug. 1976. When the book was published, however, many readers were surprised to read that, in spite of the evidence found in the letters, Wells voiced her opinion that Woolley and Marks had probably never expressed their love for each other in a specifically sexual manner. This led to another round of controversy in different circles, where it was asserted that such "historical denial" by biographers of numerous accomplished and admired women of the past serves to advance homophobia and the perpetuation of myths about lesbians as being strange, sick, and criminal and having nothing to contribute to the societal good. See Blanche Wiesen Cook, "'Women Alone Stir My Imagination': Lesbianism and the Cultural Tradition," *Signs* 4 (Summer 1979): 718–39; and Leila J. Rupp, "'Imagine My Surprise': Women's Relationships in Mid-Twentieth Century America," in Duberman, Vicinus, and Chauncey, *Hidden from History,* 395–410.

9. The claim was first made by Rebecca Patterson in *The Riddle of Emily Dickinson* (Boston: Houghton Mifflin, 1951). It is reiterated by Camille Paglia in

Sexual Personae: Art and Decadence from Nefertiti to Emily Dickinson (New York: Vintage Books, 1991). Paglia pelts her readers with phrases from Dickinson's poems and letters to prove that the Belle of Amherst was actually "Amherst's Madame de Sade," a sadomasochistic self-masculinizing homosexual voyeur "gaming at sexual inclusiveness" (p. 673). A list of other scholars who have discussed the possibility of Dickinson's erotic interest in women is found in Martha Nell Smith, "Gender Issues in Textual Editing of Emily Dickinson," *Women Studies Quarterly* 19, no. 3/4 (Fall/Winter 1991): 108 n. 20.

10. Poem 249 in *The Complete Poems of Emily Dickinson*, ed. Thomas H. Johnson (Boston: Little, Brown, 1960), 114.

11. Lillian Faderman's massive study of "romantic friendships"—close attachments between women that were common and societally accepted in past periods of history—was sparked by her examination of Emily Dickinson's love poems and letters to Sue Gilbert. See Faderman, *Surpassing the Love of Men*. Faderman suggests that Dickinson and Gilbert's relationship seems to fit into the "romantic friendship" category. Such relationships, says Faderman, "were love relationships in every sense except perhaps the genital, since women in centuries other than ours often internalized the view of females as having little sexual passion." She continues:

> Thus they might kiss, fondle each other, sleep together, utter expressions of overwhelming love and promises of eternal faithfulness, and yet see their passions as nothing more than effusions of the spirit. If they were sexually aroused, bearing no burden of visible proof as men do, they might deny it even to themselves if they wished. But whether or not these relationships had a genital component, the novels and diaries and correspondence of these periods consistently showed romantic friends opening their souls to each other and speaking a language that was in no way different from the language of heterosexual love: They pledged to remain "faithful" forever, to be in "each other's thoughts constantly," to live together and even to die together. [p. 16]

Were such relationships lesbian? By some definitions, no—if the word is used solely in a sexual sense. Faderman found few hints of a sexual expression of affection recorded in the correspondence and diaries of the historical periods she focused upon, even though declarations of love between women were articulated unabashedly. On the other hand, by some definitions, yes, such relationships could be called lesbian. Faderman writes, "If by 'lesbian' we mean an all-consuming emotional relationship in which two women are devoted to each other above anyone else, these ubiquitous sixteenth-, seventeenth-, eighteenth-, and nineteenth-century romantic friendships were 'lesbian'" (p. 19). Elsewhere, Faderman demonstrates the difference between what Emily Dickinson really wrote in her letters to Sue Gilbert and the less passionate versions published by her niece (who was also Gilbert's daughter), Martha Dickinson Bianchi. Faderman explains, "As anxious as [Bianchi] was to prove that Sue played a great part in making Emily a poet and to show that they were closest of friends, she was even more anxious to prove that Emily and Sue were *only* friends." See Lillian Faderman, "Who Hid Lesbian History?" in *Lesbian Studies Present and Future*, ed. Margaret Cruikshank (New York: Feminist Press, 1982), 119. For a more detailed account, see Lillian Faderman, "Emily Dickinson's Letters to Sue Gilbert," *Massachusetts Review* 18, no. 2 (Summer 1977): 197–225.

12. William Shakespeare, Sonnet 20.

13. *The Poetical Works of Christina Georgina Rossetti,* ed. William Michael Rossetti, 4th ed. (London: Macmillan, 1908), app. B, xlii.

14. John T. Shawcross, "Milton and Diodati: An Essay in Psychodynamic Meaning," *Milton Studies* 7 (1975): 127–63.

15. Margaret Evening, *Who Walk Alone* (Downers Grove, IL: InterVarsity Press, 1974), 63–64. This passage was greatly altered in the second printing. The publisher explained to us in personal correspondence that he had received many complaints about the section on homosexuality.

16. W. H. Auden, *Collected Longer Poems* (New York: Random House, 1969), 181, 183–84.

17. Matthew R. Brown, "Gerard Manley Hopkins: Exploding into Christ," *Christianity Today* 21 (7 Jan. 1977): 388–90.

18. Wendell Stacey Johnson, "Sexuality and Inscape," *Hopkins Quarterly* 3 (July 1976): 59–66. See also the review of E. E. Phare's book on Hopkins in *Criterion* 13 (April 1934): 497–500, in which W. H. Auden flatly asserted that Hopkins's feelings were homosexual. And see the delicately worded discussion of Hopkins's homosexual condition in Peter Milward, *Hopkins' Poetry* (Grand Rapids, MI: Eerdmans, 1975), 91–92. Robert Bernard Martin provides ample proof of Hopkins's same-sex orientation in his highly acclaimed biography, *Gerard Manley Hopkins: A Very Private Life* (New York: Putnam, 1991). Martin describes Hopkins's meeting with Digby Dolben as "the most momentous emotional event of Hopkins' undergraduate years, probably of his entire life" (p. 80).

19. *The Norton Anthology of English Literature* (New York: Norton, 1974), 2:1742.

20. "The Lesbian Priest," *Time,* 24 Jan. 1977, 58.

21. Elizabeth Moberly, "Homosexuality and the Church," *Christian* 4 (Annunciation 1977): 151.

22. Moberly, "Homosexuality and the Church," 151.

23. Joe Wakalee-Lynch, "Should I Stay or Go?: Christian Gays and Lesbians Debate Their Place in the Church," *Utne Reader,* January/February 1992, 40, 42.

24. *New York City Presbytery News,* May 1977, 2, 4.

25. *New York City Presbytery News,* May 1977, 2, 4.

26. John J. McNeill, *The Church and the Homosexual,* 3d ed. (Boston: Beacon Press, 1988).

27. John J. McNeill, *Taking a Chance on God: Liberating Theology for Gays, Lesbians, and Their Lovers, Families, and Friends,* (Boston: Beacon Press, 1988).

28. Edward Schillebeeckx, *Christ: The Experience of Jesus as Lord* (New York: Crossroad, 1983), 785, as quoted in McNeill, *Taking a Chance on God,* 88.

29. The publishers of the bimonthly *Second Stone* describe it as "the national newsjournal for gay and lesbian Christians and their families, friends and supporters." Its address is P.O. Box 8340, New Orleans, LA 70182. *Open Hands* is published quarterly by the Reconciling Congregation Program (United Methodist), More Light Churches Network (Presbyterian), Open and Affirming Program (United Church of Christ), and Reconciled in Christ Program

(Lutheran). The mailing address is 3801 N. Keeler Ave., Chicago, IL 60641. The address for *Christus Omnibus,* another bimonthly magazine for gay and lesbian Christians, is 146 E. Duarte Road, Suite 213, Arcadia, CA 91006. Christian Lesbians Out Together (CLOUT), an organization of Christian lesbians, has declared three major objectives: "claiming spiritual and sexual wholeness," proclaiming "the goodness of our lives, our ministries, and our relationships," and "empower[ing] ourselves and each other to challenge the churches to which we belong." *CLOUTreach,* a quarterly newsletter for members, is available from CLOUT, c/o Selisse Berry, P.O. Box 460808, San Francisco, CA 94146.

30. Chris Glaser, *Uncommon Calling: A Gay Man's Struggle to Serve the Church* (San Francisco: Harper & Row, 1988).

31. Chris Glaser, *Come Home! Reclaiming Spirituality and Community as Gay Men and Lesbians* (San Francisco: Harper & Row, 1990).

32. Rose Mary Denman, *Let My People In: A Lesbian Minister Tells of Her Struggles to Live Openly and Maintain Her Ministry* (New York: William Morrow, 1990), 168.

33. Denman, *Let My People In,* 168.

34. Denman, *Let My People In;* quoted on the book jacket from records of the ecclesiastical trial of Rose Mary Denman.

35. Karen Thompson and Julie Andrzejewski, *Why Can't Sharon Kowalski Come Home?* (San Francisco: Spinsters/Aunt Lute, 1988), 11.

36. Thompson and Andrzejewski, *Sharon Kowalski,* 108.

37. Malcolm Boyd, *Am I Running with You, God?* (New York: Doubleday, 1977), 23. Reprinted by permission of Doubleday & Company, Inc.

CHAPTER 4 ▼ STIGMA AND STEREOTYPING

1. "*Playboy* Interview: Jimmy Carter," *Playboy* 23 (November 1976), 69.

2. Paul Rock, *Deviant Behaviour* (London: Hutchinson, 1973), 28.

3. Peter Berger and Thomas Luckmann, *The Social Construction of Reality* (Garden City, NY: Doubleday Anchor Books, 1967), 33.

4. Personal interview, February 1976. See Letha Scanzoni, "Conservative Christians and Gay Civil Rights," *Christian Century* 93 (13 Oct. 1976): 858.

5. Felice Yeskel, "The Price of Progress," *Women's Review of Books,* February 1992, 21.

6. Carolyn J. Mooney, "Homosexuals in Academe: Fear of Backlash Clouds Reactions to Increased Tolerance," *Chronicle of Higher Education,* 23 Sept. 1992, A17–19.

7. Quoted in "Gay-rights Group Signs Up to Clean Roadside Near CBN," *Virginian-Pilot,* 21 May 1992, D3. This report tells of the work of the Hampton Roads Lesbian and Gay Pride Coalition, an umbrella group comprising various gay and lesbian organizations from cities in the Hampton Roads Harbor region of southeastern Virginia. The group asked to be assigned to the section of highway in front of the Christian Broadcasting Company headquarters and Regent University (formerly called CBN University) as a statement to Christians who have judged homosexual persons so harshly. The statement was especially intended for television preacher Pat Robertson, founder of CBN

and host of the "700 Club," who has repeatedly spoken out against homosexuality. Three times, due to vandalism, the highway department had to replace the $150 signs that identified the lesbian and gay group as the designated clean-up volunteers for that section of the interstate. Although CBN officials denounced the vandalism, the spray-painting incidents continued, causing the highway department to announce it could no longer afford to replace the signs. The coalition then decided to pay for new signs out of its own budget. See "Gay Rights Group's Adopt-a-Highway Signs Vandalized," *Virginian-Pilot and the Ledger-Star,* 1 Nov. 1992, B-3.

8. Isobel Miller, *Patience and Sarah* (New York: McGraw-Hill, 1969; originally published under the title *A Place for Us*).

9. Laura Z. Hobson, *Consenting Adult* (New York: Doubleday, 1975). *Gentleman's Agreement* was published by Simon and Schuster in 1947.

10. According to an article distributed by the *New York Times* News Service at the time of Hobson's death in 1986, Hobson's younger son, Christopher, had publicly revealed his homosexuality in an essay written around the time *Consenting Adult* was published. Hobson declined to say whether her book was autobiographical but spoke of it as "a 'true' novel." See "'Gentleman's Agreement' Author Laura Z. Hobson Dies," *Greensboro* [North Carolina] *News and Record,* 2 Mar. 1986, C-4.

11. Nancy Garden, *Annie on My Mind* (New York: Farrar, Straus and Giroux, 1982).

12. Howard Brown, M.D., *Familiar Faces, Hidden Lives* (New York: Harcourt Brace Jovanovich, 1976).

13. An article by John O'Connor in the *New York Times* (9 Mar. 1976) pointed out that only recently have there been less embarrassment and more public acceptance of the fact of Whitman's homosexuality. In the past, writes O'Connor, "that fact bubbled up into public controversy whenever a proposal was presented to name a bridge, a school, or an auditorium in honor of the poet. . . . More often than not, the proposal would be shelved."

14. Alex Davidson, *The Returns of Love* (London: InterVarsity Press, 1970), 18.

15. Rock, *Deviant Behaviour,* 30.

16. N. K. Denzin, "Rules of Conduct and the Study of Deviant Behavior," in *Deviance and Respectability,* ed. J. Douglas (New York: Basic Books, 1970), 121, as quoted in Rock, *Deviant Behaviour,* 31.

17. "I Choose to Dislike Queers," *Virginian-Pilot,* 17 June 1992, Letters section (A-8).

18. Armand Nicholi II, "Homosexualism and Homosexuality," *Baker's Dictionary of Christian Ethics,* ed. Carl F. H. Henry (Grand Rapids, MI: Baker Book House, 1973), 296.

19. Reported in the *Love Line* (Newsletter of Spatula Ministries, La Habra, CA; Barbara Johnson, ed.), March 1992, 3.

20. Comment of a survey respondent, as quoted in Peggy Halsey and Lee Coppernoll, "Survey Report: Crisis Experiences of *Response* Readers," *Response* (official program journal of United Methodist Women), January 1982, 23.

21. Erving Goffman, *Stigma* (Englewood Cliffs, NJ: Prentice-Hall, 1963), 28.

22. Erik F. Strommen, "'You're a What?': Family Member Reactions to the Disclosure of Homosexuality," *Journal of Homosexuality* 18, no. 1/2 (1989): 40.

23. The theory of cognitive dissonance was first set forth by Leon Festinger in his book *A Theory of Cognitive Dissonance* (Stanford, CA: Stanford Univ. Press, 1957).

24. Ascanio Condivi, "Michelangelo Buonarroti," in *The Portable Renaissance Reader,* ed. James Bruce Ross and Mary Martin McLaughlin (New York: Viking Press, 1953), 509.

25. Brown, *Familiar Faces, Hidden Lives,* 32.

26. W. H. Auden, *The Dyer's Hand and Other Essays* (New York: Random House, 1962). See especially pp. 27, 71, 131–32, and 158.

27. From "The Age of Anxiety," in *W. H. Auden: Collected Poems,* ed. Edward Mendelson (New York: Random House, 1976), 408. Used by permission of Random House, Inc.

CHAPTER 5 ▼ WHAT DOES THE BIBLE SAY?

1. D. Sherwin Bailey, *Homosexuality and the Western Christian Tradition* (Hamden, CT: Shoe String Press Archon Books, 1975; unaltered, unabridged reprint of original 1955 edition), 1–28. See also the discussion of this interpretation in John Boswell, *Christianity, Social Tolerance, and Homosexuality: Gay People in Western Europe from the Beginning of the Christian Era to the Fourteenth Century* (Chicago: Univ. of Chicago Press, 1980), 94–96.

2. "Homosexuality," in *Towards a Quaker View of Sex,* rev. ed. (London: Friends Home Service Committee, 1964), 33.

3. See the Editors of the Harvard Law Review, *Sexual Orientation and the Law* (Cambridge: Harvard Univ. Press, 1990), 9–10. These authors note that, in some cases, courts have construed their particular state's sodomy statutes to be inapplicable to oral-genital acts. Howver, even in these states, there often exist other classifications prohibiting "lewd and lascivious acts," including oral-genital sex. Although a number of states have revoked sodomy laws in recent years, as of 1989 twenty-four states and the District of Columbia still had statutes making sodomy a crime. In seven of these states, sodomy statutes were applicable only to persons of the same gender. But in the remaining states, sodomy statutes were considered applicable to both heterosexual and homosexual persons who engage in oral-genital or anal-genital contact, even (with the exception of one state, Alabama) if the two persons are husband and wife.

4. Susan Brownmiller, *Against Our Will: Men, Women, and Rape* (New York: Simon & Schuster, 1975).

5. George R. Edwards, *Gay/Lesbian Liberation: A Biblical Perspective* (New York: Pilgrim Press, 1984), 42–46.

6. Alan J. Davis, "Sexual Assaults in the Philadelphia Prison System and Sheriff's Vans," *Transaction* 6, no. 2 (1968), as reprinted in Chad Gordon and Gayle Johnson, eds., *Readings in Human Sexuality: Contemporary Perspectives* (New York: Harper & Row, 1976), 155–56.

7. The man is described in this passage as the woman's husband and a son-in-law to her father, even though the woman is called a *concubine*. It must be kept in mind that a concubine was legally recognized in the polygamous society of that time as, in a sense, a secondary wife whose status was inferior to that of the

principal wife. Phyllis Trible points out that, in essence, the woman in this story is nothing more than a slave under the control of her master, a man who regarded her as property to do with as he wished. See Trible's commentary on this tragic incident in *Texts of Terror: Literary-Feminist Readings of Biblical Narratives* (Philadelphia: Fortress Press, 1984), chap. 3.

8. John L. McKenzie, S.J. *The World of the Judges* (Englewood Cliffs, NJ: Prentice-Hall, 1966), 165.

9. John J. McNeill, *The Church and the Homosexual,* 3d ed. (Boston: Beacon Press, 1988), 50.

10. L. William Countryman, *Dirt, Greed, and Sex: Sexual Ethics in the New Testament and Their Implications for Today* (Philadelphia: Fortress Press, 1988), 134 n. 11.

11. McNeill, *The Church and the Homosexual,* 68–75. See also Countryman, *Dirt, Greed, and Sex,* 133–34; Boswell, *Christianity, Social Tolerance, and Homosexuality,* 97; Edwards, *Gay/Lesbian Liberation,* 101–2; and Robin Scroggs, *The New Testament and Homosexuality: Contextual Background for Contemporary Debate.* (Philadelphia: Fortress Press, 1983), 100 n. 3.

12. Edwards, *Gay/Lesbian Liberation,* 101.

13. Scroggs, *The New Testament and Homosexuality,* 100 n. 3.

14. Paul Enns, *Approaching God: Daily Readings in Systematic Theology* (Chicago: Moody Press, 1991), reading for October 7.

15. Boswell, *Christianity, Social Tolerance, and Homosexuality,* 99.

16. Edwards, *Gay/Lesbian Liberation,* 58.

17. See Roland de Vaux, *Ancient Israel,* trans. John McHugh (London: Darton, Longman & Todd, 1961), 460; Mary Douglas's section on "The Abominations of Leviticus" in her *Purity and Danger: An Analysis of Pollution and Taboo* (London: Penguin Pelican Books, 1970), 54–72; Countryman, *Dirt, Greed, and Sex,* chaps. 1 and 2; and Martin Samuel Cohen, "The Biblical Prohibition of Homosexual Intercourse," *Journal of Homosexuality* 19, no. 4 (1990): 3–20.

18. Cohen, "Homosexual Intercourse," 6.

19. Cohen, "Homosexual Intercourse," 13.

20. Cohen, "Homosexual Intercourse," 15.

21. Shabbath 65a and Yebamoth 76a, *The Babylonian Talmud,* 34 volumes, translated into English with notes, glossary, and indexes, ed. I. Epstein (London: Soncino Press, 1935–48), 7:311, 16:513.

22. Norman Pittenger, "The Homosexual Expression of Love," in *Is Gay Good?,* ed. W. Dwight Oberholtzer (Philadelphia: Westminster Press, 1971), 237.

23. McNeill, *The Church and the Homosexual,* 172.

24. Morton Scott Enslin, *The Ethics of Paul* (Nashville, TN: Abingdon Press, 1957), 45.

25. Arthur E. R. Boak and William G. Sinnigen, *A History of Rome to A.D. 565,* 5th ed. (New York: Macmillan, 1965), 311–331.

26. Enslin, *The Ethics of Paul,* 9 n. 24.

27. See Edwards, *Gay/Lesbian Liberation,* chap. 4; Victor Paul Furnish, *The Moral Teaching of Paul* (Nashville, TN: Abingdon Press, 1979), 73–78; Hendrik Hart, "Romans Revisited," *The Other Side* 28 (July/August 1992): 56–62; Scroggs, *The New Testament and Homosexuality,* 90–94, 102, 117.

28. This position is taken by various scholars, including Countryman in his *Dirt, Greed, and Sex.* "Rather than confronting Jewish Christians directly," he writes, "[Paul] begins with a critique of the dirtiness of Gentile culture in which he expects that they will silently join him. He then questions whether this condemnatory attitude toward Gentiles is justified by unimpeachable virtue in the critic" (p. 121). Edwards, in *Gay/Lesbian Liberation,* makes a similar point, emphasizing that "Romans 1:26–27 stands in a rhetorical context wherein Paul uses a traditional Jewish pattern of ideas directed against Gentile depravity in order to turn the accusation against the accuser, just as the prophets turned the ethnocentric accusations against the Canaanites in on Israel itself and gave rise thereby to the moral depth of prophetic religion." See Edwards, *Gay/Lesbian Liberation,* 93.

29. See Countryman, *Dirt, Greed, and Sex,* 120–23.

30. Countryman, *Dirt, Greed, and Sex,* 61

31. Countryman, *Dirt, Greed, and Sex,* 62.

32. Countryman, *Dirt, Greed, and Sex,* 62.

33. Margaret Evening, *Who Walk Alone* (Downers Grove, IL: InterVarsity Press, 1974), 57.

34. Enslin, *The Ethics of Paul,* 146.

35. Jack Wyrtzen, as quoted in "Battle over Gay Rights," *Newsweek,* 6 June 1977, 22.

36. Alfred Kinsey et al., *Sexual Behavior in the Human Female* (New York: Pocket Books, 1965), 449.

37. Suzanne Chevalier-Skolnikoff, "Homosexual Behavior in a Laboratory Group of Stumptail Monkeys (*Macaca arctoides*): Forms, Contexts, and Possible Social Functions," *Archives of Sexual Behavior* 5 (November 1976): 511–27.

38. Paul Gebhard, "Mammalian Sexual Behavior" (Lecture presented at the Institute for Sex Research, Indiana Univ., Bloomington, 20 July 1977). (The Institute for Sex Research was later renamed the Kinsey Institute for Research in Sex, Gender, and Reproduction. It has always been known popularly as the Kinsey Institute, after its founder, Alfred C. Kinsey.)

39. See Furnish, *The Moral Teaching of Paul,* 77–78; Edwards, *Gay/Lesbian Liberation,* 91–98.

40. James Graham-Murray, *A History of Morals* (London: Library 33 Limited, 1966), 64–66.

41. David Halperin, "Sex Before Sexuality: Pederasty, Politics, and Power in Classical Athens," in *Hidden from History: Reclaiming the Gay and Lesbian Past,* ed. Martin Bauml Duberman, Martha Vicinus, and George Chauncey, Jr. (New York: New American Library, 1989), 49–50.

42. Polybius, *The Histories,* trans. Mortimer Chambers (New York: Washington Square Press, 1966), 306.

43. Furnish, *The Moral Teaching of Paul,* 65–66.

44. Scroggs, *The New Testament and Homosexuality,* 144.

45. Virginia Ramey Mollenkott, "Critical Inquiry and Biblical Inerrancy," *Religion and Public Education: The Journal of the National Council on Religion and Public Education,* Winter 1990, 87. Dr. Mollenkott used the penultimate draft of the New Revised Standard Version as well as the published version during the preparation of this article.

46. Scroggs, *The New Testament and Homosexuality,* 106.

47. McNeill, *The Church and the Homosexual,* 53. See also Boswell, *Christianity, Social Tolerance, and Homosexuality,* 107, 344–345.

48. Boswell, *Christianity, Social Tolerance, and Homosexuality,* 344.

49. Petronius, *The Satyricon,* trans. William Arrowsmith (New York: New American Library, Mentor Books, 1959), 223.

50. Suetonius, *The Twelve Caesars,* trans. Robert Graves (Middlesex, England: Penguin Books, 1957), 223.

51. Scroggs, *The New Testament and Homosexuality,* 120.

52. Scroggs, *The New Testament and Homosexuality,* chap. 3.

53. McNeill, *The Church and the Homosexual,* 52; Edwards, *Gay/Lesbian Liberation,* 82; Scroggs, *The New Testament and Homosexuality,* 62.

54. Enslin, *The Ethics of Paul,* 147. See also Scroggs, *The New Testament and Homosexuality,* 62–65.

55. Countryman, *Dirt, Greed, and Sex,* 202 n. 10. Countryman draws upon Paul Veyne, ed., *A History of Private Life* (Cambridge: Harvard University Press, Belknap Press, 1987), vol. 1, *From Pagan Rome to Byzantium,* trans. Arthur Goldhammer.

56. Countryman, *Dirt, Greed, and Sex,* 117 n. 26.

57. John Milton, *Paradise Lost,* book 11, lines 632–34 and their context; see also *Paradise Regained,* book 2, lines 220–30.

58. *The Compact Edition of the Oxford English Dictionary,* s.v. "effeminate."

59. See Virginia Ramey Mollenkott, *Sensuous Spirituality* (New York: Crossroad, 1992), 126.

60. Michael G. Maudlin, "John Stott Speaks Out," *Christianity Today,* 8 Feb. 1993, 37–38.

61. Isaac Bashevis Singer, "Genesis," in *Congregation: Contemporary Writers Read the Jewish Bible,* ed. David Risenberg (New York: Harcourt Brace Jovanovich, 1987), 8.

62. J. Rinzema, *The Sexual Revolution: Challenge and Response,* trans. Lewis B. Smedes (Grand Rapids, MI: Eerdmans, 1974), 105.

CHAPTER 6 ▼ WHAT DOES SCIENCE SAY?

1. Paul H. Gebhard, "Incidence of Overt Homosexuality in the United States and Western Europe," in *National Institute of Mental Health Task Force on Homosexuality: Final Report and Background Papers,* ed. John Livingood (Rockville, MD: National Institute of Mental Health, 1972), 22–29. In subsequent notes, this report will be referred to as Livingood, *NIMH Report.*

2. Gebhard, "Incidence of Overt Homosexuality," 26; also see Alfred Kinsey et al., *Sexual Behavior in the Human Female* (New York: Pocket Books edition, 1965), 469–72.

3. Three researchers in psychology have pointed out that, by failing to examine sexual orientation over the entire course of a person's life, many studies have especially overlooked *bisexuality* as a distinct category. These scholars have therefore developed a more detailed measurement of sexuality (the Multidimensional Scale of Sexuality, or MSS) to help us better understand some of the

situations in which people appear to change from one orientation to another at some time in their lives. (Examples would be the person who has been in a longtime heterosexual relationship, perhaps married, but who falls in love with someone of the same sex. Or someone who has been considered homosexual because of past same-sex relationships but who at some point surprises acquaintances—and perhaps even himself or herself—by becoming romantically involved with a person of the opposite sex.) See Braden Robert Berkey, Terri Perelman-Hall, and Lawrence A. Kurdek, "The Multidimensional Scale of Sexuality," *Journal of Homosexuality* 19, no. 4 (1990), 67–87.

4. Gebhard, "Incidence of Overt Homosexuality," 27–28.

5. Berkey, Perelman-Hall, and Kurdek, "The Multidimensional Scale of Sexuality," 69.

6. Gebhard, "Incidence of Overt Homosexuality," 26.

7. Alan Bell, "The Homosexual as Patient," in *Sex Research Studies from the Kinsey Institute,* ed. Martin S. Weinberg (New York: Oxford Univ. Press, 1976), 203.

8. See Alan P. Bell, Martin S. Weinberg, and Sue Kiefer Hammersmith, *Sexual Preference: Its Development in Men and Women* (Bloomington: Indiana Univ. Press, 1981), chaps. 9 and 16.

9. Joseph Harry, "Sexual Orientation as Destiny," *Journal of Homosexuality* 10, no. 3/4 (Winter 1984): 122.

10. Bell, "The Homosexual as Patient," 203; Gebhard, "Incidence of Overt Homosexuality," 27–28.

11. R. W. Ramsay, M. Heringa, and I. Boorsma, "A Case Study: Homosexuality in the Netherlands," in *Understanding Homosexuality: Its Biological and Psychological Bases,* ed. J. A. Loraine (New York: American Elsevier, 1974), 136.

12. Phone interview with Paul Gebhard, conducted by Letha Dawson Scanzoni, 10 Feb. 1978.

13. William Paul and James D. Weinrich, "Whom and What We Study: Definition and Scope of Sexual Orientation," in *Homosexuality: Social, Psychological, and Biological Issues,* ed. William Paul et al. (Beverly Hills, CA: Sage Publications, 1982), 25.

14. Tom W. Smith, "Adult Sexual Behavior in 1989: Number of Partners, Frequency of Intercourse and Risk of AIDS," *Family Planning Perspectives* 23 (May/June 1991): 102–7.

15. See Anne Fausto-Sterling, "Why Do We Know So Little About Human Sex?" *Discover* 13 (June 1992): 28–30.

16. This estimate was arrived at by calculating 5 percent of the population figure given in the 1990 United States Census for people eighteen years of age and older.

17. *Towards a Quaker View of Sex,* rev. ed. (London: Friends Service Committee, 1964), 26.

18. Ramsay, Heringa, and Boorsma, "Homosexuality in the Netherlands," 132.

19. John Money, "Statement on Antidiscrimination Regarding Sexual Orientation," *SIECUS Report* 6 (September 1977): 3.

20. Wilhelm Stekel, *The Homosexual Neurosis* (New York: Emerson Books, 1949), 290–91.

21. Martin S. Weinberg and Colin J. Williams, *Male Homosexuals: Their Problems and Adaptations* (New York: Penguin Books edition, 1975), 18.

22. Edward Carpenter, *Homogenic Love and Its Place in a Free Society* (London: Redundancy Press, n.d.; originally published, Manchester, England: Labour Press, 1894), as quoted in James D. Weinrich, "Task Force Findings," in Paul et al., *Homosexuality*, 381.

23. David Lester, *Unusual Sexual Behavior: The Standard Deviations* (Springfield, IL: Charles C. Thomas, 1975), 71–72.

24. Bell, Weinberg, and Hammersmith, *Sexual Preference*, 191–92.

25. Bryan E. Robinson, Patsy Skeen, Carol Flake Hobson, and Margaret Herrman, "Gay Men's and Women's Perceptions of Early Family Life and Their Relationships with Parents," *Family Relations* 31 (January 1982): 79–83.

26. Bryan E. Robinson, Lynda Henley Walters, and Patsy Skeen, "Response of Parents to Learning That Their Child Is Homosexual and Concern over AIDS," *Journal of Homosexuality* 18, no. 1/2 (1989): 59–80.

27. George W. Brown, *Sociological Research: How Seriously Do We Take It?* (London: Bedford College, Univ. of London, 1974), 10.

28. Lester, *Unusual Sexual Behavior*, 71–72.

29. Richard Green, *Sexual Identity Conflict in Children and Adults* (New York: Penguin Books, 1975), 237.

30. In 1970, the American Anthropological Association passed resolutions recognizing "the legitimacy and immediate importance" of anthropological research on the topic of homosexuality and denouncing discrimination against those who undertake such research. A summary of some of the pioneering anthropological studies of homosexuality can be found in Thomas K. Fitzgerald, "A Critique of Anthropological Research on Homosexuality," *Journal of Homosexuality* 2, no. 4 (Summer 1977): 385–97.

31. Paul Chance, "Facts That Liberated the Gay Community," *Psychology Today* 9 (December 1975): 52–55, 101; this article is an interview with Evelyn Hooker. See also Evelyn Hooker, "The Adjustment of the Male Overt Homosexual," *Journal of Projective Techniques* 21 (1957): 17–31. A concise summary of Hooker's study appears in John C. Gonsiorek, "Results of Psychological Testing on Homosexual Populations," in Paul et al., *Homosexuality*, 78–79.

32. Paul Gebhard, "Human Sexual Research and Its Impact on Values" (Lecture presented at the Ad Hoc Committee for Humanistic Affairs Forum, Indiana Univ., Bloomington, 12 Mar. 1977). Also see Livingood, ed., *NIMH Report*.

33. For a discussion of the term *healthy homosexual*, see George Weinberg, *Society and the Healthy Homosexual* (New York: Doubleday Anchor Books, 1973).

34. American Psychiatric Association (Washington, DC), news release, 15 Dec. 1973. The "sexual orientation disturbance" category came under much criticism for its vagueness and was replaced in 1978 by the category "ego-dystonic homosexuality," which referred to cases where a person engaging in homosexual behavior desired "to acquire or increase heterosexual arousal." Many professionals saw just as many, if not more, problems with this terminology and its implications. As John Gonsiorek has written, "Current psychiatric diagnosis concepts are useless at best and, at worst, a potentially dangerous avenue

for justifying continued labelling of homosexuals as ill despite the lack of evidence for that designation." See Gonsiorek's introduction to the "Mental Health" section in Paul et al., *Homosexuality,* 60.

35. Gebhard, "Human Sexual Research."
36. Quoted in Gerald C. Davison, "Politics, Ethics, and Therapy for Homosexuality," in Paul et al., *Homosexuality,* 90.
37. For a review of studies specifically focused upon lesbian women, see Barbara Sang, "Lesbian Research: A Critical Evaluation," in *Our Right to Love: A Lesbian Resource Book,* ed. Ginny Vida (Englewood Cliffs, NJ: Prentice-Hall, 1978), 80–87; and Kristiann Mannion, "Psychology and the Lesbian: A Critical Review of the Research," in *Female Psychology: The Emerging Self,* ed. Sue Cox, 2d ed. (New York: St. Martin's Press, 1981), 248–74.
38. See Paul et al., *Homosexuality,* sec. 2, "Mental Health" (55–161).
39. Weinberg and Williams, *Male Homosexuals.* See especially the preface and chapters 1, 11, and 22.
40. Michael Schofield, *Sociological Aspects of Homosexuality* (Boston: Little, Brown, 1965), summarized in Evelyn Hooker, "Homosexuality," in Livingood, *NIMH Report,* 18.
41. Elizabeth D. Gibbs, "Psychosocial Development of Children Raised by Lesbian Mothers: A Review of Research," in *Loving Boldly: Issues Facing Lesbians* (reprint of *Women and Therapy* 8, no. 1/2), ed. Esther D. Rothblum and Ellen Cole (New York: Harrington Park Press, 1989), 67. See also n. 37 above.

CHAPTER 7 ▼ FROM HOMOPHOBIA TO UNDERSTANDING

1. George Weinberg, *Society and the Healthy Homosexual* (Garden City, NY: Doubleday Anchor Books, 1973), chap. 1.
2. Reported in the Bloomington (Indiana) *Daily Herald-Telephone,* 13 Apr. 1977.
3. Weinberg, *Society and the Healthy Homosexual,* chap. 1.
4. Jeremy Seabrook, *A Lasting Relationship* (London: Allen Lane, 1976), 231, 17.
5. Deborah Zera, "Coming of Age in a Heterosexist World: The Development of Gay and Lesbian Adolescents," *Adolescence* 27 (Winter 1992): 852. See also R. F. C. Kournay, "Suicide Among Homosexual Adolescents," *Journal of Homosexuality* 13, no. 4 (1987): 111–16; and Shira Maguen, "Teen Suicide: The Government's Cover-Up and America's Lost Children," *Advocate,* 24 Sept. 1991, 40–47. Maguen reports that one of the studies commissioned by a 1989 Department of Health and Human Services task force on youth suicide was squelched because of a conservative backlash in reaction to its findings on teenage gay and lesbian suicides. The study, conducted by social worker Paul Gibson, indicated that homosexual adolescents are two to three times more likely to attempt to end their lives than are other young people. Further, according to this report, it is estimated that nearly one-third of the teenagers who actually do commit suicide are homosexual. The Gibson report's call for acceptance and support for homosexual adolescents so that they will not feel that suicide is the only answer to their struggles was perceived by some politicians to be undermining the institution of the family. In another study, Gary

Remafedi and his professional colleagues in adolescent medicine found that 41 out of a sample of 137 self-identified gay and bisexual males between the ages of fourteen and twenty-one had attempted suicide and that nearly half of those who had attempted suicide had tried more than once. See Gary Remafedi, James A. Farrow, and Robert W. Deisher, "Risk Factors for Attempted Suicide in Gay and Bisexual Youth," *Pediatrics* 87 (June 1991): 869–75.

6. Eli Coleman, "Developmental Stages of the Coming-Out Process," in *Homosexuality: Social, Psychological, and Biological Issues,* ed. William Paul et al. (Beverly Hills, CA: Sage Publications, 1982), 150.

7. Reported in the *National NOW Times,* August 1982.

8. Reported in *Working Together* (Publication of the Center for the Prevention of Sexual and Domestic Violence, Seattle, Washington), July/August 1982, 3. The editors wrote, "The real issue at stake is whether or not Congressmen have been involved in child sexual abuse, i.e. sexual exploitation of teenagers over whom the Congressmen have authority. Unfortunately, the public outrage in response to these allegations will undoubtedly focus on homosexual contact. This homophobic response clouds the public's willingness to understand and address the sexual abuse of teenagers whether they are male or female."

9. Summary of a statement by Paul Gebhard during a discussion following a paper presented by Alan Bell, "Research in Homosexuality: Back to the Drawing Board," as part of a conference on sex research held at the State University of New York at Stony Brook, 5–9 June 1974. The paper and discussion summary were reprinted in *Archives of Sexual Behavior* 4 (July 1975): 431.

10. William Paul, "Social Issues and Homosexual Behavior: A Taxonomy of Categories and Themes in Anti-Gay Argument," in Paul et al., *Homosexuality,* 49–50.

11. C. A. Tripp, *The Homosexual Matrix* (New York: McGraw-Hill, 1975), 209–10.

12. Reported in Paul, "Social Issues and Homosexual Behavior," 39–40.

13. Paul, "Social Issues and Homosexual Behavior," 51.

14. C. Everett Koop, *Koop: The Memoirs of America's Family Doctor* (New York: Random House, 1991), 198.

15. Newark, NJ, *Star-Ledger,* 27 Aug. 1993, 4.

16. For a summary of studies on homophobia, see Paul Siegel, "Homophobia: Types, Origins, Remedies," *Christianity and Crisis* 12 (November 1979): 280–84.

17. Tripp, *The Homosexual Matrix,* 211.

18. Richard Green, *Sexual Identity Conflict in Children and Adults* (New York: Penguin Books, 1974), 74.

19. Evelyn Hooker, "Homosexuality," in *National Institute of Mental Health Task Force on Homosexuality: Final Report and Background Papers,* ed. John Livingood (Rockville, MD: National Institute of Mental Health, 1972), 11.

20. William Fitch, *Christian Perspectives on Sex and Marriage* (Grand Rapids, MI: Eerdmans, 1971), 133.

21. Paul D. Meier, *Christian Child-Rearing and Personality Development* (Grand Rapids, MI: Baker Book House, 1977), 52.

22. Berkeley Rice, "Coming of Age in Sodom and New Milford," *Psychology Today* 9 (September 1975), 64–66.

23. Meier, *Christian Child-Rearing,* 52–53.

24. Meier, *Christian Child-Rearing,* 52.

25. Suzanne Pharr, *Homophobia: A Weapon of Sexism* (Little Rock, AR: Chardon Press, 1988).

26. Richard Green, "Atypical Sex Role Development in Children" (Lecture presented at the Institute for Sex Research, Indiana Univ., Bloomington, 26 July 1976). See also Green, *Sexual Identity Conflict.*

27. In her research on matched samples of lesbian women and female transsexuals (women who wanted to become men), Dr. Anke Ehrhardt found that the transsexuals had fantasies that they were males while having sex relations with other women. This was not true of the lesbians, who were very much aware that they themselves were, like their partners, female. Reported by Dr. Ehrhardt at the Institute for Sex Research, Indiana Univ., Bloomington, 28 July 1977. For further information on transsexualism, see Green, *Sexual Identity Conflict;* Deborah Heller Feinbloom, *Transvestites and Transsexuals* (New York: Dial Press/Delacorte Press, 1976); and Thomas Kando, *Sex Change: The Achievement of Gender Identity Among Feminized Transsexuals* (Springfield, IL: Charles C. Thomas, 1973).

28. William Shakespeare, Sonnet 116 (emphasis added).

29. Robert Brain, *Friends and Lovers* (London: Hart-Davis, MacGibbon, 1976), 223, 259–60.

30. Alfred Kinsey et al., *Sexual Behavior in the Human Female* (New York: Pocket Books, 1965), 457.

31. See John Money and Anke Ehrhardt, *Man and Woman, Boy and Girl* (Baltimore: Johns Hopkins Univ. Press, 1972), chap. 11; Green, *Sexual Identity Conflict;* Hooker, "Homosexuality"; James D. Weinrich, ed. "Biology," in Paul et al., *Homosexuality,* sec. 3 (163–211).

32. Mary Calderone, "Of Dade County, Homosexuals, and Rights," *SIECUS Report* 6 (September 1977): 2.

33. Alan Bell, discussion following his "The Appraisal of Homosexuality" (Lecture presented at the Institute for Sex Research, Indiana Univ., Bloomington, 23 July 1976). See also Alan Bell, Martin S. Weinberg, and Sue Kiefer Hammersmith, *Sexual Preference: Its Development in Men and Women* (Bloomington: Indiana Univ. Press, 1981), 101.

34. William Simon and John Gagnon, "The Lesbians: A Preliminary Overview," in *Sexual Deviance,* ed. John Gagnon and William Simon (New York: Harper & Row, 1967), 255.

35. Parker Rossman, "The Pederasts," *Transaction/Society* 10 (March/April 1973), reprinted in *Sexual Deviance and Sexual Deviants,* ed. Erich Goode and Richard Troiden (New York: William Morrow, 1974), 396–409.

36. For an honest and compelling first-person account of a self-acknowledged pedophile who tells of experiencing God's grace, see Paul Evans [pseud.], "Old Lies and New Beginnings: A Child Molester Shares His Journey Toward Recovery," *Other Side,* January/February 1993, 57–63. Evans had been a much-loved teacher and later a school principal before his arrest after fifteen years of sexual involvement with children. From prison, he writes, "My old life was full of kids. My new life is, and will be, child-free. I still love children, but I know that to form relationships with them is unwise. . . . Never again do I need to be

sexual with a child, nor do I plan to or want to. But memories, associations, and arousals will probably always be a part of my life, even if to smaller degrees. Like an alcoholic, I will always be a 'recovering' pedophile" (p. 63).

37. Pat Griffin, "From Hiding Out to Coming Out: Empowering Lesbian and Gay Educators," *Journal of Homosexuality* 22, no. 3/4 (1991): 182.

38. Quoted in Griffin, "From Hiding Out to Coming Out," 183.

39. Roger H. Ard, "Why the Conservatives Won in Miami," *Christian Century* 94 (3-10 Aug. 1977): 678.

40. Larry Hugick, "Public Opinion Divided on Gay Rights," *Gallup Poll Monthly,* June 1992, 2–6. In the first edition of this book, we cited the June 1977 Gallup Poll, in which only 56 percent of Americans favored equal job opportunities for homosexual persons (as compared with the 74 percent figure fifteen years later). And only 27 percent of Americans were willing for homosexual people to be hired as elementary school teachers (as compared with 41 percent in 1992). Clearly, public opinion is changing on the topic of homosexuality, and acceptance of homosexual people has gradually increased. But at the same time, Americans continue to be wary of homosexual teachers on the elementary school level. There is slightly more openness to the hiring of homosexual teachers on the high school level, with 47 percent of respondents to the 1992 Gallup Poll expressing such willingness. (The 1977 poll had not included a question on the hiring of homosexual high school teachers.) An August 1992 *Newsweek* poll yielded slightly higher figures. Seventy-eight percent of those polled felt homosexual people should have equal rights in job opportunities, with 51 percent approving the hiring of homosexual people as elementary school teachers. Fifty-four percent approved of hiring homosexual high school teachers. See *Newsweek,* 14 Sept. 1992, 36.

41. Personal interview, 5 Feb. 1976. See Letha Scanzoni, "Conservative Christians and Gay Civil Rights," *Christian Century* 93 (13 Oct. 1976): 860.

42. Anke Ehrhardt, "Gender Development, Homosexuality, and Transsexualism" (Lecture presented at the Institute for Sex Research, Indiana Univ., Bloomington, 28 July 1977). See also Money and Ehrhardt, *Man and Woman.*

43. Sharon L. Huggins, "A Comparative Study of Self-Esteem of Adolescent Children of Divorced Lesbian Mothers and Divorced Heterosexual Mothers," *Journal of Homosexuality* 18, no. 1/2 (1989), 124.

44. Elizabeth D. Gibbs, "Psychosocial Development of Children Raised by Lesbian Mothers: A Review of Research," in *Loving Boldly: Issues Facing Lesbians* (reprint of *Women and Therapy* 8, no. 1/2), ed. Esther D. Rothblum and Ellen Cole (New York: Harrington Park Press, 1989), 70.

45. Richard Green, "Atypical Sex Role Development in Children" (Lecture presented at the Institute for Sex Research, Indiana Univ., Bloomington, 28 July 1977). For his full report, see his "Sexual Identity of 37 Children Raised by Homosexual or Transsexual Parents," *American Journal of Psychiatry* 135 (1978): 692–97.

46. Green, "Atypical Sex Role Development."

47. Heino F. L. Meyer-Bahlburg, "Sex Hormones and Male Homosexuality in Comparative Perspective," *Archives of Sexual Behavior* 6 (July 1977): 321.

48. The results were reported in two volumes. See Alan P. Bell and Martin S. Weinberg, *Homosexualities: A Study of Diversity Among Men and Women*

(New York: Simon and Schuster, 1978); and Bell, Weinberg, and Hammersmith, *Sexual Preference*.

49. Bell, Weinberg, and Hammersmith, *Sexual Preference*, 220. In the early 1990s, two California studies suggested certain physiological differences in the brains of homosexual and heterosexual men. Dr. Simon Levay, a neurobiologist at the Salk Institute of Biological Studies, studied brain samples obtained from autopsies of homosexual and heterosexual men. He found that a section of the hypothalamus (which, on the basis of data from animal studies, may have some effect on the sexual behavior of males) was smaller in homosexual men than in heterosexual men. In 1992, a year after Levay's study, Laura Allen and Roger Gorski, biological researchers at the UCLA School of Medicine, found that another portion of the brain (the anterior commissure structure of nerve cells) was about one-third larger in homosexual men than in heterosexual men. Other studies that have led to the conclusion that biological factors may play a part in sexual orientation have been studies concentrating on gay male twins and lesbian twins, which indicate the possibility of a strong genetic component. Such studies have been undertaken by Northwestern University psychologist Michael Bailey and Boston University School of Medicine psychiatrist Richard Pillard. For a concise overview of these studies, see David Gelman et al., "Born or Bred: The Origins of Homosexuality," *Newsweek*, 24 Feb. 1992, 46–53. See also Natalie Angier, "The Biology of What It Means to Be Gay," *New York Times*, 1 Sept. 1991, sec. 4, p. 1; Associated Press, "Brain Trait Common in Gay Men," *Virginian-Pilot and the Ledger-Star*, 1 Aug. 1992, A-3; "Gay Genes," *Discover*, January 1993, 55; and "Study Suggests Genes Play Role in Lesbianism," Associated Press report, *Virginian-Pilot and the Ledger-Star*, 12 Mar. 1993, A-6.

50. For a detailed historical review of case law on homosexual teachers as well as current trends, see Karen M. Harbeck, "Gay and Lesbian Educators: Past History/Future Prospects," *Journal of Homosexuality* 22, no. 3/4 (1991): 121–39.

51. Russell Baker, "Sunday Observer: Role Models," *New York Times Magazine*, 26 June 1977, 10.

52. Earl V. Pullias and James D. Young, "A Model: An Example," in *A Teacher Is Many Things* (Bloomington: Indiana Univ. Press, 1968), 72–73.

53. Theodore Isaac Rubin, *Compassion and Self-Hate: An Alternative to Despair* (New York: Ballantine Books, 1975), 5.

54. Weinberg, *Society and the Happy Homosexual*, chap. 4. See also John Boswell, *Christianity, Social Tolerance, and Homosexuality: Gay People in Western Europe from the Beginning of the Christian Era to the Fourteenth Century* (Chicago: Univ. of Chicago Press, 1980), 41–46.

55. Hooker, "Homosexuality," *NIMH Report*, 19–20; Maurice Leznoff and William Westley, "The Homosexual Community," *Social Problems* 3 (April 1957): 257–63; Evelyn Hooker, "The Homosexual Community," in Gagnon and Simon, *Sexual Deviance*, 167–84.

56. Laud Humphreys, *Tearoom Trade: Impersonal Sex in Public Places* (Chicago: Aldine, 1970).

57. Letter to the Bloomington (Indiana) *Daily Herald Telephone*, 8 Feb. 1977.

58. Dennis Altman, *Homosexual Oppression and Liberation* (New York: Discus/Avon Books, 1971), 66.

59. Bell and Weinberg, *Homosexualities,* 299. After this study was conducted in the San Francisco Bay area in 1970, seven years were spent analyzing the massive amount of data obtained from the nearly one thousand homosexual people interviewed. For further discussion of the differences between gay men and lesbian women in seeking out casual sexual encounters, see Paul et al., *Homosexuality,* 220–26, 244.

60. Alan Bell, "The Homosexual as Patient," in *Sex Research: Studies from the Kinsey Institute,* ed. Martin S. Weinberg (New York: Oxford Univ. Press, 1976), 208. On the basis of his studies in West Germany, sociologist Siegrid Schafer suggests that while homosexual women "have internalized the sociosexual norms of combining love and sexuality equally as much as heterosexual women," with the result that lesbian partners tend to reinforce these norms in one another, males (both homosexual and heterosexual) have been socialized to view sex quite differently. "Males learn from the beginning of puberty, or even earlier, to conceive of sexuality in and of itself," he explains. Among heterosexual men, tendencies to detach sex from the context of love and emotional involvement are restrained through the influence of their female partners and the institutions of marriage and family. "These inhibiting conditions do not exist among homosexual males," Schafer points out, adding that the situation is compounded by the standards of the male homosexual subculture, where "sexual success is an important status symbol." See Siegrid Schafer, "Sociosexual Behavior in Male and Female Homosexuals: A Study in Sex Differences, *Archives of Sexual Behavior* 6 (September 1977): 360–62.

61. Evelyn Hooker, "Homosexuality," *NIMH Report,* 19. See also Nancy Achilles, "The Development of the Homosexual Bar as an Institution," in Gagnon and Simon, *Sexual Deviance and Sexual Deviants,* 228–44; Richard Troiden, "Homosexual Encounters in a Highway Rest Stop," in Goode and Troiden, *Sexual Deviance,* 211–28; Humphreys, *Tearoom Trade;* Martin S. Weinberg and Colin J. Williams, "Gay Baths and the Social Organization of Impersonal Sex," *Social Problems* 23 (December 1975): 124–36.

62. See "The Young and the Reckless," *Newsweek,* 11 Jan. 1993, 60–61.

63. See Ralph Blair, *Ex-Gay* (New York: HCCC, 1982). For information on the degree of success of "ex-gay" ministries, write to Dr. Ralph Blair, Evangelicals Concerned, 311 East 72nd Street, New York, NY 10021.

64. See the preceding note for the address of Evangelicals Concerned.

65. Hooker, "Homosexuality," *NIMH Report,* and Hooker, "The Homosexual Community." See also the "Gay Marriage" section in Letha Dawson Scanzoni and John Scanzoni, *Men, Women, and Change* (New York: McGraw-Hill, 1976, 1981, and 1988), 185–94 (1st ed.); 235–62 (2d ed.); 178–202 (3d ed.).

66. Personal interview with student, 17 January 1977.

67. Tim LaHaye and Beverly LaHaye, *The Act of Marriage* (Grand Rapids, MI: Zondervan, 1976), 264.

68. Carl F. H. Henry, "In and Out of the Gay World," in *Is Gay Good?,* ed. W. Dwight Oberholtzer (Philadelphia: Westminster Press, 1971), 111–12.

CHAPTER 8 ▼ THE DEBATE IN AMERICAN CHRISTENDOM

1. Howard Brown, *Familiar Faces, Hidden Lives* (New York: Harcourt Brace Jovanovich, 1976), 89–95.

2. Brown, *Familiar Faces, Hidden Lives*, 81.

3. Sylvia Rudolph, "One of Our Family Is Gay," *Christian Home* 9 (May 1977): 16–18.

4. Lewis Penhall Bird, "Deviance vs. Variance in Sexual Behavior," *Christian Medical Society Journal* 6 (Summer 1975): 9–17.

5. See William V. D'Antonio, "The American Catholic Family: Signs of Cohesion and Polarization," in *The Religion and Family Connection: Social Science Perspectives,* ed. Darwin L. Thomas (Provo, UT: Brigham Young Univ. Religious Studies Center, 1988), 88–106; and T. R. Balakrishnan, Karol Krotki, and Evelyne Lapierre-Adamcyk, "Contraceptive Use in Canada, 1984," *Family Planning Perspectives,* September/October 1985, 209–15.

6. See David M. Kennedy, *Birth Control in America: The Career of Margaret Sanger* (New Haven, CT: Yale Univ. Press, 1970).

7. Ed Wheat, *Sex Problems and Sex Techniques in Marriage* (Springdale, AR: Bible Believers Cassettes, 1975), cassette no. 2, side 1.

8. Herbert J. Miles, *Sexual Happiness in Marriage* (Grand Rapids, MI: Zondervan, 1967), 81.

9. Tim LaHaye and Beverly LaHaye, *The Act of Marriage* (Grand Rapids, MI: Zondervan, 1976), 275.

10. H. L. Ellison, *Ezekiel: The Man and His Message* (Grand Rapids, MI: Eerdmans, 1956), 89. See also Ezek. 18:5–13.

11. Maurice Lamm, *The Jewish Way in Love and Marriage* (San Francisco: Harper & Row, 1980), 191.

12. For a detailed listing of such gay/lesbian-positive groups, including their objectives and addresses, see the 1990 edition of *Christians and Homosexuality* (a booklet compiled by the editors of the magazine *The Other Side*), 46–47. The Gay and Lesbian Religious Caucus compiles a frequently revised list of relevant organizations and addresses, available from Martin Rock, Box 1540, Washington, DC 20003-0440.

13. Brochure published by Evangelicals Concerned (311 East 72nd Street, New York, NY 10021).

14. Maurice R. Irvin, "What the Bible Says About Sex," *Alliance Witness* 110 (16 July 1975): 5.

15. Ralph Blair, *An Evangelical Look at Homosexuality,* rev. ed. (New York: Evangelicals Concerned, 1977), 15.

16. The Reverend Troy Perry is the founder of the Universal Fellowship of Metropolitan Community Churches (UFMCC), a denomination that welcomes gay and lesbian people and provides one of the few public places where they can meet in a social and spiritual atmosphere instead of in the more specifically sexual atmosphere of the bars, bathhouses, and sex clubs. Founded in 1968 in Los Angeles, the Universal Fellowship of Metropolitan Community Churches now has nearly three hundred congregations in the United States and seventeen other countries. The UFMCC offers its congregants not only worship services and Bible studies but also discussion groups, fellowship hours, covered-dish

dinners, and even holiday dinners for those whose families are far away. In his homespun autobiography, Troy Perry explains that he does not believe there should be a segregated church for homosexual people, but that anti-gay discrimination practiced by the churches of the United States forced him to found the UFMCC. It was founded, he says, so that "gays would have a place to worship God in dignity, and not as lepers and outcasts"—a place where they could be recognized as people created by God, God's own children. See Troy Perry, *The Lord Is My Shepherd and He Knows I'm Gay* (Los Angeles: Nash Publishing, 1972), 221–22.

17. Various authors have independently concluded that such a spectrum of views exists, though its component parts have been described differently. In "Conservative Christians and Gay Civil Rights" (*Christian Century* 93 [13 Oct. 1976]: 857–62), Letha Scanzoni described five views held by Christians: (1) the "sin perspective," which holds that homosexuality is a sin—period; (2) the "dichotomized view," which distinguishes between the sinfulness of homosexual *acts* and the moral indifference of the homosexual *orientation* (which is considered not the person's "fault"); (3) a "compassionate, questioning view," which seeks more information, recognizes God's love for all people, and refuses to judge and condemn; (4) a "cautious accommodation" view, which is willing to grant the possibility that monogamous same-sex relationships may be within the will of God for some people if celibacy is not possible; and (5) a full, unqualified acceptance of committed homosexual relationships as being wholly compatible with the Christian faith. In his book *Embodiment* (Minneapolis: Augsburg, 1978), Christian ethicist and theological-seminary professor James B. Nelson has described a range of four views: (1) the *rejecting-punitive* stance, in which there is unrestricted denunciation of homosexuality and a punitive attitude toward homosexual people; (2) the *rejecting-nonpunitive* stance, which holds that "homosexuality must be condemned, but in the light of grace the homosexual *person* must not" (p. 190); (3) the "qualified acceptance" stance, which sees heterosexuality as the creation ideal but accepts scientific evidence of constitutional homosexuality and suggests ethically responsible relationships for those who cannot either change or sublimate their homosexual desires; and (4) the "full acceptance" stance, which views "the homosexual orientation as more of a given than a free choice" and "rests on the conviction that same-sex relationships can richly express and be the vehicle of God's humanizing intentions" (p. 197). In *Homosexuality and Ethics* (New York: Pilgrim Press, 1980), Episcopal priest and university chaplain Edward Batchelor, Jr., categorized the perspectives of various Protestant, Roman Catholic, and Jewish scholars of the past and present under four headings based on attitudes toward same-sex sexual acts: (1) "Homosexual acts are 'intrinsically evil'"; (2) "Homosexual acts are 'essentially imperfect'"; (3) "Homosexual acts are to be evaluated in terms of their relational significance"; and (4) "Homosexual acts are natural and good." In her book on sex education for the Christian home, *Sex Is a Parent Affair,* rev. ed. (New York: Bantam, 1982), Letha Dawson Scanzoni used four C's to summarize basic attitudes found among Christians with regard to homosexual people: *condemnation* (the belief that gay and lesbian people are especially singled out for God's wrath), *change* (an insistence that gay and lesbian people can and should be changed or healed through the power of Christ and

enabled to live heterosexually), *celibacy* (a belief that if change is not possible, homosexual people are called to live celibate lives), and *committed couple relationships* (endorsement of monogamous covenantal unions between same-sex persons who love each other and desire a permanent relationship).

18. Resolution adopted by the Continental Congress on the Family, St. Louis, MO, 1975: "Affirmation on the Family."

19. Joseph Bayly, "The Bible and Two Tough Topics," *Eternity* 25 (August 1974): 41–42.

20. Margaret Evening, *Who Walk Alone* (Downers Grove, IL: InterVarsity Press, 1974), 62.

21. From the tenth American Lutheran Church Convention, as quoted by Carol Kasabah, director of the Lutheran Office of Governmental Ministry in New Jersey, in a letter to state legislators urging passage of a bill designed to protect the civil rights of gay and lesbian people, 29 Oct. 1991.

22. See the journal *Manna for the Journey* (later retitled *Open Hands*), Winter 1986, 15.

23. James B. Nelson, *Embodiment: An Approach to Sexuality and Christian Theology* (Minneapolis: Augsburg, 1978), 205.

24. John J. McNeill, *The Church and the Homosexual*, 3d ed. (Boston: Beacon Press, 1988), 198.

25. Louie Crew, "View from a Gay Person's Pew," *Witness* 66 (August 1983), 18.

26. Darrell J. Doughty, "Homosexuality and Obedience to the Gospel" (Paper presented at the hearings of the Special Task Force to Study the Issue of the Ordination of an Avowed Homosexual, Presbytery of New York City, March 1977).

27. See John E. Wagner, "Psychological Studies: From Gothard to Gay," *Christianity Today* 19 (9 May 1975): 811.

CHAPTER 9 ▼ PROPOSING A HOMOSEXUAL CHRISTIAN ETHIC

1. Lewis B. Smedes, *Sex for Christians* (Grand Rapids, MI: Eerdmans, 1976). See especially pp. 70–73.

2. Charles Curran, "Moral Theology and Homosexuality," in *Homosexuality and the Catholic Church*, ed. Jeannine Gramick (Mt. Ranier, MD: New Ways Ministry, 1983), 162–63, 165–66.

3. Charles E. Curran, "Homosexuality and Moral Theology: Methodological and Substantive Considerations," *Thomist* 35 (July 1971): 447–81; reprinted in *Homosexuality and Ethics*, ed. Edward Batchelor, Jr. (New York: Pilgrim Press, 1980), 94.

4. Curran, "Moral Theology and Homosexuality," 162.

5. Norman Pittenger, *Time for Consent: A Christian's Approach to Homosexuality* (London: SCM Press, 1970), 116–17.

6. John J. McNeill, *The Church and the Homosexual*, 3d ed. (Boston: Beacon Press, 1988), app. 1.

7. Helmut Thielicke, *The Ethics of Sex*, trans. John W. Doberstein (Grand Rapids, MI: Baker Book House, 1975), 269–92. All quotations in our discussion of Thielicke's views are taken from these pages.

8. J. Rinzema, *The Sexual Revolution* (Grand Rapids, MI: Eerdmans, 1974), 106.

9. R. W. Ramsay, M. Heringa, and I. Boorsma, "A Case Study: Homosexuality in the Netherlands," in *Understanding Homosexuality: Its Biological and Psychological Bases,* ed. J. A. Loraine (New York: American Elsevier, 1974), 121–39.

10. Ramsay, Heringa, and Boorsma, "Homosexuality in the Netherlands," 128.

11. Alex Davidson, *The Returns of Love* (Downers Grove, IL: InterVarsity Press, 1970).

12. Daniel C. Maguire, "The Vatican and Sex," *Commonweal* 103 (27 Feb. 1976): 138–39. See also his essay "The Morality of Homosexual Marriage," in *A Challenge to Love: Gay and Lesbian Catholics in the Church,* ed. Robert Nugent (New York: Crossroad, 1983), 118–34.

13. Dr. John Boswell, professor of history at Yale University, has presented this material in numerous speeches and will document his discoveries in the forthcoming *Same-sex Unions in Premodern Europe* (New York: Villard at Random House, 1994).

14. David A. Fraser, "Sensuous Theology," *Reformed Journal* 27 (February 1977): 24.

15. John Stott, "Homosexual 'Marriage': Why Same-Sex Partnerships Are Not a Christian Option," *Christianity Today,* 22 Nov. 1985, 24–25.

16. Theodore W. Jennings, "Homosexuality and the Christian Faith," *Christian Century* 94 (16 Feb. 1977): 138.

17. Rosemary R. Ruether, "The Personalization of Sexuality," in *From Machismo to Mutuality,* ed. Rosemary R. Ruether and Eugene C. Bianchi (New York: Paulist Press, 1976), 83.

18. McNeill, *The Church and the Homosexual,* 32, 197.

19. James Nelson, "Homosexuality and the Church," *Christianity and Crisis* 37 (4 Apr. 1977): 63–69. See also his *Embodiment* (Minneapolis: Augsburg, 1978), especially chap. 8, "Gayness and Homosexuality: Issues for the Church."

20. Ramsay, Heringa, and Boorsma, "Homosexuality in the Netherlands," 126.

21. Walter Barnett, *Sexual Freedom and the Constitution* (Albuquerque: Univ. of New Mexico Press, 1973), 11.

22. Erving Goffman, *Stigma* (Englewood Cliffs, NJ: Prentice-Hall, 1963), 30.

23. McNeill, *The Church and the Homosexual,* 158. McNeill himself has experienced the "social and psychological stigma" he writes about. Within a year of the August 1976 publication of the first edition of his book, a directive from the Vatican's Sacred Congregation of the Faith ordered him to cease lecturing on the topic of homosexuality or any other area of sex ethics. Furthermore, future editions of *The Church and the Homosexual* would not be allowed to carry the *imprimi potest* (a notation of the Roman Catholic Church's official permission to print a book as worthy of discussion even though the views set forth may not be those officially endorsed by the church). The matter culminated in the ousting of John McNeill from the Jesuits in January 1987, on the grounds of "public dissent from the church's teaching on homosexuality." See "Jesuit Theologian Silenced," *Christian Century* 94 (21 Sept. 1977): 809; and "Jesuits to Expel Rebel Gay Priest," *National Catholic Reporter,* 14 Nov. 1986, 1, 6. A full account of these events is provided in McNeill, *The Church and the Homosexual,* app. 3 (217–41).

24. Richard Lettis et. al., eds., *Huck Finn and His Critics* (New York: Macmillan, 1962), 187.

25. Jacqueline G. Wexler, "Introduction," in Laura Z. Hobson, *Gentleman's Agreement* (New York: Arbor House, 1983; originally published in 1947).

26. Hobson, *Gentleman's Agreement,* 189–90.

27. Paul Oestreicher, "Thought for the Day," BBC broadcast, 17–20 May 1976; reprinted as "Aspects of Freedom" in *Christian,* Annunciation 1977, 188.

28. *An Inclusive-Language Lectionary: Readings for Year B,* rev. ed. (New York: National Council of Churches, 1987), 138.

CHAPTER 10 ▼ THE CONTINUING CHALLENGE

1. Thomas Merton, "The Good Samaritan," in *A Thomas Merton Reader,* ed. Thomas McDonnell, rev. ed. (Garden City, NY: Doubleday Image Books, 1974), 348–456. The quotations are from page 349.

2. Gordon W. Allport, *The Nature of Prejudice,* abr. ed. (Garden City, NY: Doubleday Anchor Books, 1958), 9–10.

3. Allport, *The Nature of Prejudice,* 8.

4. Allport, *The Nature of Prejudice,* 23.

5. Allport, *The Nature of Prejudice,* 23–24.

6. The perception that much more variability exists within one's own group (the "we" or "in-group") than among members of a group with which one does not identify (the "they" or "out-group") has been labeled by social psychologists "the out-group homogeneity effect." In other words, people tend to view members of what they consider outsider groups as being more consistently similar to one another than is true of their own group, where individual differences are recognized and acknowledged. See the special issue of *Social Cognition* 11, no. 1 (Spring 1993).

7. Tracy W. J. Thorne, "The Fun-House Mirror Image of Gays in the Military," *Virginian-Pilot and the Ledger-Star,* 9 May 1993, C-3; reprinted from the *Los Angeles Times.* See also Kerry DeRochi, "'Golden Boy' Turns Political Leper," *Virginian-Pilot,* 8 July 1992. For an account of Thorne's dismissal and the navy's refusal to hear or consider evidence based upon both his superlative record and the cost to the nation, see "Navy Won't Let Gay Flier Challenge Ban" and "Navy Pushes to Discharge Gay Flier," *Virginian-Pilot and the Ledger-Star,* 24 and 25 July 1993, respectively.

8. Thorne's testimony was given before the Senate committee during public hearings held at the Norfolk Naval Base, Norfolk, Virginia, 10 May 1993.

9. Quoted in Jeffrey Schmalz, "Difficult First Step: Promises and Reality Clash As Clinton Is Moving to End Military's Gay Ban," *New York Times,* 15 Nov. 1992, national edition, 22. See also Margo Harakas, "Gay Veterans Hopeful About Changes," *Virginian-Pilot,* 11 Nov. 1992, A-7; reprinted from the *Fort Lauderdale Sun-Sentinel.*

10. "Gay-Troop Ban Under Fire," *Virginian-Pilot,* 19 June 1992, A-1.

11. The material on Matlovich is derived from various news sources, including "The Sergeant v. the Air Force," *Time,* 8 Sept. 1975, 34; "USAF Is Back in Court over Policy on Gays," *Washington Post,* 9 Sept. 1980; "Air Force Will

Pay Matlovich $160,000 to Settle Gay Suit," *Washington Post,* 25 Nov. 1980; and "Gay Vet Buried with Full Honors," *Greensboro* [North Carolina] *News and Record,* 3 July 1988. More detailed information on Matlovich may be found in Randy Shilts, *Conduct Unbecoming: Gays and Lesbians in the U.S. Military* (New York: St. Martin's Press, 1993).

12. Earl Swift, "Another Year, Another Gay; but the Same Sad Navy Tune," *Virginian-Pilot,* 29 July 1992, D-1.

13. Margo Harakas, "Gay Veterans Hopeful About Changes," *Virginian-Pilot,* 11 Nov. 1992, A-7; reprinted from the *Fort Lauderdale Sun-Sentinel.* For a full discussion of types of discharges given to military personnel accused of homosexuality and the practical and psychological consequences when such charges become part of a person's permanent record, see Martin S. Weinberg and Colin J. Williams, *Homosexuals and the Military: A Study of Less than Honorable Discharge* (New York: Harper & Row, 1971); and Shilts, *Conduct Unbecoming,* 1993), 163–64. Shilts describes the elaborate code of Separation Program Numbers (SPN, or "spin," numbers) typed onto discharge papers, indicating several types of gay-related discharge, which were no secret to employers (see pp. 164, 198, and 745 n. 20).

14. Shilts, *Conduct Unbecoming,* 377–80.

15. For a richly detailed account, see Shilts, *Conduct Unbecoming.*

16. Kerry DeRochi, "Gays in the Military: Battling the Ban," *Virginian-Pilot and the Ledger-Star,* 23 Aug. 1992, C-1; "Navy Forced to Reinstate Gay Sailor," *Virginian-Pilot,* 11 Nov. 1992, A-1; "The Colonel Is a Lesbian," *Virginian-Pilot,* 2 June 1992, A-10; "Gay Gulf Veteran Goes Public, Awaits Army Repercussions," *Virginian-Pilot and the Ledger-Star,* 25 Apr. 1993, A-5; and "Award Winning Gay Sergeant Is Discharged," *Virginian-Pilot and the Ledger-Star,* 12 May 1993, A-7.

17. "Military Wins Challenge by Homosexuals," *Virginian-Pilot,* 27 Feb. 1990; Jane Gross, *New York Times* News Service, "Secrecy Remains Their Creed," *Virginian-Pilot and the Ledger-Star,* 15 Apr. 1990, C-1.

18. Associated Press, "Hoping to Aid Aviator, Senator Seeks to End Military's Ban on Gays," *Virginian-Pilot,* 29 July 1992, A-3.

19. Shilts, *Conduct Unbecoming,* 15.

20. Shilts, *Conduct Unbecoming,* 16–17.

21. Shilts, *Conduct Unbecoming,* 377–80.

22. Shilts, *Conduct Unbecoming,* 17, 104–8, 378–79.

23. Shilts, *Conduct Unbecoming,* 17.

24. April Witt, "Gays in the Military: Fighting to Serve," *Virginian-Pilot,* 1 Feb. 1991, B-4.

25. Quoted in Kay Longcope, "Gays, Lesbians Struggling for Military's Acceptance," *Boston Globe,* 19 Feb. 1991, 8.

26. Shilts, *Conduct Unbecoming,* 281–82.

27. Theodore R. Sarbin and Kenneth E. Karols, "Nonconfoming Sexual Orientations and Military Suitability." Report prepared for the Defense Personnel Security Research and Education Center, Monterey, CA, December 1988, p. 33. An unabridged reprint of this report and the internal memoranda surrounding its publication may be found in Kate Dyer, ed., *Gays in Uniform: The Pentagon's Secret Reports* (Boston: Alyson Publications, 1990), 1–49.

28. Gerry Studds, "Introduction," in Dyer, *Gays in Uniform*, ix–xi.

29. Michael A. McDaniel, "Preservice Adjustment of Homosexual and Heterosexual Military Accessions: Implications for Security Clearance Suitability." Report prepared for the Defense Personnel Security Research and Education Center, Monterey, CA, January 1989, p. iii. An unabridged reprint of this report may be found in Dyer, *Gays in Uniform*, 109–35.

30. As quoted in editorial, "Gay Soldiers, Good Soldiers," *New York Times*, 1 Sept. 1991, sec. 4, p. 10.

31. For a full account, see Shilts, *Conduct Unbecoming*, 647–49.

32. As quoted in Witt, "Gays in the Military," B-4.

33. Phyllis W. Jordan, "When the Military Mixed," *Virginian-Pilot and the Ledger-Star*, 14 Mar. 1993, C-1, C-3.

34. James O. Eastland (D-Miss.), during Senate debates, June 1948, as quoted in Jordan, "When the Military Mixed," C-3.

35. See, for example, Julianne Malveaux, "Not an Apt Parallel," *Virginian-Pilot*, 28 Jan. 1993, A-9. Malveaux is a syndicated columnist and an associate professor of African-American studies at the University of California at Berkeley. Although she favors nondiscrimination toward homosexual people in the military or anywhere else, she writes, "Gays have taken the tools that African-Americans have fashioned for our advancement, like affirmative action, and sought to push their own agendas, often to the exclusion of ours."

36. Barbara Smith, "Homophobia: Why Bring It Up?" *Interracial Books for Children Bulletin* 14, no. 3/4 (1983): 7–8.

37. Audre Lorde, "There Is No Hierarchy of Oppressions," *Interracial Books for Children Bulletin* 14, no. 3/4 (1983): 9.

38. Mark O'Keefe, "Congregation Leader Quits After Church Accepts Gay Couple," *Virginian-Pilot and the Ledger-Star*, 20 May 1993, A-1. In the end, the two men were warmly received into the church membership by many in the congregation. A small number refused to participate in the membership welcoming ritual, and still others boycotted the ceremony altogether. A number of influential families said they would leave the church, prompting one woman to warn that the pastor had apparently not considered the fact that this would mean "$40,000 walking out the door." Both the pastor and the bishop were supportive of the new gay members. Selland himself regretted the media attention, saying he had intended his decision to be private but that opponents of his membership had leaked the matter to the media. See Mark O'Keefe, "Church Formally Inducts 2 Gay Men," *Virginian-Pilot and the Ledger-Star*, 31 May 1993, A-1; and Richard Dirk Selland's letter to the editor, "Religion Is Privacy Issue, Says Gay Officer," *Virginian-Pilot and the Ledger-Star*, 28 May 1993, A-14.

39. James Davison Hunter, *Culture Wars: The Struggle to Define America* (New York: Basic Books, 1991), 194.

40. For detailed discussions of how misinterpretations of Scripture have fostered gender inequality within Christianity, see Virginian Ramey Mollenkott, *Women, Men, and the Bible*, rev. ed. (New York: Crossroad, 1988); and Letha Dawson Scanzoni and Nancy A. Hardesty, *All We're Meant to Be: Biblical Feminism for Today*, 3d ed. (Grand Rapids, MI: Eerdmans, 1992).

41. Quoted in Peter Gabriel Filene, *Him/Her/Self: Sex Roles in Modern America* (New York: New American Library Mentor Book, 1975), 107.

42. Shilts, *Conduct Unbecoming*, 491.

43. New York Times News Service, "End of Military Ban on Gays May Help Women Most," *Virginian-Pilot and the Ledger-Star*, 4 May 1993, A-6.

44. Shilts, *Conduct Unbecoming*, 414.

45. Shilts, *Conduct Unbecoming*, 5.

46. Jane Gross (New York Times News Service), "Navy Must Root Out Lesbians, Admiral Says," *Virginian-Pilot and the Ledger-Star*, 2 Sept. 1990, A-1. See also Shilts, *Conduct Unbecoming*, 719–20.

47. B. D. Clark, "How the Navy Uses the 'Lesbian' Label to Hold Back Women," *Virginian-Pilot and the Ledger-Star*, 21 Oct. 1990, C-6.

48. Suzanne Pharr, *Homophobia: A Weapon of Sexism* (Little Rock, AR: Chardon Press, 1988), 19.

49. Pharr, *Homophobia*, 18.

50. Pharr, *Homophobia*, 19.

51. Susan Ager, "Tailhook: 'Enough!' of 'Men Being Men' and Using Women," *Virginian-Pilot and the Ledger-Star*, 2 May 1993, C-1.

52. It is interesting to note the observation of a former army intelligence officer, who has written that if it is conduct, not simply sexual orientation, that should determine a person's fitness for military service, then the fact must be acknowledged that gay and lesbian people who served in the Persian Gulf war were "much less of a disciplinary problem than heterosexual males preying on women." Under the Freedom of Information Act, he obtained the files of the army's Criminal Investigation Division, which carried out hundreds of investigations related to the nearly two hundred thousand troops taking part in Operations Desert Shield and Desert Storm between August 1990 and July 1991. There were sixteen complaints from women reporting sexual harassment by men and six court-martials for heterosexual rape. Only four cases of homosexual activity were prosecuted, and three of them involved sex acts by consenting adults. See Jeff Stein, "Gays in the Gulf," *Virginian-Pilot and the Ledger-Star*, 6 Dec. 1992, C-1; reprinted from the *Washington Post*. Prosecutions for homosexual rape in the military are extremely uncommon, and the rare cases that have occurred are no more cause for labeling all gay and lesbian people sexual predators than are the sex escapades by participants in the Tailhook scandal a reason to label all heterosexual navy pilots sex offenders.

53. Ann L. Page and Donald A. Clelland, "The Kanawha County Textbook Controversy: A Study in the Politics of Life Style Concern," *Social Forces* 57, no. 1 (September 1978): 265.

54. These sentiments were expressed during a discussion of gay and lesbian rights broadcast on National Public Radio's *Fresh Air*, 26 Aug. 1992.

55. During Anita Bryant's campaign against homosexual rights in the mid-seventies, syndicated columnist Patrick Buchanan wrote that her efforts aroused the "passions associated with a religious war." His use of religious-warfare terminology during his speech at the 1992 Republican National Convention prompted writer Molly Ivins to comment satirically that Americans could now experience the "fun" of heretic hunts and slaughter in God's name and would

be able "at long last to enjoy the charming ambience of Northern Ireland and Lebanon." See Patrick Buchanan, "What Does Anita Bryant Threaten?," *Greensboro* [North Carolina] *Record,* 2 Oct. 1978; and Molly Ivins, "A Feast of Hate and Fear," *Newsweek,* 31 Aug. 1992, 32.

56. See "No 'Special Rights' for Gays," *Newsweek,* 23 Nov. 1992, 32. The American Civil Liberties Union, the three cities whose gay-rights ordinances were repealed by the amendment, and several other groups advocating nondiscrimination on the basis of sexual orientation joined together to file suit in federal court, arguing that the amendment violates constitutional rights. See "Gay-Rights Vote Challenged," *New York Times,* 15 Nov. 1992, 20. During the summer of 1993, the Colorado Supreme Court refused to lift a lower court injunction that prevented the amendment from taking effect before a civil lawsuit could be brought to trial in October of that year. The Colorado Supreme Court said that the amendment is probably unconstitutional and emphasized that a majority vote by the citizens of Colorado could not invalidate the fourteenth amendment to the United States Constitution with its guarantee of equal protection for all citizens. The justices ruled, "One's right to life, liberty and property . . . and other fundamental rights may not be submitted to vote; they depend on the outcome of no elections." Associated Press report, "Colorado High Court Won't Lift Ban on Gay Amendment," *Virginia-Pilot and the Ledger Star,* 20 July 1993, A-4. An appeal to the United States Supreme Court appeared to be on the horizon as we went to press.

57. Timothy Egan, "Oregon Measure Asks State to Repress Homosexuality," *New York Times,* 16 Aug. 1992, 1; Joye Mercer, "Oregon Proposal Would Require Higher Education to Fight Homosexuality As 'Abnormal, Wrong, Perverse,'" *Chronicle of Higher Education,* 16 Sept. 1992, A27.

58. Told during a radio interview on the Canadian Broadcasting Corporation's *As It Happens,* 7 Oct. 1992.

59. As quoted in Timothy Egan, "Chief of Police Becomes the Target in an Oregon Anti-Gay Campaign," *New York Times,* 4 Oct. 1992, L-22.

60. Jack Fincher, *Lefties: The Origins and Consequences of Being Left-Handed* (New York: Barnes and Noble, 1993), 190. Originally published as *Sinister People* (New York: G. P. Putnam's Sons, 1977).

61. Fincher, *Lefties,* 18.

62. Don ("Lefty") Duncan, "Left Out?," *Virginian-Pilot and the Ledger-Star,* 5 Jan. 1991, E-1.

63. Duncan, "Left Out?," E-2; Barbara Palmer, "Left Out: Post Office May Fire Banfield Because He Works Left-handed," Bloomington (Indiana) *Herald-Telephone,* 3 June 1977, 13, reprinted from the *Washington Star;* Marilynn Mansfield, "Lefties with Rights on the Mind," *Greensboro* [North Carolina] *News and Record,* 12 Aug. 1984, F-1.

64. Duncan, "Left Out?," E-2.

65. Peter L. Berger and Thomas Luckmann, *The Social Construction of Reality* (Garden City, NY: Doubleday Anchor Books, 1967), 108.

66. This point is well illustrated in a letter written to a newspaper after a judge awarded custody of a baby to the child's grandmother. The judge had ruled

that the baby's mother was an unfit parent for no other reason than that she lived in a committed lesbian relationship. The letter writer said, "This conduct also renders one an unfit person, in my humble opinion. The judge and I share the same opinion; that makes at least three of us who do, the third being God." "Moral It Is Not," *Virginian-Pilot and the Ledger-Star*, 14 Sept. 1993, Letters section (A-22).

67. Kai T. Erikson, *Wayward Puritans: A Study in the Sociology of Deviance* (New York: Wiley, 1966), 52, 57.

68. Michael D. Guinan, "Homosexuals: A Christian Pastoral Response Now," in *A Challenge to Love*, ed. Robert Nugent (New York: Crossroad, 1983), 68–69.

69. Erikson, *Wayward Puritans,* 48.

70. Quoted in Page and Clelland, "Kanawha County Textbook Controversy," 276.

71. Mary Douglas, *Purity and Danger* (New York: Penguin Books, 1966), 50–53.

72. As we went to press, Congress had made clear its dissatisfaction with President Clinton's suggested compromise policy of "don't ask, don't tell, and don't pursue," and had signaled its preference for a stricter policy that would go beyond not perceiving the presence of homosexual people. The Senate and House voted for a statement declaring homosexuality to be an "unacceptable risk" to military morale and thereby indicated the upholding of conventional attitudes of condemnation and censure. At the same time, separate federal court rulings halted the dismissal from military service of Lt. J. G. Dirk Selland and Petty Officer Keith Meinhold and raised questions about the constitutionality of the military's traditional discriminatory policy against gay and lesbian people. As a result, the Pentagon was forced to put its action against gays on hold and decided to seek "extraordinary relief" from the United States Supreme Court. Implementation of the restrictive version of the "don't ask, don't tell" policy endorsed by Congress was delayed past the 1 October 1993 target date as the Pentagon pursued the case further.

73. Thomas S. Szasz, *Manufacture of Madness* (New York: Harper & Row, 1970), 154, in Harper Colophon edition.

74. Winthrop D. Jordan, *White over Black* (Baltimore: Penguin Books Pelican paperback edition, 1969), 517–21.

75. Jordan, *White over Black,* 520.

76. Douglas, *Purity and Danger,* 51.

77. Weinberg and Williams, *Male Homosexuals,* 21–22; Edwin M. Schur, *The Politics of Deviance* (Englewood Cliffs, NJ: Prentice-Hall, 1980).

78. William Paul, "Minority Status for Gay People," in Paul et al., *Homosexuality,* 351–69.

79. Sherry E. Woods and Karen M. Harbeck, "Living in Two Worlds: The Identity Management Strategies Used by Lesbian Physical Educators," *Journal of Homosexuality* 22, no. 3/4 (1991): 141–66.

80. Joseph Julian, *Social Problems,* 3d ed. (Englewood Cliffs, NJ: Prentice-Hall, 1980), 12–13.

81. Weinberg and Williams, *Male Homosexuals,* 22.

82. Louis Wirth, "The Problem of Minority Groups," in *Science of Man in the World Crisis,* ed. R. Linton (New York: Columbia Univ. Press, 1945), 347, as quoted in Paul, "Minority Status for Gay People," 358.

83. "Reason to Retain the Gay Ban," *Virginian-Pilot and the Ledger-Star,* 14 Apr. 1993, Letters section (A-10).

84. Schur, *Politics of Deviance,* 4.

85. Erikson, *Wayward Puritans,* 13.

86. Erikson, *Wayward Puritans,* 195.

87. Rev. Jane Adams Spahr, as quoted in Ari L. Goldman, "Presbyterians Forbid Hiring of Homosexual Ministers," *New York Times,* 8 Nov. 1992, E-4.

88. Quoted in Jorge Aquino, "Gay Issues Kept Alive for Presbyterians," *Christian Century,* 5–12 Feb. 1992, 118–19. See also "PCUSA Rules Against Lesbian Pastor," *Christian Century,* 18–25 Nov. 1992.

89. *New York Times* News Service, "Presbyterians Retain Ban on Gay Clerics," *Virginian-Pilot and the Ledger-Star,* 9 June 1993, A-6.

90. Dennis Hevesi, "Gay Church Again Rejected by National Council Group," *New York Times,* 15 Nov. 1992, 22.

91. "ABC: Homosexuality is 'Incompatible,'" *Christian Century,* 4 Nov. 1992, 993.

92. *Washington Post* News Service, "Vatican Declares Support for Discrimination Against Gays," *Virginian-Pilot and the Ledger-Star,* 18 July 1992, A-4; Robert A. Bernstein, "Gays and the Vatican: A Religious Call to Hate," *San Francisco Examiner,* 24 July 1992; "Rome on Gay Rights," *Christian Century,* 12–19 Aug. 1992, 739.

93. *Washington Post* News Service, "Baptists OK Amendment for Ousting Congregations Condoning Homosexuality," *Virginian-Pilot and the Ledger-Star,* 16 June 1993, A-2.

94. "Lame-Duck Group Issues Homosexuality Report," *Christian Century,* 11 Nov. 1992, 1024.

95. "SBC Church Withdraws from Convention," *Christian Century,* 24 Feb. 1993, 202.

96. Woods and Harbeck, "Living in Two Worlds," 146.

97. John O. G. Billy et al., "The Sexual Behavior of Men in the United States," *Family Planning Perspectives* 25, no. 2 (March/April 1993): 52–60; see also in the same issue Koray Tanfer, "National Survey of Men: Design and Execution," 83–86. The results may have been affected by the fact that the interviewers were female and also by the refusal of 27 percent of the men (selected through random probability sampling) to consent to an interview. For an insightful critique of serious methodological flaws in this and other research on the incidence of homosexuality in the 1990s, see Paul H. Gebhard, "Kinsey's Famous Figures," Indiana Alumni, September/October 1993, 64.

98. "The Impact of Gay Political Power," *Newsweek,* 26 Apr. 1993, 57.

99. Overlooked Opinions, a marketing research firm that gathers demographic information on gay and lesbian people, reported in 1993 that gay and bisexual men reported an annual household income of $42,689; for lesbian women, the figure was $36,072. The researchers also found that a majority in their survey held college degrees and were employed as professionals. See Kara Swisher,

"Targeting the Gay Market," *Washington Post*, 25 Apr. 1993. See also Thomas Stewart, "Gay in Corporate America," *Fortune*, 16 Dec. 1991, 42–56.

100. Such arguments were heard on the popular syndicated Christian radio program *Focus on the Family*, hosted by Dr. James Dobson, 9 Dec. 1992.

101. Paul Tsongas, speech before the Senate to introduce an amendment to Title VII of the Civil Rights Act of 1964, *Congressional Record*, 96th Cong., 1st sess., 5 Dec. 1979, vol. 125, no. 172, p. 1.

102. Jay Lucas and Mark Kaplan,"What Do Gays Want? Out of the Closet," *Virginian-Pilot and the Ledger-Star*, 1 May 1993, A-13. See also Stewart, "Gay in Corporate America."

103. See *SIECUS Report*, February/March 1993, 19. The cities were Boston, Chicago, Minneapolis/St. Paul, New York, and San Francisco.

104. Patrick J. Buchanan, "What Does Anita Bryant Threaten?" *Greensboro* [North Carolina] *Record*, 2 Oct. 1978.

105. Bell and Weinberg, *Homosexualities*, 24.

106. The researchers wrote that they used the term *close-coupled* for this category because the word *close* has two senses (as well as two pronunciations). These social scientists found that "first, the partners in this kind of relationship are closely bound together. Second, the partnership is closed in that the Close-Couples tend to look to each other rather than to outsiders for sexual and interpersonal satisfactions." Both gay and lesbian couples in this category were found to be "more self-accepting and less depressed or lonely than any of the others, and they were the happiest of all." Bell and Weinberg, *Homosexualities*, 219–20.

107. For a summary of such diversity, see Letha Dawson Scanzoni and John Scanzoni, *Men, Women, and Change: A Sociology of Marriage and Family*, 3d ed. (New York: McGraw-Hill, 1988), 178–203.

108. See Virginia Ramey Mollenkott, *Sensuous Spirituality* (New York: Crossroad, 1992), 163–64; "The Age of Outing," *Newsweek*, 12 Aug. 1991, 22–23; Fred Friendly, "Gays, the News Media and All Americans' Right to Privacy," *Virginian-Pilot and the Ledger-Star*, 14 Apr. 1990, A-8; "'Outing': An Unexpected Assault on Sexual Privacy," *Newsweek*, 30 Apr. 1990, 66.

109. A helpful discussion is found in Pat Griffin, "From Hiding Out to Coming Out: Empowering Lesbian and Gay Educators," *Journal of Homosexuality* 22, no. 3/4 (1991): 167–95.

110. "SIECUS Fact Sheet: Sexual Orientation and Identity," *SIECUS Report*, February/March 1993, 19.

111. Lindsay Van Gelder, "The 'Born That Way' Trap," *Ms.*, May/June 1991, 86.

112. Beverly Burch, *On Intimate Terms: The Psychology of Difference in Lesbian Relationships* (Urbana: Univ. of Illinois Press, 1993). See also the review of this book by Irene Elizabeth Stroud, "Equal and Opposite," *Women's Review of Books* 10, no. 9 (June 1993), 20–21.

113. Barbara Ponse, *Identities in the Lesbian World: The Social Construction of Self* (Westport, CT: Greenwood Press, 1978), 160–68.

114. See Jeffrey Schmalz, "Gay Politics Goes Mainstream," *New York Times Magazine*, 11 Oct. 1992, 18ff.; Stephen Burd, "AIDS Activists, Frustrated by Failure of Drugs, Make Greater Effort to Improve Federal Research Policies,"

Chronicle of Higher Education 23 (September 1992): A-28; "The Power and the Pride" (cover story on lesbians), *Newsweek*, 21 June 1993, 54–60.

115. The story of Michael Gottlieb, a young immunologist who saw connections missed by others, perceived a medical emergency, and reported his findings about the illness to the Centers for Disease Control, is told in Jeremy Schlosberg, "Diagnosis AIDS," *Rochester Review* (University of Rochester alumni magazine), Spring/Summer 1993, 26–30.

116. See Geoffrey Cowley, "The Future of AIDS," *Newsweek*, 22 Mar. 1993, 47–52; and Geoffrey Cowley and Mary Hager, "What If a Cure Is Far Off?" *Newsweek*, 21 June 1993, 70.

117. Cowley and Hager, "What If a Cure?" See also Associated Press, "New U.S. AIDS Report Has Focus on Women," *Virginian-Pilot and the Ledger-Star*, 11 June 1993, A-6; and Gena Corea, *Invisible Epidemic: The Story of Women and AIDS* (New York: HarperCollins, 1992).

118. Cowley, "The Future of AIDS," 47.

119. See Bernard Gavzer's article on long-term survivors of AIDS, "What Keeps Me Alive," *Parade*, 31 Jan. 1993, 4–7.

120. C. Everett Koop, *Surgeon General's Report on Acquired Immune Deficiency Syndrome* (Washington, DC: U.S. Department of Health and Human Services, October 1986), 6.

121. David L. Schiedermayer, M.D., "Choices in Plague Time," *Christianity Today*, 7 Aug. 1987, 20.

122. "How Far Will the Flame Reach?," *Bulletin of Weston Priory*, December 1992, 4.

▼▼▼▼▼▼▼▼▼▼

Recommended for Further Reading

THE LIST THAT FOLLOWS is highly selective. We urge interested readers to search the Notes for other helpful books and articles.

▼ FOR GENERAL INFORMATION

Abelove, Henry, Michèl Aina Barale, and David Halperin. *The Lesbian and Gay Studies Reader*. New York: Rutledge, 1993. A serious introduction to a wide range of scholarship in the emerging discipline of gay and lesbian studies.

Bell, Alan P., and Martin S. Weinberg. *Homosexualities: A Study of Diversity Among Men and Women*. New York: Simon & Schuster, 1978. Nearly one thousand interviews and seven years of studying data went into this Kinsey Institute study, which shows the great variation among homosexual adults.

Bell, Alan P., Martin S. Weinberg, and Sue Kiefer Hammersmith. *Sexual Preference: Its Development in Men and Women*. Bloomington: Indiana Univ. Press, 1981. A thorough and trustworthy study of contributing factors in the development of both the homosexual and the heterosexual orientations.

Blumstein, Philip, and Pepper Schwartz. *American Couples*. New York: William Morrow and Company, 1983. A massive in-depth study of couple relationships—both married and unmarried heterosexual couples and gay and lesbian couples—as the partners go about their everyday lives.

Duberman, Martin Bauml, Martha Vicinus, and George Chauncey, Jr., eds. *Hidden from History: Reclaiming the Gay and Lesbian Past*.

New York: New American Library, 1989. A set of essays surveying the topic, many of them brilliant and essential.

Marcus, Eric. *Is It a Choice?* San Francisco: HarperSanFrancisco, 1993. Cogent answers to three hundred of the most frequently asked questions about gay and lesbian people.

Mendola, Mary. *The Mendola Report: A New Look at Gay Couples.* New York: Crown, 1980. A discussion of the everyday lives and concerns of committed gay and lesbian couples, covering topics ranging from dividing up household chores to planning for retirement and losing a life partner through death. Based on a nationwide survey by a professional writer.

Paul, William, James D. Weinrich, John Gonsiorek, and Mary E. Hotvedt. *Homosexuality: Social, Psychological, and Biological Issues.* Beverly Hills, CA: Sage Publications, 1982. This book comprises the final report of the Task Force on Sexual Orientation of the Society for the Psychological Study of Social Issues. An excellent overview.

Pharr, Suzanne. *Homophobia: A Weapon of Sexism.* Little Rock, AR: Chardon Press, 1988. A straightforward analysis of the connectedness of all oppression, including the linkage between societal hatred of lesbian women and of women in general.

Shilts, Randy. *Conduct Unbecoming: Gays and Lesbians in the U.S. Military.* New York: St. Martin's Press, 1993. Comprehensive, accurate, and indispensable.

Weinberg, George. *Society and the Healthy Homosexual.* Garden City, NY: Doubleday Anchor Books, 1973. An illuminating discussion of homophobia, the injustices involved in trying to change homosexuals into heterosexuals, self-acceptance, and communication with parents.

▼ MATERIALS SPECIFICALLY DEALING WITH RELIGION
AND HOMOSEXUALITY

Bailey, Derrick Sherwin. *Homosexuality and the Western Christian Tradition.* London: Longmans, Green and Company, 1955. Reprint. Hamden, CT: Shoestring Press, Archon Books, 1975. Still the pioneering study of homosexuality against a background of biblical interpretation, theology, and church history.

Batchelor, Edward, Jr., ed. *Homosexuality and Ethics.* New York: Pilgrim Press, 1980. Insightful essays from a variety of viewpoints.

Blair, Ralph. *An Evangelical Look at Homosexuality.* Rev. ed. New York: Evangelicals Concerned, 1977. (Available from Evangelicals Concerned, 311 East 72nd Street, New York, NY 10021.) This pamphlet frankly examines both evangelical attitudes and the message of the Bible concerning homosexuality.

Boswell, John. *Christianity, Social Tolerance, and Homosexuality: Gay People in Western Europe from the Beginning of the Christian Era to the Fourteenth Century.* Chicago: Univ. of Chicago Press, 1980. A Yale history professor demonstrates that intolerance of homosexuality was not an essential feature of early Christianity.

Countryman, L. William. *Dirt, Greed, and Sex: Sexual Ethics in the New Testament and Their Implications for Today.* Philadelphia: Fortress Press, 1988. Direct, clear discussion.

Edwards, George R. *Gay/Lesbian Liberation: A Biblical Perspective.* New York: Pilgrim Press, 1984. An emeritus professor of New Testament at Louisville Presbyterian Theological Seminary demonstrates that religious intolerance of gays and lesbians has no biblical basis.

Gramick, Jeannine, ed. *Homosexuality and the Catholic Church.* Mt. Rainier, MD: New Ways Ministry, 1983. A collection of thoughtful essays presented at the First National Symposium on Homosexuality and the Catholic Church.

Jones, Clinton R. *Homosexuality and Counseling.* Philadelphia: Fortress Press, 1974. An Episcopal priest offers excellent advice for pastors, counselors, and general readers.

McNeill, John J. *The Church and the Homosexual.* 3d ed. Boston: Beacon Press, 1988. A thoughtful discussion of the Scriptural handling of homosexuality by a Jesuit priest who "took a chance on God."

———. *Taking a Chance on God: Liberating Theology for Gays, Lesbians, and Their Lovers, Families, and Friends.* Boston: Beacon Press, 1988. Guidance for the spiritual development of gay and lesbian Christians.

Mollenkott, Virginia R. *Sensuous Spirituality: Out from Fundamentalism.* New York: Crossroad, 1992. A lesbian Christian discusses biblical hermeneutics, spiritual practices, and interpretive communities.

Nugent, Robert, ed. *A Challenge to Love: Gay and Lesbian Catholics in the Church.* New York: Crossroad, 1983. Insightful essays covering societal, biblical-theological, pastoral, and vocational perspectives on homosexuality.

Scroggs, Robin. *The New Testament and Homosexuality: Contextual Background for Contemporary Debate.* Philadelphia: Fortress Press, 1983. A professor of New Testament at Union Theological Seminary (New York) demonstrates that because the current homosexual model of consenting adults is so different from the man-boy model attacked in the New Testament, apparent biblical judgments against homosexuality are not relevant to the contemporary debate.

Christians and Homosexuality: A Discussion of Biblical and Ethical Issues. Philadelphia: The Other Side, 1990. A compilation of articles from the magazine *The Other Side* on "coming out," coping with AIDS, lesbian/gay ordination, and whether orientational change is possible or desirable.

▼ COUNSEL FOR GAY AND LESBIAN PEOPLE AND THEIR PARENTS

Borhek, Mary V. *Coming Out to Parents: A Two-Way Survival Guide for Lesbians and Gay Men and Their Parents.* New York: Pilgrim Press, 1983. (Revised edition in press.) Helpful guidance from the mother of a gay son.

Fairchild, Betty, and Nancy Hayward. *Now That You Know: What Every Parent Should Know About Homosexuality.* New York: Harcourt Brace Jovanovich, 1979. A classic book for parents who have just learned of a son's or daughter's homosexuality. Written by two mothers who were instrumental in forming Parents of Gays, one of the earliest support groups for parents of gay and lesbian children, now affiliated with the Federation of Parents, Families, and Friends of Lesbians and Gays.

COMPREHENSIVE LISTS of books, articles, cassette tapes, and videotapes designed to aid in understanding homosexuality are available from Parents, Families, and Friends of Lesbians and Gays (P-FLAG), 1012 14th St., N.W., Suite 700, Washington, DC 20005. For information about the nearest P-FLAG chapter or help line in the United States and Canada, call 1-800-4-FAMILY.

Index of Names and Subjects

Index of Scripture References